Safety and Health for the Stage

Safety and Health for the Stage: Collaboration with the Production Process is a practical guide to integrating safety and health into the production process for live entertainment in the context of compliance with applicable codes, standards, and recommended practices.

This book explores the need for safety and health to become an integral aspect of theatre production and live entertainment, focusing on specific steps to take and policies to employ to bring a safety and health program into full collaboration in the production process. Readers will learn how to comply with legal codes and standards as they initiate and implement an effective safety and health program in their theatre production organization or academic theatre department. The book includes references and links to other industry-specific safety and health resources, as well as a Glossary of Safety and Health Terms to navigate safety and health jargon in the context of theatre and live entertainment. *Safety and Health for the Stage: Collaboration with the Production Process* provides links to electronic versions of sample safety and health programs, industry-specific policies and recommended practices, and forms and templates related to many of the topics covered in the book.

Written for practitioners who are engaged in all aspects of theatre production and live entertainment, as well as educators who train and influence the next generations of these practitioners, this book is an essential resource for creating a positive culture of safety in live entertainment.

William J. Reynolds joined the faculty of Yale School of Drama in 1982 and continues to teach occasional workshops in theatre safety for Yale School of Drama and other theatre organizations. In June 2017 he retired from the Yale School of Drama/Yale Repertory Theatre as the Director of Theatre Safety and Occupational Health. An OSHA Authorized Outreach Trainer, he is the USITT Safety and Health Vice-Commissioner for Education and the Student Alliance Program.

Safety and Health for the Stage

Collaboration with the Production Process

William J. Reynolds

NEW YORK AND LONDON

First published 2020
by Routledge
605 Third Avenue, New York, NY 10017

and by Routledge
2 Park Square, Milton Park, Abingdon, Oxon, OX14 4RN

Routledge is an imprint of the Taylor & Francis Group, an informa business

© 2020 Taylor & Francis

The right of William J. Reynolds to be identified as author of this work has been asserted by him in accordance with sections 77 and 78 of the Copyright, Designs and Patents Act 1988.

All rights reserved. No part of this book may be reprinted or reproduced or utilised in any form or by any electronic, mechanical, or other means, now known or hereafter invented, including photocopying and recording, or in any information storage or retrieval system, without permission in writing from the publishers.

Trademark notice: Product or corporate names may be trademarks or registered trademarks, and are used only for identification and explanation without intent to infringe.

Library of Congress Cataloging-in-Publication Data
A catalog record for this title has been requested

ISBN 13: 978-0-8153-5325-6 (hbk)
ISBN 13: 978-0-8153-5326-3 (pbk)
ISBN 13: 978-1-351-13698-3 (ebk)

DOI: 10.4324/9781351136983

Typeset in Arial
by Apex CoVantage, LLC

Visit the eResources: www.routledge.com/9780815353263

The love and support of my family has made my life in theatre possible.

To Sharon, my wife: I have deep and humble gratitude for your love, patience, and encouragement. You provide me a safe place to be myself, and allowed us to fulfill our dreams together.

To Steve and Fred, our sons: I am honored to be your father. You taught me confidence in self, and the importance of integrity in relationships.

Dedicated in Honor and in Memory of
Pierre-André Salim

CONTENTS

List of Figures   viii

Acknowledgements   x

Foreword   xiii

Preface   xv

CHAPTER 1   *Introduction and Overview   1*

CHAPTER 2   *Safety Evolves Within the Theatre Industry   11*

CHAPTER 3   *Safety and Health Programs   38*

CHAPTER 4   *Compliance   66*

CHAPTER 5   *Industry Standards, Recommended Practices, Training, and Certifications   109*

CHAPTER 6   *Policies and Procedures: Specific Hazards   129*

CHAPTER 7   *Borrowing Safety Strategies   156*

CHAPTER 8   *Putting It All Together: Safety Culture   188*

APPENDIX   *Additional Resources   201*

Glossary of Safety and Health Terms   216

Bibliography   232

Index   234

LIST OF FIGURES

Figure P.1 2017 Event Structures and Staging Accidents xviii

Figure 3.1 W. Edwards Deming's Plan–Do–Study–Act Cycle 40

Figure 3.2 OSHA Safety and Health Programs Core Elements 41

Figure 3.3 Facilities Hazards Inspection Form 49

Figure 3.4 Hierarchy of Controls 51

Figure 3.5 Hazard Control Plan Management Cycle 53

Figure 3.6 Lagging and Leading Indicators 59

Figure 4.1 Hierarchy of Safety Controls: Codes 68

Figure 4.2 29 CFR 1910, Subparts F, H, N, O 73

Figure 4.3 29 CFR 1910, Subpart Z—Toxic and Hazardous Substances 74

Figure 4.4 29 CFR 1904, Partially Exempt Industries 81

Figure 5.1 Hierarchy of Safety Controls: Industry Standards 110

Figure 5.2 Hierarchy of Safety Controls: Recommended Practices, Training, and Certifications 111

Figure 6.1 Hierarchy of Safety Controls: Policies and Procedures 130

Figure 6.2 Sample Live Flame and Smoking Incidents Form 143

Figure 6.3 OSHA 300 Log Required Data Fields 146

Figure 6.4 Relationship of Hazardous Conditions to Injuries and Fatalities 150

Figure 7.1 Typical Theatre Organizational Chart (simplified) 158

Figure 7.2 A Checklist for Checklists 161

Figure 7.3 Production Hazards Identification Checklist—Props 166

Figure 7.4 Hierarchy of Controls—PtD   170

Figure 7.5 Risk Assessment Matrix (adapted from ANSI E1.46—2016)   174

Figure 7.6 Sample Risk Assessment Documentation Form   175

Figure 7.7 Field Level Hazard Assessment Symbol   178

Figure 7.8 Sample FLHA Potential Hazards Checklist   178

Figure 7.9 H. W. Heinrich Safety Pyramid   181

Figure 8.1 Listening Skills   189

ACKNOWLEDGEMENTS

This book is grounded in my concern for safety and health, and reflects my passion to ingrain safety and health into the fabric of the production process for theatre and live events. My Mother, Elinor Reynolds, is responsible in part for the first aspect—my concern for safety and health. She earnestly looked out for our well-being as kids, but made sure we knew we bore responsibility for our own safety. "Hang on tight," she would admonish me high in a tree (not "Don't fall!"), showing her concern for my safety while putting the onus on me to be safe. My passion for theatre was most influenced by two people: Jack Watkins and John Vestal. Jack Watkins, English teacher and drama director at Monroe High School in Rochester, NY, was not only a mentor, but he instilled in me a deep and abiding passion for the collaboration of artists in theatre making. John Vestal, Lighting Design and Technical Director at SUNY Geneseo, NY, nurtured the practical side of theatre production and established a model of commitment and professionalism centered on his mantra of "neatness and thought." My interest in theatre safety emerged during my years as an MFA graduate student in Technical Design and Production (TD&P) at Yale School Drama (YSD) in the 1970s. John Hood, TD&P department chair, and Ben Sammler, a recent MFA graduate and technical director for Yale Repertory Theatre (YRT), developed and implemented the first written safety rules for theatre production I had seen. My return to YSD in 1982 as a faculty member in TD&P provided an environment in which to cultivate and evolve my passion for safety in theatre production. Ben Sammler, then both the chair of the TD&P department and the technical director for YRT, effectively encouraged and uplifted safety by the required theatre safety class which I taught. Ben and the faculty of the TD&P department also expanded the previous basic safety rules into comprehensive safety policies. An additional thank-you goes to the YSD/YRT senior leadership, faculty, and staff who embraced the integration of safety and health policies into the curriculum and production activities at the School and the Yale Rep. Among the people whom I single out with profound gratitude is Ben Sammler, not only for his foresight in integrating safety and health training into the TD&P curriculum at YSD, but importantly for his friendship in the decades of sharing work and family during and after our time together at YSD/YRT.

I must also give tribute to many people with whom I worked, or who have been mentors. In the arena of safety and health, I am deeply grateful for the staff of Yale University's Environmental Health and Safety (EHS) office, particularly EHS Director Pete Reinhardt. Many members of the Yale EHS staff contributed their time and expertise both to me and to the YSD/YRT safety and health program. I am particularly thankful to: Asst. EHS Director Kevin Charbonneau; Cathy King (industrial hygienist); Ben Fontes (biological safety); Paula Castagna (chemical hygiene); John Campbell (safety engineer); and JoAnn Farrell (safety advisor to YSD/YRT). In the area of fire and life safety, I owe a debt of thanks to the staff of fire inspectors at Yale's Office of the Fire Marshal, and the inspectors at the New Haven Fire Department's Office of Pubic Assembly.

As attention to safety and health in the entertainment industry has grown, many professionals focused energy on creating an expectation for integrating safety and health into theatre production, and for compliance with codes and standards within the industry. Monona Rossol and Randy Davidson were early advocates for safety and health, and are prominent among this group to whom thanks is due. A result of this focus was the establishment of the Safety and Health Commission within the United States Institute for Theatre Technology (USITT). My work with this Commission has been educational and fulfilling particularly because of the theatre professionals who over the years have committed their time and expertise to its goals. I am grateful to several USITT members with whom I shared the work of the Commission: Dave Glowacki, Bryan Huneycutt, Greg Petruska, Ross Rauschkolb, and Adam Tackett.

Anna Glover (Dir. of Theatre Safety and Occupational Health, YSD/YRT) has also been active in the USITT S&H Commission, but I extend to Anna additional appreciation for her professional support. Anna has provided encouragement and expertise as she helped me to gain confidence in my work in theatre safety. I am especially thankful for her editorial review of this book as a subject-matter expert.

I am grateful to have been able to turn to theatre professionals from around the world to assist in the development of several sections of this book. My text describing various professional organizations in the industry benefited from review by: James Mountcastle (Actors Equity Association [AEA]); Erin Grabe (Entertainment Services and Technology Association [ESTA]); Steven Adelman (Event Safety Alliance [ESA]); Hannah D'Amico (International Alliance of Theatrical Stage Employees [IATSE]); and Dave Glowacki (USITT). I thank the following people for their time in allowing me to interview them about their theatre organizations' safety and health programs: Abby Rodd (Glimmerglass Festival); Scott Conn (Goodman Theatre); Jared Clarkin and Kaitlyn Anderson (Milwaukee Repertory Theater); Alys Holden and Hazel Wheeler (Oregon Shakespeare Festival); and Anna Glover (Yale School of Drama/Yale Repertory Theatre). The section in Chapter Four about compliance with codes from a sampling of countries other than the United States benefited from sources, and suggestions for resources from several theatre professionals. I thankfully recognize the contributions of: Martin Montaner (Chile); Janet Sellery (Canada); Sayantee Sahoo (India); Barbara Tan-Tiongco (Philippines); Cheng heng Lee (Singapore); Jeong-Sik Yoo (South Korea [Republic of Korea]); Tien Sung Ma (Taiwan [R.O.C.]); and Anna Glover and Greg Petruska (United Kingdom).

FOREWORD

It was Monday, September 19, 2011. Surrounded by a team of doctors in the hospital ICU, I was awoken after eight days in an induced coma. They were asking me routine questions. I was answering, and while I had no memory of what had brought me here, I could sense that everyone around me was extremely surprised. They were expecting signs of permanent damage. I was exhibiting none!

The details of what had transpired on the afternoon of September 11 were shared with me over the next several days, weeks, and years, by those who were there. I had suffered a sudden heart attack while playing the fourth volleyball game of the day. It was in my back yard during our beginning of the school year party. I'd collapsed while surrounded by over a hundred students, faculty, staff, and alumni of Yale's Technical Design and Production Department (TD&P). I had no pulse, and Bill Reynolds (YSD '77) immediately initiated CPR. Bill was assisted by Rick Silvestro ('75) with Shaminda Amarakoon ('12) monitoring my pulse for quite a while until the paramedics arrived. I apparently died at least three times during the entire ordeal—I have no recollection.

And thus, the doctor's surprise at my revival. Statistically the survival rate for someone receiving CPR for as long as I had was 2 percent. And they had warned my family that should I survive it was certain that I would have permanent disabilities. I have none.

It was primarily due to the actions of Bill Reynolds that I am here to write this foreword eight years after that heart attack. But on reflection I've realized that almost everyone around me that day was capable of saving my life. Mandatory CPR training for our department is just one small part of the comprehensive Safety and Health Program that Bill developed and oversaw during his tenure at the Yale School of Drama.

Bill and I both retired from the Yale School of Drama/Yale Repertory Theatre in 2017. During my retirement speech I mentioned several books that had been written by our alumni and faculty over the course of my tenure as chair of the TD&P Department. As

I ended the list of publications I noted that I soon expected to see a Theatre Safety book by Bill. Luckily for all of us, Bill had already come to the same conclusion.

The book that follows is far more than a safety manual. Bill began his career as a technical manager with extensive production experience. He was drawn to considering safety procedures for theatre just as the notion of safety practice in our industry was emerging. He developed protocols throughout his long career with a fine eye toward the needs of our industry, while incorporating practices and regulations as they evolved. His book appropriately demonstrates the integration of safety and health within the production process. It is a must read for anyone considering creating a Safety and Health Program for any Academic or Professional Theatre Organization.

Bronislaw J. Sammler
Henry McCormick Professor Emeritus of
Technical Design and Production
Yale School of Drama

PREFACE

Theatre[1] safety requires the effective integration of safety and health into the theatre production process in compliance with applicable codes, standards, and recommended practices.[2] I wrote this book to provide guidance to theatre practitioners, creative collaborators, and instructors in academic theatre programs to make this integration possible. This book's contents, recommendations, and ideas are based on a theatre safety curriculum I developed and taught at the Yale School of Drama for over 30 years, and the theatre safety program I developed in my role as Director of Theatre Safety and Occupational Health for the Yale School of Drama/Yale Repertory Theatre. The text provides readers with strategies for the identification of hazards in theatre production, methods for risk assessment, and the mitigation of hazards. I include theatre-specific policies, procedures, and recommended practices which can effectively reduce the level of risk and assure code compliance when integrated into a theatre safety and health program. These ideas are bound together by the conceptualization of safety and health as an active participant in the theatre production process. Where will this take us? The goal is to develop, implement, and nurture a positive safety culture in a theatre producing organization or an academic theatre department which is supportive of the organization's mission.

I will demonstrate that safety and health can effectively contribute to the theatre production process while reducing risk and assuring compliance as productions evolve. Regional theatres and academic theatre production organizations are typically time-constrained, and under-resourced. Because of this, the integration of safety and health into the production process might be viewed as a positive goal, but perceived to be financially challenging, a factor that will limit creativity, or an impediment to maintaining an already short time-line. To counter such perceptions, I will examine how safety and health in collaboration with other aspects of the theatre production process promotes creative solutions, helps to maintain schedules, and achieves artistic goals by supporting a positive safety culture within the organization.

Significant and well-publicized accidents, injuries, and deaths related to theatre production since the 1980s have focused attention on the need for a positive culture of safety within the industry. Statistics are difficult to compile, but a few examples will suffice to illustrate the point:

Accidents, Injuries, and Deaths in Theatre Production

1984—Cast, crew, and musicians experience headaches and nausea from exposure to trichloroethane, a component of the cleaning agent used on costumes at the time.

1993—Actor killed by mistakenly loaded stage weapon during filming.

1995—Stagehand fell into an orchestra pit; suffered severe spinal cord injury.

1998—Twelve undergraduate students injured from the collapse of an elevated platform on stage during a performance.

2003—Stage technician died from a 30-foot fall from a catwalk.

2005—An actor fell through a trap door during a performance and broke a rib.

2006—Stage technician had crushing injuries to chest and stomach, and other injuries to face, ear, and jaw, while operating an under-stage elevator-like apparatus in which he got stuck.

2007—An actor broke his leg in three places during a preview performance.

2008—Graduate student killed while unloading scenery from a trailer.

2008—Undergraduate student injured from 25-foot fall from an open section of a tension-wire grid.

2009—Actor injured backstage; hit in the head by a large backdrop during an awards ceremony.

2009—Stage technician died from injuries in a fall from a 30-foot high catwalk while working at a performing arts center.

2010 to 2013—At least six cast members injured during the previews and performances of a show on Broadway.

2010—Lighting designer received serious injuries when an elevated aerial lift without outriggers fell over when moved during focus.

2012—Band drum technician killed and three other stage crew were injured when the temporary roof structure over the stage collapsed.

2013—Participating patron suffered brain and physical injuries from a fall during a performance of a magic act.

2013—Performer died from a fall during a performance.

2013—Conductor died from a fall into unprotected orchestra pit during rehearsal.

2014—Camera operator killed when hit by a train during filming on location.

2014—Employee at university campus arena killed when the 30-foot Genie TWP (lift) tipped over.

2018—Lead singer nearly hit by falling cover from a lighting unit.

2018—Stagehand fell to his death from a balcony on location during the filming of a movie.

2019—Lead rigger fell 60 feet from a lighting scaffold during load-in for an outdoor festival.

Facilities incidents and stage collapses have impacted the industry over the decades. The number of such incidents in a single year highlights their frequency.[3]

2017 Event Structures and Staging Accidents
6-Months: January to June

DATE	WHAT HAPPENED	CAUSE	CITY, NATION
2-Jan	Truss Stage Roof Collapse	High Winds	?, Brazil
20-Feb	Stage Roof Total Collapse	Wind	Sao Miguel, Barzil
20-Feb	Stage Roof Total Collapse	Wind	Belem, Brazil
28-Feb	Stage Roof Skin Ripped Loose	Rain Storm	Minas Geris, Brazil
1-Mar	Lighting Grid Collapse	Crane Towing	Mendoza, Argentina
1-Apr	Scaffolding Tower Collapse	Bad Vertical Joints	?, Mexico
12-Apr	Truss Roof Collapse	Wind	?, China
16-Apr	Stage Roof Collapse	Rain Storm	Cebu, Philipines
16-Apr	Tent Collapse	Wind; Storm	W. Cape, South Africa
20-Apr	Scaffolding Tower & P.A. Collapse	?	?
23-Apr	Stage Floor Collapse	?	Brazil
10-May	Roof Ladder Failed and Canopy Ripped	?	Russia
12-May	LED-Screen Structure Toppled	Wind	Grand Canary Islands
24-May	Audio Scaffolding Tower Collapse	Wind	Perm, Russia
3-Jun	Stage Roof Skin Ripped Off	Wind	Estonia
20-Jun	Stage Roof Collapse	Wind + Rain	Perorinho, Brazil
24-Jun	Stage Roof Collapse	Wind + Rain	Sotocje, Slovenia

FIGURE P.1 2017 Event Structures and Staging Accidents

Fortunately, since the 1980s the integration of safety and health into theatre production has grown in scope and effectiveness. Concepts of hazard identification, risk assessment, and job hazard analysis are implemented in many aspects of production. Industry-based consensus standards for safety and health are becoming the norm in our day-to-day activities. The academic environment has embraced the need to effectively integrate theatre safety and health into their curricula and student training. This book identifies and documents these trends, and is a charge to the industry to build on successes while it continues on the path toward the comprehensive and consistent merging of safety and health into all aspects of theatre production. To paraphrase Arthur Ashe, among others:

> Safety is a journey; a journey as important as the destination. Focus on the journey as you anticipate the destination.[4]

I begin this book's journey by looking more deeply into what is at stake and who is affected by an organization's safety culture. To provide better context for the situation in the industry as of this book's publication, I will provide a representative sampling of theatre organizations and academic institutions with developed and developing theatre safety and health programs. Lest we make assumptions related to what is meant by the term "safety and health program", I will define the term, and discuss what makes a safety and health program successful. (Additional safety and health terms and concepts are defined in the Glossary.) At the core of any safety and health program is compliance with applicable codes and adherence to industry-specific policies, procedures, and recommended practices. These will be identified, and noted with specific reference to their sources and applications. Live theatre production has its own suite of hazards unique to the industry: stage fog; stage weapons; staged violence; live flame; indoor pyrotechnics; and life safety exposures to both employees and patrons. My discussion of policies, procedures, and recommended practices will include specific examples to address these unique hazards along with examples of their successful implementation into the theatre production process. An active, effective, and positive culture of safety will be presented as a means for success on your safety journey that is fully supportive of theatre and the performing arts.

Let's begin.

NOTES

1. Throughout this book I use the term "theatre" to be inclusive of such aspects of the performing arts as drama, ballet, opera, music, and dance performed live before a proximate audience.
2. I use the term "recommended practice" in lieu of "best practice" in this book. I draw guidance from the aviation industry and their definition

of recommended practice: "any specification for physical characteristics, configuration, material, performance, personnel or procedure, the uniform application of which is recognized as desirable in the interest of safety, regularity or efficiency." Wikipedia, "Standards and Recommended Practices," accessed March 26, 2019, https://en.wikipedia.org/wiki/Standards_and_Recommended_Practices.

3 Event Safety Alliance, "2017 Event Structure and Stage Accidents," list compiled by Rinus Bakker, Rhino Staging Company, accessed May 23, 2019, https://www.eventsafetyalliance.org/news/2018/1/5/2017-event-structure-and-stage-accidents.

4 "Success is a journey not a destination. The doing is usually more important than the outcome. Not everyone can be Number 1," Arthur Ashe, accessed November 27, 2018, https://www.goodreads.com/author/quotes/149539.Arthur_Ashe. Also see references to similar citations, accessed November 27, 2018, https://quoteinvestigator.com/2012/08/31/life-journey/.

CHAPTER 1

Introduction and Overview

William J. Reynolds

The activities involved with the development and presentation of a play, an opera, or a live performance event are inherently hazardous. To quote Monona Rossol:

> Theatrical, motion picture, television, and entertainment productions are hazardous endeavors. In fact, it would be hard to imagine an industry with more hazards.[1]

You might be able to name some industries which are more hazardous than theatre,[2] but one of the unique aspects of theatre is our intention to explore risk in all forms as an essential component of what we do. Think of how many theatre mission statements include words such as "challenging," or "experimental," or "innovative," or "fearless," or "risk." Gordon Rogoff gives context to risk in theatre in the Preface to his book of critical essays, *Theatre Is Not Safe*:

> Is there anything better than the theatre when it shines with the actor's presence and the playwright's intelligence? The dream, unfortunately, keeps running out of control. Even so, the risks are worth taking. Theatre is a fugitive form, a completely unprivate art where natural harbors, meditative sanctuaries, and safe places can't be found.[3]

As a collaborator in the theatre production process, your theatre safety and health program must be empowered to encourage theatre productions that are artistically risky, but effectively safe. I write this book to provide tools to identify these hazards, and means and methods to eliminate or mitigate them. My audience is the artistic and technical collaborators who make theatre productions and live entertainment possible.

As this book is being written, the legacy of decades of theatre production related injuries and deaths resonates among theatre practitioners. In addition to the incidents listed in my Preface, I sadly can add:

- The Station nightclub fire in Rhode Island
"A fire occurred on the night of Feb. 20, 2003, in The Station nightclub at 211 Cowesett Avenue, West Warwick, Rhode Island. A band that was on the platform that night, during its performance, used pyrotechnics that ignited polyurethane foam insulation lining the walls and ceiling of the platform. The fire spread quickly along the walls and ceiling area over the dance floor. Smoke was visible in the exit doorways in a little more than one minute, and flames were observed breaking through a portion of the roof in less than five minutes. Egress from the nightclub, which was not equipped with sprinklers, was hampered by crowding at the main entrance to the building. One hundred people lost their lives in the fire."[4]

- Indiana State Fair collapse
"On August 13, 2011, nearly 12,000 people were awaiting the start of the Sugarland performance at the Grandstand Stage at the Indiana State Fairgrounds. At approximately 8:46 p.m., the temporary structure supporting spotlights and other equipment mounted on top of the Grandstand Stage collapsed."[5] "A wind gust from an approaching severe thunderstorm hit the stage's temporary roof structure, causing it to collapse. The structure landed among a crowd of spectators, killing seven people and injuring 58 others."[6]

- Ringling Bros. and Barnum & Baily Circus hair-hang accident
"On May 4, 2014, an incident occurred at the Dunkin' Donut Center in Providence, Rhode Island during the 11:00 a.m. performance of 'Ringling Bros. and Barnum & Bailey Presents Legends'. At the time of the incident, the 'Hang Hair Act' was being enacted. The 'Hang Hair Act' involved eight performers in an aerial act where the

performers, aka hairialists, were suspended from their hair alone with their hands and feet free to perform swinging and spinning motions in a choreographed acrobatic manner. Suddenly, during the act, the metal apparatus supporting the performers plummeted in excess of 20 feet to the floor below along with the performers injuring all eight performers to varying degrees. Two of the performers sustained critical injuries. A dancer on the floor was also caught in the mishap, and was also injured. In total, there were injuries to nine employees. Rescue workers and police immediately responded to the call, and the injured performers were taken to the nearby hospital."[7]

The theatre industry has responded to these accidents, injuries, and deaths with the development of theatre-specific safety and health standards, workplace recommended practices,[8] theatre-focused safety training programs, more comprehensive adoption of safety and health practices from other industries, and increasing compliance with national safety codes. The breadth of the industry's responses can be seen in the gains made in fall protection practices, stage fog exposure limits, and control technologies for automation systems, to name only a few. In spite of these gains, we must acknowledge the need for more effective integration of safety and health programs into our daily theatre production operations.

This book will address the integration of safety and health programs in theatre production activities for those theatre professionals actively engaged in live entertainment outside of an academic setting. I will also provide the educators and mentors of the next generation of theatre practitioners with practical guidance on the safety and health knowledge and skills their students must have for success in their future employment. As awareness and focus on safety and health continues to grow in the industry, so too will the expectation for expertise and skills in the areas of safety and health of those working in theatres.

The safety, health, and well-being of those involved in all aspects of a theatre production, as well as of the patrons who attend these live events, depends to a large extent on a positive and effective safety culture in the producing organization or academic department. Over the ensuing chapters of this book, I will investigate and detail many aspects of theatre safety and health programs. Those who manage theatre productions, producing organizations, and academic theatre departments can utilize these aspects to develop a robust safety culture appropriate to their organization. My goal is to give the reader an awareness of what is possible for safety and health in theatre production, and provide examples of techniques to effectively integrate safety and health into their theatre production process.

A theatre production is the result of the effective integration of many diverse elements: script or concept, direction, creative talent, management, design, technology, and resources. This integration is achieved through the active collaboration of individuals with unique skills in specific areas who work together to create the whole: a live theatre production or performance event.

> This type of interdependence among everyone within the organization signals the needs for everyone to be part of the collaborative process; awareness of this is intrinsic to possible success in the theatre.[9]

The effectiveness of a theatre organization's safety culture is dependent on the extent to which safety and health takes a seat as a collaborator at the production table. Individually and collectively within each department's focus, safety and health must be integrated as an element of the collaborative process. Over the several chapters of this book I will examine the ways a positive culture of safety evolves from this collaboration.

To start, we need to investigate who is most affected by the lack of an effective safety and health program in a theatre producing organization, and who within these organizations is best positioned to develop and integrate such programs into their production environment. There is much at stake when the risks involved in theatre production are misunderstood, ignored, or minimized. Generalizing the potential hazards of production may blur our ability to focus on each hazard specifically and may reduce the effectiveness of our planning and response. Because of this, I will present a conceptualization of the hazards into two broad categories: fixed (routine production activities) and fluid (hazards unique to each production). This dichotomy will assist our discussion of theatre safety and health programs by establishing a slightly different focus of attention toward the identification of hazards and the reduction of risk.

But first, let's address the question, "Who is affected by the lack of effective safety and health programs in theatre production?" One answer might be, "Everyone." Certainly the case can be made that anyone connected to an incident (a near-miss or a serious accident) is affected by its consequences. If Everyone is affected by the lack of safety and health programs, it follows that Everyone benefits from the integration of such programs into the theatre production process. It is essential to determine who is most directly affected by this lack and, then, who is in the best position to implement measures to either prevent accidents or mitigate negative consequences. The primary audience for this book is the latter group: administrative and technical managers in theatre production companies and academic theatre departments. They are in positions of power and influence within their organizations. They can identify the needs, and take the steps necessary to develop and implement a safety and health program in their organizations. In academia, this group of influencers is comprised of the educators who develop curricula, conduct classes, and train subsequent generations of theatre administrators and practitioners. For theatre students and early-career theatre professionals, this book will further their education by providing an overview of the theatre safety and health knowledge required for their employment and success in their chosen careers.

Given the variety of risks inherent in the production of live theatre, we should acknowledge what is at stake. The list of incidents already noted contains many of the most serious of these consequences: death or life-altering serious injury. Another negative outcome is an interruption of the production process. An interruption in the plan for a theatre production (work stoppage caused by an accident or injury) will require an unanticipated demand for additional resources, loss of human resources through injury, time required to stop, assess, regroup, and correct the problem, and material resources to correct deficiencies or repair damaged equipment. Even a near-miss can result in the need to alter the carefully planned schedule, and might require additional resources to maintain a production time-line constrained by a deadline we call Opening Night:

> The last few tasks of a show's load-in are being completed before the start of technical rehearsals onstage. Just before "places" is called, an unsecured piece of equipment falls from the mid-rail catwalk. No one is injured by the falling equipment, but the up-stage cyc [cyclorama] was torn, making it unusable for setting lighting cues. The technical rehearsal proceeds once the scene is made safe, but an additional cue-setting session for the entire cast and crew must be scheduled once the cyc is repaired or replaced. In addition, resources of time, expertise, and money must be identified for repairs, or to purchase and replace the cyc.

Potential financial risks go beyond those related to scenery. Our most precious resource—the people involved (euphemistically called human capital)—is the most challenging to replace. The initial response to an injury requires at minimum a work stoppage, medical attention to those directly involved, assessment of hazards, and a determination of the ability to continue work. The latter entails an assessment of your human capital on two levels. One: is the production's personnel emotionally capable of "moving-on"? Another: can the production continue with the remaining staff? There may be an understudy to replace an injured cast member, or an assistant electrician who might stand in for an injured lighting board operator, but most under-resourced theatre organizations do not have access to people who are adequately trained and readily available to fill a critical role left empty by an injury.

Finally, the lack of an effective safety and health program can have the effect of limiting the career longevity of those who expect lifelong work in the theatre. The impact of multiple minor injuries, inadequate ergonomic workplaces, or exposures to hazardous chemicals or air contaminants can result in a talented theatre practitioner having to change careers, or to leave employment in the theatre altogether. A more subtle but equally consequential impact of limited attention to safety and health in the workplace is low morale and burn-out. A safety and health program by its very implementation sends many important messages to your staff, employees, students, and volunteers. A statement of caring about them is implicit in the program's mission; in the stepping forward by leaders and senior managers supporting the safety program; in the allocation of resources toward safety and health; and in employee (and/or student) participation in the development and success of the program.

Correlating employee participation and job satisfaction is important in many organizations, and is a positive consequence of an effective safety and health program. A research report by the Society for Human Resource Management noted that in their survey of employee job satisfaction: "Fifty percent of employees reported that feeling safe in the work environment was very important to their job satisfaction."[10] Our theatre organizations and academic departments are typically limited in their ability to provide adequate salary or benefits as rewards for excellence. While salary and benefits are important, employee engagement and participation in an active safety and health program form a dynamic means to assure a positive safety culture.[11]

The division of hazards into the two broad categories of fixed and fluid will assist us in our ensuing discussion of the hazards in theatre production, and their risks. The fixed hazards are related to routine production activities and typical fabrication processes. Such things as the hazards associated with inadequate flooring surfaces in the rehearsal hall, machine tool hazards in the fabrication shops, and fall hazards during load-in are considered fixed. Other examples are health exposures to hazardous chemicals in the paint and costume shops, and hazards related to permanent stage machinery or equipment (lifts, winches, counterweight systems, company switches, etc.). Tasks required during load-ins and strikes often involve repeated activities utilizing carts, trucks, manual lifting, fork lifts, ladders, scaffolding, and mobile elevated work platforms (MEWPs), among other materials handling equipment. All of these fixed hazards require specific assessment and the mitigation of their risks through training, equipment maintenance, and documentation of related safety policies and procedures. For instance, water on the floor around the sinks and dye vats in a costume shop crafts room can be evaluated as a slip and fall hazard, which can be mitigated with floor drains, and a raised flooring for the work surface. Once assessed and their mitigation integrated into the safety and health program, fixed hazards do not typically require frequent revaluation.

On the other hand, each theatre production introduces a unique set of hazards, which I will call fluid hazards. These fluid hazards must be assessed, evaluated, and mitigated for each production, or for each staging concept added to an ongoing production. To do so, a collaboration between safety and health concerns and the rest of the production's creative and technical team is required. An example is water onstage in a production, which presents unique hazards. For one production I worked on, we identified the slip and fall hazard of a wet stage floor. This hazard was mitigated by adding anti-slip floor treatment to the paint finish. In addition, due to the storing and recycling of the water during the run of the show, we had to evaluate the potential for bacterial growth in the water, and the likelihood of contact infection by actors and stage personnel. A small amount of bleach and recirculating the water within the storage tanks proved be a successful mitigation for this "fluid" hazard. Electrical hazards were identified due to the adjacency of water to stage electrical equipment. These hazards were mitigated with extensive use of GFCI (ground-fault circuit interrupter) protection. Other hazards might be identified when water is included as a design element for a show, such as slippery walking surfaces requiring slip-resistant footwear for actors and techical staff, or floor damage due to the tracking of water through backstage areas. Only through the careful assessment of these fluid hazards as part of the organization's safety and health program can the risk be brought to an acceptable level.

I will explore the ideas related to fixed and fluid hazards in subsequent chapters. In the next chapter I will review examples of how safety and health programs are currently being integrated into theatre production organizations and theatre departments of academic institutions. From these examples, and discussions of different aspects of their theatre safety and health programs, we'll be able to discern how such hazards are addressed by their programs, policies, and procedures.

NOTES

1. Monona Rossol, *The Health and Safety Guide for Film, TV, and Theater*, 2nd edition (New York: Allworth Press, Inc., 2011), xv.
2. Throughout this book I use the term "theatre" to include such aspects of the performing arts as drama, ballet, opera, music, and dance performed live before a proximate audience.
3. Gordon Rogoff, *Theater Is Not Safe: Theatre Criticism 1962–1986* (Evanston, IL: Northwestern University Press, 1987), xiii.
4. NIST NCSTAR 2: Vol. I, *Report of the Technical Investigation of The Station Nightclub Fire*, page iii, accessed April 12, 2019, https://ws680.nist.gov/publication/get_pdf.cfm?pub_id=100988.
5. Witt Associates, *Assessment of 2011 Indiana State Fair Collapse Incident, Part I. Executive Summary*, page 7, accessed April 12, 2019, https://www.wittobriens.com/wp-content/uploads/2017/09/171758_1883990_3448726_1_6041423_Witt-Associates-Indiana-State-Fair-Report-April-2012.pdf.
6. Wikipedia, "Indiana State Fair Stage Collapse," accessed April 12, 2019, https://en.wikipedia.org/wiki/Indiana_State_Fair_stage_collapse.
7. Occupational Safety and Health Administration (OSHA), *Investigation of the May 4, 2014 Incident at the Ringling Bros. and Barnum & Bailey Performance in Providence, RI, October, 2014*, page 6, accessed April 12, 2019, https://www.osha.gov/doc/engineering/2014_r_05.html.
8. I will consistently use the term "recommended practice" in lieu of "best practice." For doing this, I draw guidance from the aviation industry and their definition of recommended practice: "any specification for physical characteristics, configuration, material, performance, personnel or procedure, the uniform application of which is recognized as desirable in the interest of safety, regularity or efficiency," Wikipedia, "Standards and Recommended Practices," accessed March 26, 2019, https://en.wikipedia.org/wiki/Standards_and_Recommended_Practices.
9. Robert I. Sutherland, *Introduction to Production: Creating Theatre Onstage, Backstage, & Offstage* (New York: Routledge, 2018), 2.
10. Christina Lee, Society for Human Resource Management, *Employee Job Satisfaction and Engagement: Revitalizing Changing Workforce*, page 32, accessed June 18, 2019, https://www.shrm.org/hr-today/trends-and-forecasting/research-and-surveys/Documents/2016-Employee-Job-Satisfaction-and-Engagement-Report.pdf.

11 Karen Price, "Employee Engagement Improves Safety," accessed May 23, 2019, https://www.coverys.com/knowledgecenter/Articles/Employee-Engagement-Improves-Safety. And, Jeff Ross, "Improving Safety through Employee Engagement," accessed May 23, 2019, https://www.cashort.com/blog/employee-engagement-is-key-to-improving-workplace-safety.

BIBLIOGRAPHY

Barylick, John. *Killer Show: The Station Nightclub Fire, American's Deadliest Rock Concert*. Lebanon, NH: University Press of New England, 2012.

Rogoff, Gordon. *Theater Is Not Safe: Theatre Criticism 1962–1986*. Evanston, IL: Northwestern University Press, 1987.

Rossol, Monona. *The Health and Safety Guide for Film, TV, and Theater*, 2nd edition. New York: Allworth Press, 2011.

Sutherland-Cohen, Robert I. *Introduction to Production: Creating Theatre Onstage, Backstage & Offstage*. New York: Routledge, 2018.

CHAPTER 2

Safety Evolves Within the Theatre Industry

William J. Reynolds

In the Fall of 2017, I presented several conference sessions and a keynote address at the Minnesota Theater Alliance Statewide Theater Conference in Minneapolis. In preparation for my keynote, I did a brief survey of the then-current state of safety and health programs in theatre production in the United States. Through internet searches, responses to email inquiries sent to theatre practitioners, and a review of documents collected over years of teaching theatre safety, I found much had been implemented in theatre programs at colleges and universities, as well as in the production processes of theatre organizations. Over 16 college or university theatre departments responded that they include theatre safety and health in their curricula. Most augmented in-class teaching with specific safety training; 13 had developed and implemented theatre safety and health manuals or handbooks. Eight colleges or universities had such programs managed by their Environmental Health and Safety Office on a campus-wide basis. Over 10 theatre producing organizations were acknowledged to have safety programs as part of their operations. At the time, I took this list to represent the tip of the theatre safety iceberg, and further research has borne out this assumption. (A list of such colleges, universities and organizations as of the date of publication is included in the Appendix at the end of this book.)

These growing numbers are an acknowledgement of the integration of safety and health programs into the training and production activities in the industry. While there has been progress, we do not have to look back very far to recognize the deficiencies that previously existed in the training of theatre practitioners, and in the production of live theatre events. Any of us who were active in the industry in the 1970s can attest to the lack of fall protection, the cavalier use of hazardous materials, the limited use of PPE (personal protective equipment), and the presence of flammable if not explosive materials in stage effects.

By way of example, consider that the Occupational Safety and Health (OSH) Act was passed by the U.S. Congress and signed into law by then-president Richard M. Nixon in December 1970. The Occupational Health and Safety Administration (OSHA) was established the following year on April 28, 1971. OSHA's Asbestos Standard was issued in 1972.[1] In the same year, as an undergraduate theatre student, I was tossing handfuls of loose asbestos fibers from a 20-pound bag into a 5-gallon bucket to mix with scene paint to create texture. I was wearing neither gloves, nor protective eyewear, nor any respiratory protection and was working in a paint area that had no industrial ventilation and was not separated from the fabrication space.

During OSHA's initial decades, the theatre industry was admittedly slow to adopt or even acknowledge its applicable standards. I can remember in the 1980s earnest conversations among theatre practitioners questioning whether OSHA even applied to us, "There are no OSHA standards for theatre production? Right?" Subsequent decades, though, provide examples of an accelerating catching-up within the industry:

- The integration of OSHA standards into theatre production operations.
- Safety and health training required of theatre production staff.
- The utilization of risk-based assessments of hazards.
- The creation of consensus-based theatre safety and health standards.
- The development and implementation of recommended practices for safety and health within the industry.

The impetus for this growth in theatre safety and health programs since the 1970s has come from several directions. Applying OSHA standards to the activities and workplaces of the entertainment industry gained clarity and acceptance in the decades after OSHA's inception. In 1997, in a Letter of Interpretation OSHA replied to an inquiry from an IATSE senior stage rigger related to fall protection in the entertainment industry. Among the specifics included in OSHA's reply is an affirmation of OSHA standards applicability to the industry: "the entertainment industry would be covered under the general industry standards . . . there are some construction jobs [in the entertainment industry that] would be required to follow the construction standards."[2] This assertion is followed by a statement clarifying OSHA's expectation for compliance with OSHA standards at workplaces in the theatre:

> OSHA is concerned with the safety and health of all workers in the entertainment industry. Although OSHA recognizes it is not appropriate to put guardrails at the edges of stages, theatrical employees need to be protected from all occupational safety and health hazards. The fall protection standards for general industry . . . as well as the personal protection equipment standards are the appropriate standards for your situation.[3]

Possibly the most public impetus toward this growth in safety and health programs was increased awareness of the hazards inherent in theatre productions from high-profile accidents, injuries, and deaths, some of which were noted earlier in this text. Such incidents resulted in a number of inspections, investigations, citations, and fines from OSHA.[4] In 2010, then-director of OSHA, David Michaels, highlighted this awareness when he was interviewed after the death of a stagehand from a fall at a performing arts center in Florida:

> "We've seen several examples of employers in the entertainment industry that have not provided precautions adequate to protect workers. And we've seen fatalities as a result of that," Assistant Labor Secretary and OSHA Director David Michaels said Thursday during a conference call with reporters for the Orlando Sentinel. "There's a tremendous amount of risky work in these facilities and safety is often not considered the highest priority in these cases," Michaels said.[5]

Within the theatre industry, safety and health evolved as a priority through the efforts of several entertainment industry organizations. These organizations and their members contributed ideas and resources to this evolution. I will cite just a few of these organizations to illustrate the decades-long growth of safety and health from within the industry:

- Actors' Equity Association (AEA).
- Entertainment Services and Technology Association (ESTA).
- Event Safety Alliance (ESA).
- International Alliance of Theatrical Stage Employees (IATSE).
- United States Institute for Theatre Technology (USITT).

Members of these organizations identified the need for industry-generated safety and health standards and recommended practices. They responded by developing specific standards and recommended practices for the industry over the past several decades. The dates related to these developments coincide with the 30-plus years of growth in safety and health programs within the entertainment industry.

- The Actors' Equity Association (AEA), often referred to as Equity, was founded in 1913. The union was established to represent and protect the rights of actors and stage mangers in the entertainment industry. The beginning of the 20th century was a period when "exploitation had become a permanent condition of an actor's employment."[6] AEA responded to this exploitation through its efforts on behalf of AEA members to improve working conditions, and provide health and pension plans. The safety and health of AEA members continues to be an essential aspect of AEA activities. Since the 1960s, to assure the healthcare of AEA members, producers are required to contribute to the Equity-League Pension and Health Trust Funds.[7] Equity contracts contain AEA's Safe and Sanitary Workplace Rules, which cover areas of safety and health for performers and stage managers including: first aid kits, exposure to theatrical smoke and haze, evaluation of toxic materials and emergency evacuation and fire safety procedures. Venues are subject to inspection by an AEA representative to confirm compliance with Equity's safe and sanitary contract provisions.[8] AEA members participated in the research and exposure testing, which resulted in guidelines for stage fog and haze exposures developed by ENVIRON in 2000.[9] To mitigate ergonomic injuries caused by repeatedly performing on an inclined surface, the angle of raked stages is regulated by certain Equity contracts, and a qualified raked stage instructor may be required to train AEA members who work on such stages.

- The Entertainment Services and Technology Association's vision (ESTA) is to, "Build the business of show business through networking, safe practices, education, and representation."[10] ESTA published its first consensus ANSI-compliant standard in 1999: ANSI E1.1—1999—Entertainment Technology—Construction and Use of Wire Rope Ladders.[11] In the intervening years, over 65 entertainment industry consensus standards, guidelines, and recommended practices have been published and made freely available online. In 2003, ESTA established a personnel certification program for technicians in the entertainment industry. ESTA collaborated with "an unprecedented group of industry organizations, businesses, and subject matter experts to craft a program of rigorous assessments for professional technicians."[12] Entertainment Technician Certification Program (ETCP) Certified Technicians are recognized throughout the industry as riggers and electricians whose knowledge, skills, and capabilities have been evaluated through rigorous examination and experiential requirements. As of March, 2019, there were over 2,780 ETCP-certified practitioners in the entertainment industry.

- The Event Safety Alliance (ESA) website states that the organization is, "dedicated to promoting 'life safety first' throughout all phases of event production and execution. ESA's mission is to help event professionals and our guests be *Empowered*, *Safe*, and *Aware* of the reasonably foreseeable risks around them."[13] In 2011, the stage roof collapse at the Indiana State Fair, which left seven people dead and more than 50 injured,[14] directed public and industry attention to the need to emphasize safe practices related to the planning and management of live events. ESA was established in 2012 in direct response to the horrors of Indiana and the three other outdoor stage roof collapses that occurred within a few weeks of each other during the Summer of 2011. ESA's annual Event Safety Summit provides the entertainment industry with networking and training related to the planning and management of live performance events in a variety of venues. The ESA Severe Weather Summit, held each year, focuses attention on potential weather disruption of live events "to aid event and venue professionals of all types in preparing for and responding to dangerous weather conditions."[15] Training is a core component of ESA's mission. Several event safety training and credentialing programs are sponsored by ESA, including Crowd Safety Symposium, Event Safety University, and Event Safety Access Training. In addition to promoting event and life safety training, and coordination of activities among event managers, promoters, and technicians, ESA publishes *The Event Safety Guide*. As described on the ESA website, "*The Event Safety Guide* compiles the best operational practices currently available in the live event industry in a single easily-referenced manual."[16] As of this writing, ESA is collaborating with ESTA to expand upon key chapters of *The Event Safety Guide* to turn them into ANSI standards for the industry, beginning with a first-of-its-kind standard for Crowd Management. ESA has broadened its outreach in the years since its inception by partnering with international affiliates in the entertainment industry, including organizations in Canada, Germany, China, and South Africa.[17]

- The International Alliance of Theatrical Stage Employees (IATSE)[18] traces its roots back to the 1880s; the first Local One member's card was issued in 1886.[19] Training in stage technical skills and industry recommended practices has been part of its activities on behalf of its members since the beginning. Focused efforts in safety and health training for

IATSE members were strengthened toward the end of the 20th century. In 2009, the IATSE Craft Advancement Program (ICAP) was created.[20] The implementation of this Program helped shape the 2011 creation of the IATSE Entertainment and Exhibition Industries Training Trust Fund (TTF).[21] The IATSE mission includes safety as an essential value among its Four Pillars of Success for the Union:

The nature of IATSE members' entertainment-industry jobs means working for many different employers, making a consistent expectation of safety a challenge. Through training, safety committees, safety programs, and participating in standards writing, the IATSE International leadership is committed to making the jobs members show up for daily as safe as possible.[22]

The TTF supports a range of safety and health courses, training, and digital resources. The outreach of TTF for IATSE members, and non-members working under an IATSE contract, includes funding to defray the cost of safety training and certifications. TTF benefits, such as the Safety First! Online Courses,[23] are available free to IATSE members. Other IATSE safety and health initiatives include:

- The IATSE Safety Hotline,[24] created in 2015 to enable IATSE members to report hazards on the job.
- The IATSE Safety Info App, an information and hazard reporting tool for IATSE members.
- The OSHA-USIIT-IATSE Alliance,[25] created in 2013 and renewed in 2018, as part of OSHA's National Alliance Program to coordinate safety and health within the entertainment industry through training and education.

- The United States Institute for Theatre Technology (USITT) was established in 1960 to support entertainment industry designers, technicians, practitioners, and educators through networking and advocacy.

The health and safety of theatrical designers and technicians has been a core concern of USITT since its birth as a professional organization. As early as 1964 a committee was formed to work on theatre related portions of New York City's Building Code.[26]

USITT is organized around several design, technical, and management Commissions that coordinate the planning of annual conference sessions, and promote the ongoing work of the Institute through each Commission's outreach activities. In 1973, the USITT Safety and Health Commission was established as one of 11 USITT Commissions, and remains active within the Institute.[27] For example, in addition to the conference sessions programmed by the Safety and Health Commission, each of the other USITT Commissions is required to program a safety- or health-related session as part of its offerings at the USITT Annual Conference and Stage Expo. In 1986, one of the first industry recommended practices, USITT DMX512, was developed by a USITT Committee. This recommended practice evolved through industry input and updating of technical data into ANSI E1.11—2008 (USITT DMX512-A), a standard which continues to define the communication protocol between stage lighting dimmers and lighting control boards.[28]

The collective efforts of these and other entertainment industry organizations have resulted in the theatre production industry moving into the 21st century with a much stronger and more comprehensive theatre safety culture than that of the mid-20th century.

The existence of theatre industry–specific safety and health standards and recommended practices does not automatically result in the reduction of risk, the elimination of hazards, or the prevention of accidents. Indeed, even the improper utilization of a single piece of rigging hardware can result in a significant incident, as witnessed by the hair-hang accident during a performance of an aerial act in the 2014 Barnum & Baily Circus. To quote from the OSHA news release at the time: "this incident occurred because the carabiner used to support the performers failed from being improperly loaded."[29] To be effective, safety and health standards, recommended practices, and training must be adopted, implemented, and integrated into the operation of theatre production organizations, and academic institutions.

Many theatre organizations have adopted industry standards and recommended practices, and effectively integrated safety and health into their operations. Their continued artistic and organizational success while doing so is an acknowledgement that a safety and health program is not an impediment to the creative and collaborative process required for a theatre to thrive. From many possible examples of this, let's take a closer look at several theatre organizations where safety and health is effectively integrated into the production process. Their safety and health programs assure compliance with codes and standards, provide for the safety and health of employees and audiences, identify hazards and reduce risks, all while collaborating in support of the creative process for each production. The following was developed from interviews with the production leadership, and a review of the safety and health program documents and policies for:

- Glimmerglass Festival
- Goodman Theatre
- Milwaukee Repertory Theater
- Oregon Shakespeare Festival
- Yale Repertory Theatre.

GLIMMERGLASS FESTIVAL

The Glimmerglass Festival's first production was in 1975 (*La Bohème*).[30] The Festival's current seasons include four major productions performing in rotating repertory plus concerts, production of new works, lectures, and youth performances: all condensed into a summer season of performances that start in July and end in the third week of August. Located in Cooperstown, upstate New York, the theatre has benefited from strong and diverse support from the local community. Like many summer theatre operations, Glimmerglass Festival faces the challenge of the rapid expansion of production activity and staff from the relative calm of the off-season months (with around 30 people employed) to the energy and engagement of preparation, fabrication, and rehearsals beginning in May of each year as the staff grows over several weeks to around 400. This annual cycle has had a profound effect on the evolution of the Festival's safety and health program.

A move to a new theatre for the Festival's productions in 1987,[31] a commensurate expansion of production activity, and the hiring of a new production management team combined to focus efforts on the expansion and codification of its safety and health program. Outreach to several funding sources resulted in the Festival obtaining grants that permitted the hiring of safety professionals to provide guidance, inspections, and training in areas related to industrial hygiene (such as chemical safety and health exposures), stage rigging, and fabrication processes such as welding. The New York State OSHA On-site Consultation Program[32] was tapped as an adjunct to this process. The Consultation Program provided safety consultants for advice and guidance, and safety inspections with detailed reporting of findings and agreed-upon time-lines for the Festival to correct deficiencies. In conjunction with these safety professionals and staff from the OSHA Consultation Program, a comprehensive safety manual was developed and documented. An additional benefit from engaging these safety professionals was their authoritative documentation of hazards, recommendations to correct them, guidance on safety policies to be implemented, and safety training for the Festival's staff. This multi-pronged approach established the Festival's safety and health program as a model for other theatre organizations to emulate.

The Festival's production and staffing cycle influenced the safety and health program's emphasis on training and documentation. Each season's influx of young and early-career theatre practitioners, 40 percent of whom are new to the Festival's operations, creates both a challenge and an opportunity. The challenge is represented by the commitment of resources (time and professional staff) for three or more days of training as each department's staff and interns arrive. Each season's training cycle provides an opportunity to imprint virtually the entire Festival staff with the safety culture inherent in the organization's operations. An essential element to successfully meeting the training challenge was the establishment of the position of Safety Coordinator for the Festival. The person in this role arrives in Cooperstown two weeks before the rest of the production and operations staff to ready the Festival's facilities for the upcoming season, prepare for the ramp-up of staff and interns, and update safety training and related policies in anticipation of the production season's start. After coordinating and providing safety orientation and training for the new staff and interns in June, the Safety Coordinator's focus shifts to oversight of production-related hazards, means and methods for their mitigation, and checklists for such hazards as slips and falls, stage weapons, and live flame onstage. The hazard assessments completed by the Safety Coordinator result in a safety plan for each show to be used by that show's run crew and stage operations staff. Once the shows are open and running in repertory, the Safety Coordinator maintains oversight for safety and health for the shows in conference with each show's production team.

Community resources continue to support Glimmerglass Festival's safety and health program's ongoing effectiveness. Community support for the Festival originated in its roots when in early 1970 several community leaders gathered to "start a theatre." As the scale of production increased over the 1990s, and the safety and health program expanded to keep pace, people and organizations in Cooperstown and the local region provided support of all kinds to the Festival. This support is particularly evident in the safety and health program. Some examples:

- Health professionals from the local hospital provide fit testing and health monitoring for the respiratory protection program, and noise exposure monitoring and hearing testing for production staff.

- Staff from a gym and fitness center conduct ergonomic assessments and assist in the development of stretching exercises for several departments.

- The Festival has collaborated with a police dog training facility in the area for the use of theatre facilities for bomb and drug sniffing dog training.

- Key production department staff have been trained by local EMS (Emergency Medical Services) as first responders to allow oxygen and other response equipment to be located onsite.

Both as supporters and patrons, the local community remains very engaged in the operations of the Festival.

An important aspect to note is the interdependent relationships among the artistic success of the Festival's productions, the integration of the safety and health program in the Festival's operations, and the level of trust that exists between the artistic and production staff within the organization. Because of a strong safety and health program and the associated culture of safety in the organization, the production manager, technical director, and other key production departments heads are trusted in their assessments of hazards. Their input into creative ways to reduce the level of risk presented by a design element or production idea is welcome because they are perceived to be equal collaborators in the production process.[33]

GOODMAN THEATRE

Goodman Theatre initiated its long and successful history in the Fall of 1925 in Chicago.[34] The bequest that helped establish Goodman Theatre in the 1920s was grounded in a "vision of an ideal theatre, one that would combine professional training with the highest possible performance standards."[35] The organization continues to maintain this dual focus on training through education and performance through professional productions. Over many decades of operation, including a move to a new theatre and production facility in 2000, safety and health was a common practice incorporated in the theatre's production activities. In 2005, working with Goodman Theatre's insurance broker, the theatre's administrative and production staff began compiling the existing safety and health practices of the various departments into a formalized and cohesive program to serve the entire organization. Their broker's recommendation to do so was based on industry recommended practices, and to better manage insurance rates and workers' compensation costs. To support this effort, the insurance broker provided guidance, support, and assistance in the form of an industrial hygienist and other staff from their risk assessment department. The consultants from the insurance broker effectively engaged with the theatre's staff, and provided reassurance that this effort to develop and implement a safety and health program would take time. A core group of theatre staff worked on the program's development, consulting with key stakeholders including staff from several departments in the organization. The program took five years to complete, and was fully rolled out to the entire staff in 2011.

Among the attributes of Goodman Theatre's Health and Safety Program is its comprehensiveness. This includes engagement and support from all parts of the organization, including a review of safety and health as part of every employee's annual performance evaluation. Employees at the Goodman strongly support the program, with department supervisors providing effective oversight of health and safety in the theatre's daily operations. Communication is open and welcome at all levels, with a variety of ways for employees to make suggestions and report incidents, including an email address dedicated to the reporting of safety and health incidents, concerns, and suggestions. Goodman Theatre's safety program has benefited from a partnership formed with the Health in the Arts program, part of the School of Public Health at the University of Illinois at Chicago.[36] Doctors in occupational medicine and graduate students in the Health in the Arts program provide training and guidance to the theatre in its daily activities and fabrication processes, as well as consulting on production-related hazard assessments.

The safety culture engendered by Goodman Theatre's Health and Safety Program assures routine identification of production hazards, and evaluation of risks as each production evolves from conception to implementation. The Health and Safety Program is recognized as an essential element in the collaboration with the creative team as part of the production process for each show. Through many years of such collaboration, Goodman Theatre's production staff have strived to understand the goals of a show's creative team in order to provide creative, low-risk solutions to production challenges. Visiting artists and directors who routinely work at the Goodman have come to expect and appreciate the creative contributions related to safety and health from the theatre's technical and production departments. The Health and Safety Program has been a key element in the evolution of the organization's positive safety culture.[37]

MILWAUKEE REPERTORY THEATER

The Milwaukee Rep was established in 1954. Initially producing seasons of Broadway hits with casts of well-known performers, the Milwaukee Rep evolved in the 1960s into a regional theatre with a resident acting company. Production activities include 12 major productions each season, along with smaller projects and a variety of community and educational outreach programs.[38] Along with its peer regional theatres, the Milwaukee Rep organization increasingly integrated aspects of safety and health into its production activities. In 2009, with the establishment of the position of Assistant Production Manager (AMP), resources of time and expertise were in place for the theatre to more fully coordinate existing safety and health policies into a cohesive safety and health program. This impulse was strengthened by the confluence of several other factors, among them a realization by the theatre's senior leadership of the value of a well-documented safety and health program, and the newly hired APM's experience with theatre safety and health programs. A safety manual that codifies the safety and health program for the Milwaukee Rep was a significant outcome of this convergence of organizational support and expertise.

As is typical of any safety and health program, it is a work in progress. Activities of the program include safety training for employees, consisting of biannual training for new employees, and incremental training for all employees when updates or additions to the safety manual are implemented. These periodic training sessions cover general aspects of the program for all employees, such as accident and incident reporting, evacuation procedures, and ergonomic assessments. Staff are also trained in emergency response to such situations as an active shooter, as well as CPR training and AED use (cardio pulmonary resuscitation/automated external defibrillator). For the production department staff, additional time is scheduled to provide training in hazardous communication (haz comm), chemical safety, personnel lifts, and electrical safety, among other technical topics. Their haz comm program maintains a chemical products inventory and binders of SDS (safety data sheets) for each of the production shops. To assist with this aspect of the haz comm program, technology such as bar code readers is used to locate and update SDS and chemical safety information for the various products used in production. Technical department managers are required to submit updates to the chemical inventory as well as appropriate SDS when new chemical products are obtained. For each of the 12 shows produced in a season, the cast, crew, and creative team receive training at the start of tech rehearsals on the theatre's safety and health policies, incident reporting, emergency response, and evacuation procedures.

Organizational support for the safety and health program includes resources for staff training, such as in rigging safety, and for the hiring of a stage rigging company to conduct a comprehensive inspection and assessment of the theatre's rigging systems. The latter resulted in recommendations for repairs and improvements, which were prioritized and completed with specific monies allocated. Funds are designated in the organization's annual budget for safety and health equipment and supplies. The theatre's annual budget also supports first aid and CPR/AED training, required for specific staff (front-of-house and production staff), but open for any Milwaukee Rep employee. Other support comes from the theatre's insurance carrier(s), particularly in the form of consultation and training on ergonomics, and walk-thru safety inspections of stages and production facilities.

The production leadership of the Milwaukee Rep recognizes their safety and health program is an ongoing project. They acknowledge that they began with basic but essential parts of the program and are committed to build on these successes. While experiencing some challenges, most employees are supportive of the theatre's safety culture and participate in the program's implementation and evolution. And typical of many similar theatre producing organizations, they face issues related to older buildings (renovated not purpose-built), facilities, and legacy equipment used for fabrication and productions.[39]

OREGON SHAKESPEARE FESTIVAL

The Oregon Shakespeare Festival (OSF) in Ashland traces its beginnings to the Chautauqua Movement that thrived across the United States between 1880 and 1930. The Chautauqua Movement, patterned after the Chautauqua Institute's activities in Chautauqua, New York, established local performance centers for lectures, debates, and entertainment in hundreds of communities across the country.[40] "'Chautauqua' had a degree of cachet and became shorthand for an organized gathering intended to introduce people to the great ideas, new ideas, and issues of public concern."[41] These roots in Chautauqua provided the OSF with several of the foundations on which its over 85-year history rest. One of these was an actual foundation: the remains of the circular concrete wall of the original Chautauqua building in Ashland. This wall formed an enclosure for the OSF's first productions in 1935. (The circular concrete walls reminded the OSF founders of typical Elizabethan theatre floorplans, hence the choice of playwright for the first few decades of OSF productions.[42]) Another foundational aspect is support from the local community.

The Oregon Shakespeare Festival's performance activities have expanded from its early roots of four productions each summer season to the current 11-production season extending from March through October. In the 1950s, the season began to include works by playwrights other than Shakespeare, and current seasons provide an eclectic mix of playwrights, genres, and levels of productions. The OSF comprises three performance venues, several fabrication shops, classrooms for educational programs, and a center dedicated to rehearsal activities. One of the performance venues is an open-air amphitheatre modeled after the layout of a typical Elizabethan theatre. The company of 500 is comprised of seasonal and full-time staff, plus individual production artists and performers. The production and technical departments have a core of year-round staff, augmented by additional staff as the season ramps up each year. Since 2007 oversight and coordination of the OSF safety and health program has been provided by a full-time Safety, Health, and Wellness Manager (Safety Manager). The safety and health program at the OSF evolved over a time-line that included informal but effective practices in the company's early decades to the adoption of industry recommended practices and a focus toward compliance with OSHA, and other standards, from the 1970s on. (Oregon is an OSHA-Approved State Plan state.)

Many aspects of the OSF safety and health program are influenced by the intense nature of the OSF season. The 11 OSF major productions perform in repertory from March to October. Starting in March, on any given day between two and seven shows are in performance across their four venues. Several show changeovers occur each day, and performers switch stages and shows several times each week. This fluid schedule adds to the complexity of assuring the safety and health of the performers involved with each show, and places intense physical demands on the stage technicians who manage each venue. The OSF safety and health program addresses these risks in a variety of ways:

- Stage path marking and platform edge marking with color-coded LEDs to assist performers and technicians in navigating a changing stage plan.

- Lengthy and intense fight calls to allow the performers time and space to rehearse staged violence and fights for the different shows they perform in every couple of days.

- Specific attention to how the physical demands of 700 changeovers and running 11 shows over a nine-month season affects stage technicians and backstage crews.

An issue of more recent concern related to safety and health was the presence of wildfires in the Ashland area. This relatively new hazard prompted the OSF to develop and enforce procedures that required daily assessment of the wildfire threat (particularly related to smoke and air quality), coordination of a response plan among the OSF leadership based on the assessment, and communication within the company and among patrons and local community members of response activities. Based on each day's assessment of the wildfire hazard, the responses ranged from warnings about air quality, to restrictions on outdoor activities, to canceling performances.

The OSF's safety and health program developed to encompass fixed and fluid hazards. Related to the venue and fabrication facilities' fixed hazards, upgrades to facilities or policies implemented to mitigate these hazards include: protection of exposed areas of outdoor venues by the installation of lightning rods and grounding wire; compliant guardrails installed on technical catwalks; upgrading the stage lighting dimmer systems; and providing Petzl-type hardhats with a chin strap for the technical stage crew. The fluid hazards presented by each production's design concepts have been managed through the development of policies that require the assessment of hazards specific to each show. The need for railings to provide fall protection onstage as part of each show's design are assessed, and railings are designed into the show as needed. Other fall hazards related to a scenic design or conceptual staging are assessed, and design alterations or choreographed actor movements are implemented to reduce risk. The application of flame-retardant coatings are included as part of the scene painting process for shows.

The process the OSF uses to assess and mitigate production-related hazards includes oversight by the safety manager, and assessment by each technical department head. The safety manager serves as a safety and health resource to assist in developing control measures for identified hazards. These risk-reduction conversations are part of the design development process for each element of the show's design. Once onstage, a safety inspection for each production is conducted with the safety manager and others on the production's technical team. Having a safety professional included in the organization's staff provides a readily available resource for guidance and assistance. The visible presence of designated safety and health oversight has proven to be an effective means to grow the safety culture at the OSF.

The OSF safety manager also coordinates training for administrative staff, production technicians, and performers. CPR/AED and first aid are available for stagehands and house management staff. The company invested in stage winch repair and maintenance training for several stage technicians. Training is also coordinated with the local fire department, and first responders. The Ashland Fire Department uses the OSF venues to practice fall rescue techniques. These and other interactions with local safety professionals help maintain a positive relationship between the OSF and the local fire and police departments. Such coordination with local resources is reflective of the early history of the OSF noted above.

Safety culture at the OSF has roots in its past but is forward-looking in its support from the organization's senior leadership. The presence of a full-time safety manager, budgets for training and safety equipment, and internalized efforts within the production department point to an environment in which safety and health at OSF is nurtured and has room for growth. Much has been accomplished in the decades after the Safety, Health, and Wellness Manager position was established. The production staff are anticipating next steps to address ergonomic hazards and repetitive motion injuries (RMIs) among technical production staff, improvements to automation control systems, and continued growth in implementing policies and procedures related to fall protection and other production hazards.[43]

YALE REPERTORY THEATRE

Yale School of Drama (YSD) was initially formed as the Department of Drama in 1924 at Yale University in New Haven, Connecticut.[44] The University Theatre building was constructed, and opened in 1926 to house the fledgling theatre department. The University Theatre, which contained two theatres, academic offices, classrooms, a library, rehearsal halls, and production support facilities, was among the first purpose-built academic theatre facilities in the United States. The organization of YSD as one of Yale's professional schools in 1955, offering Master's and Doctor of Fine Arts degrees, set YSD apart from peer institutions due to its sole focus on graduate-level theatre education. Yale Repertory Theatre (YRT) was equally ground-breaking when founded in 1966 as part of YSD under the leadership of Dean Robert Brustein: "establishing a complementary relationship between conservatory and professional practice similar to that of a medical school and a teaching hospital."[45] YRT was one of the first regional theatres in the United States, with ambitious productions of new plays and the classics of world theatre. This confluence of firsts between YSD and YRT, coupled with the unique collaborative relationship among YSD students, theatre faculty, and the professional performing and creative artists of YRT, set a model for conservatory theatre making, training, and education. "To this day, theatres and training programs across the country strive to emulate the Rep's unique convergence of talented students and leading professionals in meaningful collaboration."[46] The School's academic programs encompass every theatrical discipline represented by nine academic departments at YSD. The interdependence and integration of the academic programs of YSD and the professional productions of YRT evolved over the decades to form a single education, training, and producing entity: Yale School of Drama/Yale Repertory Theatre (YSD/YRT). Along with all other aspects of this unified organization, the YSD/YRT safety and health program encompasses the education, training, and productions for all activities of YSD and YRT.

The development of the YSD/YRT safety and health program flows along a time-line starting with the establishment of OSHA in the 1970s. In 1975 and 1976, safety rules were published addressing production activities and fabrication, primarily addressing hazards in technical production. YSD/YRT safety policies requiring the use of hardhats onstage and other PPE date to 1978. (I am a 1977 graduate of YSD, so I learned and followed these safety rules during my time there.) By 1980, safety and health procedures were incorporated into the curricula for students in technical production and stage management. In addition to the inclusion of safety and health topics in many technical production classes, a separate credited class in theatre safety was added to the curriculum in 1982. (I joined the faculty at YSD in 1982, and taught this and other theatre safety classes during my 35-years at YSD/YRT.) This theatre safety class has been required of YSD graduate students in the departments of Technical Design and Production and Stage Management ever since. Modules addressing safety and health within various technical courses continued to be added to the curriculum as equipment, technologies, and practices in theatre production evolved. For instance:

- Rigging classes came to include mitigation of the hazards of motorized rigging.
- Planning and skills necessary for the safe use of contemporary fabrication technologies, such as CNC (computer numerical control) routers, and advanced welding processes, were added to shop technology classes.
- Scenic automation classes explore emerging technologies for a variety of safety devices (e.g. light curtains, presence-sensing devices, and pressure-sensitive sensors).

The supportive relationship among coursework, training, and the YSD/YRT safety and health program is one of many attributes of the positive safety culture at YSD/YRT.

The complementary relationship between conservatory and professional practice proved to be another asset in the development of other parts of the safety and health program. For instance, through mentoring in scenic fabrication techniques by the professional YRT staff in the scenic and costume shops YSD graduate students learn technical skills and safety awareness which reinforces the classroom theory YSD faculty teach them. Each department engages subject-matter experts and industry professionals to augment their full-time faculty and staff, providing students with specialized classes and unique training experiences. The same is true of the safety and health program and its related curricula, which partner with Yale University campus professionals in fire and life safety, environmental health and safety, industrial hygiene, and physical safety. Theatre safety professionals from the United States and around the world provide guidance and context in the successful integration of safety and health into the theatre production process. Access to these safety professionals and other intellectual resources facilitated the expansion of safety and health classes to include modules for a variety of departments at YSD (life safety for theatre managers; safe stage weapons use for stage managers; haz comm and chemical safety for design students). Education and training requirements grew to include CPR/AED, blood-borne pathogen awareness, and OSHA-10 Hour and OSHA-30 Hour General Industry classes.

The YSD/YRT safety and health program is clear in its scope and intent:

> The Yale School of Drama/Yale Repertory Theatre's commitment to safety, health and personal security is inclusive and pervasive. All YSD/YRT students, faculty and staff are included in its safety, health and security programs and policies, which are integrated to the fullest extent possible into all aspects of YSD/YRT education, training and production activities. The YSD/YRT safety, health and security programs and policies are intended to provide a safe, healthy and secure environment for all students, staff and faculty.[47]

In addition to the academic components described above, the commitment to the YSD/YRT safety and health program is evidenced by the verbal and visual support from all administrative levels and all departments of YSD/YRT, as well as by the funds allocated to the annual safety and health budget. The annual budget covers the expense of maintaining the School-wide training activities, and related safety and health equipment and supplies (PPE, first aid, among other items). Large and expensive safety and health projects and facilities improvements are funded by Yale central campus budgets. The YSD/YRT Director of Theater Safety and Occupational Health collaborates directly with senior leadership on the Yale campus to prioritize safety and health needs, develop project proposals, and coordinate project activities and completion.

The YSD *Safety Handbook* is routinely reviewed, updated, and provided electronically to everyone at YSD/YRT. The *Handbook* is divided into two main sections: "Safety, Health, and Security Practices," and "Technical Production Practices." Other sections cover:

- Specifics related to the use of YSD/YRT's six performance venues.
- Locations of PPE, safety, and emergency response equipment.
- Instructions for evacuation and shelter-in-place emergencies.
- A "Glossary of Terms" used in the *Handbook*.

The "How to Use This Handbook" section on page 4 makes clear the inclusive nature of the *Handbook*'s contents, noting which sections contain information related to specific department's activities:

> The Yale School of Drama/Yale Repertory Theatre (YSD/YRT) *Safety, Health, and Security Handbook* contains important and useful information applicable to all activities at YSD/YRT. Everyone at YSD/YRT should read the Commitment statement, Roles and Responsibilities, and Sections 1 through 19. Sections 20 through 28 under Technical Production Practices and the Venues sections (29–34) are specifically applicable to activities in YSD/YRT production shops and on YSD/YRT stages.

The inclusive content of the *Handbook* reflects the comprehensive nature of the YSD/YRT safety and health program.

The safety and health program is integrated into the production process for every YSD and YRT show. In a typical academic year, there are five YRT productions, six major YSD productions, and eight less-fully produced YSD projects. The Director of Theater Safety and Occupational Health, or the Associate Safety Advisor, provides safety and health coaching and support for each of the YRT/YSD productions. Production department heads (stage manager, technical director, costume shop manager, master electrician, projections engineer, etc.) identify hazards related to their area, and assess risk associated with the hazards. Risks requiring mitigation through concept or design change are discussed at design development meetings and at subsequent production meetings. Hazards that emerge during the rehearsal process are noted by the stage management team, then discussed and resolved at production meetings. Technical production department heads provide safety oversight during fabrication in their shops. This pattern continues through the entire life cycle of each production, with similar safety and health oversight being part of the planning and implementation of activities for technical rehearsals, performances, and strikes.

The YSD/YRT safety and health program is expected to function at the same high level of excellence as the rest of the programs and activities of YSD/YRT. This commitment was highlighted in the "Roles and Responsibilities" section of the 2016 YSD *Safety Handbook*:

> YSD/YRT sets high standards in theater production and training; graduates of the School will be positioned as leaders in the effective integration of safety and health into all aspects of theater production.[48]

The Yale School of Drama graduates 60 MFA students and six technical production interns in a typical academic year. These 60+ theatre artists and practitioners bring their training and experience in safety and health to their future places of employment, and to their work on theatre productions. The grounding they receive in safety and health from YSD courses and their involvement in YSD/YRT productions imbue in them an expectation of a positive safety culture. Their expectation of safety and health influences people and organizations throughout their careers. The faculty and staff at YSD/YRT are keenly aware of the responsibility this places on the safety and health programs, policies, and training. The positive safety culture at YSD/YRT reflects this commitment.[49]

Success stories can be encouraging, but an astute reader can respect the gains made by a specific theatre organization while at the same time questioning the applicability of them to her/his theatre company or academic department. Perceived differences of scale, scope, and resources among theatres and theatre departments may limit our ability to imagine the implementation of a safety and health program in our theatre's operations or theatre department's curriculum. To help overcome this possible impediment, we need a clear and well-defined understanding of what makes up a successful safety and health program, and how each aspect of such a program can be effectively developed and implemented. Only through our deliberate application of safety and health to the production activities of theatre organizations or academic departments via a safety and health program will the safety culture within the industry continue to grow. The next chapter will be an examination of how theatre safety and health programs can be integrated into academic theatre programs and theatre producing organizations.

NOTES

1. June, 1972, OSHA develops and issues its first standard limiting workplace exposure to asbestos fibers. "OSHA Celebrates 40 years of Accomplishments in the workplace," accessed February 5, 2019, https://www.osha.gov/osha40/OSHATimeline.pdf.
2. OSHA: Standard Interpretations, "Fall Protection for the Entertainment Industry under the OSH Act of 1970," accessed February 26, 2019, https://www.osha.gov/pls/oshaweb/owadisp.show_document?p_table=INTERPRETATIONS&p_id=22337
3. Ibid.
4. To research current and pending OSHA citations and fines issued to theatres and entertainment organizations, go to the OSHA website, https://www.osha.gov/pls/imis/industry.html. Use SIC code 7922 or NAICS code 711110 for theatres and theatre companies.

5 Jason Garcia, "Theme Parks 'on Notice' over the Safety of Workers," *Orlando Sentinel*, May 27, 2010, accessed October 23, 2019, https://www.orlandosentinel.com/business/os-xpm-2010-05-27-os-osha-theme-park-safety.
6 Actors' Equity Association (AEA), "History," accessed March 29, 2019, https://www.actorsequity.org/aboutequity/history/.
7 Ibid.
8 AEA, "Approval of Venues," accessed March 29, 2019, https://www.actorsequity.org/resources/Producers/safe-and-sanitary/venues/.
9 AEA, "Theatrical Smoke and Haze Regulations," accessed March 29, 2019, https://www.actorsequity.org/resources/Producers/safe-and-sanitary/smoke-and-haze/.
10 Entertainment Services and Technology Association (ESTA), "Vision Statement," accessed February 18, 2019, https://www.esta.org/ESTA/vision_mission.html.
11 ESTA Technical Standards Program, Published Documents, accessed February 18, 2019, http://tsp.esta.org/tsp/documents/published_docs.php. ANSI is the American National Standards Institute.
12 ESTA, "About ETCP," accessed March 26, 2019, https://etcp.esta.org/etcp/about.html. Also reference ESTA, Entertainment Technician Certification Program, accessed March 26, 2019, https://etcp.esta.org/.
13 Event Safety Alliance (ESA), "Who We Are," accessed March 27, 2019, https://www.eventsafetyalliance.org/ourmission.
14 Thornton Tomassetti, Projects, "Indiana State Fair Collapse Incident Report," 2011, accessed February 18, 2019, https://www.thorntontomassetti.com/projects/indiana_state_fair_commission_collapse_incident/.
15 ESA, "Severe Weather Summit," accessed March 29, 2019, https://www.eventsafetyalliance.org/severe-weather-summit-annual.
16 ESA, *Event Safety Guide* link on the ESA website; accessed February 18, 2019, http://eventsafetyalliance.org/.
17 ESA, "International Affiliates," accessed March 27, 2019, https://www.eventsafetyalliance.org/international-affiliates.
18 The IATSE's official name is the International Alliance of Theatrical Stage Employees, Moving Picture Technicians, Artists and Allied Crafts of the United States, its Territories and Canada.
19 International Alliance of Theatrical Stage Employees (IATSE), "About the IATSE, Timeline," accessed April 18, 2019, http://www.iatse.net/timeline.
20 Ibid.

21 Historical information from the International Alliance of Theatrical Stage Employees (IATSE) Training Trust Fund, accessed February 26, 2019, https://www.iatsetrainingtrust.org/about/.
22 IATSE, "IATSE Safety," accessed March 28, 2019, http://www.iatse.net/iatse-safety.
23 IATSE, TTF Safety First! Online Courses, accessed March 28, 2019, https://www.iatsetrainingtrust.org/safetyfirst/.
24 IATSE, "IATSE Launches Safety Hotline Program," accessed April 18, 2019, http://www.iatse.net/news/iatse-launches-safety-hotline-program.
25 OSHA, IATSE, USITT Alliance, "Alliance Renewal," accessed October 23, 2019, https://www.osha.gov/dcsp/alliances/usitt_iatse/usitt-iatse_renewal2017.html.
26 David Glowacki, "The Commissions: Devoted to Investigating and Research by Members of USITT: Health and Safety," *TD&T,* vol. 46, issue 1 (Winter 2010): 55–58.
27 Ibid.
28 ESTA, *Published Documents: Recommended Practice for DMX512: A Guide for Users and Installers*, 2nd edition, accessed March 28, 2019, https://tsp.esta.org/tsp/documents/published_docs.php.
29 OSHA news release dated November 4, 2014, accessed February 5, 2019, https://www.osha.gov/news/newsreleases/region1/11042014.
30 Glimmerglass Festival, "Past Productions," accessed February 25, 2019, https://glimmerglass.org/past-productions/.
31 Ibid.
32 "OSHA's On-Site Consultation Program offers no-cost and confidential occupational safety and health services to small- and medium-sized businesses in all 50 states, the District of Columbia, and several U.S. territories, with priority given to high-hazard worksites. On-Site Consultation services are separate from enforcement and do not result in penalties or citations. Consultants from state agencies or universities work with employers to identify workplace hazards, provide advice for compliance with OSHA standards, and assist in establishing and improving safety and health programs." OSHA On-Site Consultation, accessed February 11, 2019, https://www.osha.gov/dcsp/smallbusiness/consult.html.
33 Information related to the safety and health program at Glimmerglass Festival is based on an interview with Abby Rodd, Production Manager, conducted on February 7, 2019.

34 Goodman Theatre, "Our History," accessed February 5, 2019, https://www.goodmantheatre.org/About/Our-History/.
35 Ibid.
36 University of Illinois at Chicago School of Public Health, Health in the Arts program, accessed February 4, 2019, http://publichealth.uic.edu/great-lakes/health-in-the-arts-program.
37 Information related to the safety and health program at Goodman Theatre is based on an interview with Scott Conn, Production Manager, Goodman Theatre, conducted on January 31, 2019.
38 The Milwaukee Repertory Theater, "Our History," accessed February 5, 2019, https://www.milwaukeerep.com/Inside-The-Rep/Milwaukee-Rep-History/.
39 Information related to the safety and health program at the Milwaukee Repertory Theater is based on an interview conducted with Jared Clarkin, Production Manager, and Kaitlyn Anderson, Assistant Production Manager, conducted on February 1, 2019.
40 Encyclopedia Britannica, Britannica.com, "Chautauqua Movement," accessed March 5, 2019, https://www.britannica.com/topic/chautauqua-movement.
41 Chautauqua, "Chautauqua Movement History," accessed March 5, 2019, https://www.chautauqua.com/about-us/history/chautauqua-movement-history/.
42 Oregon Shakespeare Festival, "Our History," accessed March 5, 2019, https://www.osfashland.org/en/company/our-history.aspx.
43 Information related to the safety and health program at Oregon Shakespeare Festival is based on an interview with Alys Holden, Director of Production, and Hazel Wheeler, Safety, Health, and Wellness Manager, conducted on Wednesday, February 27, 2019.
44 Yale School of Drama, "About Us—History Yale School of Drama," accessed February 25, 2019, https://www.drama.yale.edu/about-us/.
45 Ibid.
46 Tom Shultz, "History of the Yale Repertory Theatre," accessed February 19, 2019, http://www.tomshultz.com/yrt2k3/history.html.
47 *Yale University School of Drama Safety Handbook*, 8.20.2018 ed., 5.
48 Ibid, 5.
49 Information related to the safety and health program at Yale School of Drama/Yale Repertory Theatre (YSD/YRT) is based in part on conversations with Anna Glover, Director of Theatre Safety and Occupational Health, and on the author's 35-year tenure at YSD/YRT.

CHAPTER 3

Safety and Health Programs

William J. Reynolds

A safety and health program represents a systematic approach to achieving the goal of a positive safety culture. A well-defined, documented, and fully implemented safety and health program is required for the successful integration of a positive safety culture into the theatre production process. What is a safety and health program?

> A health and safety program is an organized, written action plan to identify and control hazards, define safety responsibilities and respond to emergencies that result in the prevention of accidents and occupational diseases. The objective of a program is to integrate safety and health into all work practices and conditions.[1]

Or, as succinctly stated by Anna Glover, Director of Theatre Safety and Occupational Health for the Yale School of Drama/Yale Repertory Theatre,

> A safety and health program is a definite plan of action that provides guidelines, that defines procedures, and can cover a wide range of activities.[2]

One of the several correlations between a safety and health program and the activities required for the success of a theatre production is both are essentially proactive. One of the goals of a theatre production's process is to reduce or eliminate uncertainty. Through planning, preparation, rehearsal, and cross-checking, the production is expected to proceed without interruption to the desired outcome.

A safety and health program operates similarly in an organization. Through planning, documentation, training, and assessments of incidents, risks are reduced, hazards mitigated, and the number and severity of accidents and injuries are limited.

> Safety and health programs foster a proactive approach to "finding and fixing" workplace hazards before they can cause injury or illness. Rather than reacting to an incident, management and workers *collaborate* to identify and solve issues before they occur.[3]

The basic concept is that a safety and health program operates on the same terms within a theatre organization as its other production-related activities. Effective collaboration among the many elements that support the production process, including the safety and health program, is required for success. With this congruency in mind, let's look at the core elements required of a safety and health program. I will use recommendations from the Occupational Safety and Health Administration (OSHA) as a guide.

In 2016, OSHA published *Recommended Practices for Safety and Health Programs*, which is an update to its *1989 Safety and Health Program Management Guidelines*.[4] The *Guidelines*' description of a safety and health program's core elements mirror those of virtually every safety and health program I've encountered in my research. The core elements recommended by OSHA represent common aspects of safety and health programs described in books and articles, as well as successful theatre safety and health programs such as those described in the previous chapter. These core elements will provide an outline for this chapter, as will much of the content included in OSHA's recommended practices related to each of these elements. I will examine each core element of a safety and health program separately, but you should keep in mind their interrelated nature. Also, remember the cyclical and iterative nature inherent in most management practices; this is certainly applicable to a safety and health program. W. Edwards Deming succinctly defined these concepts in the 1950s with his Plan–Do–Study–Act cycle:

FIGURE 3.1   W. Edwards Deming's Plan–Do–Study–Act Cycle

The core elements of a successful safety and health program described in OSHA's *Recommended Practices* guide are:

- Management Leadership
- Employee Participation
- Hazard Identification and Assessment
- Hazard Prevention and Control
- Education and Training
- Coordination and Communication among All Employers and Employees on a Multi-employer Worksite
- Program Evaluation and Improvement.

Viewed graphically the interrelated aspect of the core elements look like Figure 3.2.

SAFETY AND HEALTH PROGRAMS 41

FIGURE 3.2 OSHA Safety and Health Programs Core Elements

MANAGEMENT LEADERSHIP

Safety and health must be embraced as a core value by an organization's leadership in order for the safety and health program to be successfully integrated into the activities of the organization:

> The commitment of an organization's leadership to health and safety is critical to its success. If a director talks with conviction and passion about health and safety, he or she will probably have a more powerful effect on advancing an organization's safety culture than any safety professional is likely to be able to achieve.[5]

The inclusion of safety in the organization's core values effectively aligns the goals of the safety and health program with the mission of the organization. For instance:

> We dedicate our best selves to both training and practices, holding ourselves accountable for a safe, sound, and respectful workplace, animated by good will.[6]

A specific policy statement communicating this commitment signed by the artistic director of the theatre or chair of the academic department should be posted and circulated to all employees, students, and volunteers. (In the United Kingdom, and in some Canadian provinces, such a commitment statement is included as part of a required safety and health policy.) Senior leadership (e.g. board of directors, upper manager, and department chairs) become safety leaders through their support of the organization's core values, which include safety and health. This organizational commitment must be apparent in all aspects of the operations of the theatre organization or academic department, including choices of shows to produce, the evaluation of products and processes to be used in fabrication, planning for facility modifications, and criteria for equipment purchases. In addition, managers at all levels must lead by example,[7] modeling the safety and health procedures expected of everyone, and maintaining their involvement in safety and health activities of the organization via review of incidents and program evaluations.

The goals of the safety and health program must align with and support the goals of the organization. For instance, for Goodman Theatre in Chicago in the "Policy Statement" section of its *Health and Safety Program* document, the program's goals are stated as:

Goodman Theatre is committed to:

a.) maintaining a safe workplace;
b.) the thorough training of its employees in proper emergency procedures; in the best methods of preventing work-related accidents and illnesses; in the safe handling, use and disposal of hazardous materials; and in the proper use of personal protective equipment (PPE), as well as shop equipment;
c.) the complete reporting and investigation of workplace accidents; and,
d.) correcting the conditions, behaviors and hazards which have led to workplace accidents and illness.[8]

Realistic and measurable goals related to incident and injury prevention can be established for each department by departmental supervisors in consultation with an organization's leadership. These goals provide a means for program evaluation through defining both departmental and individual performance expectations related to safety and health. By identifying safety and health as among an organization's core values, and implementing a safety and health program with well-defined roles and responsibilities, the regular assessment of an individual's work performance can include aspects of safety and health. Focusing on positive achievements (conducting inspections, reporting near-misses, developing and implementing safety procedures) can assist with the evolution of the safety and health program as well as encourage effective participation on a daily basis.

Management is responsible for the resources of an organization. The allocation of sufficient resources to successfully implement and sustain the safety and health program is essential to the program's success. One of the key initial steps required for the establishment of a safety and health program is a thorough assessment of current conditions, and the identification of deficiencies related to safety and health in the workplace. Doing so will provide data via a gap analysis of what exists, based on the assessment, and what should exist, based on codes, standards, and recommended practices. The results of this analysis will inform the scope and scale of resources required for the program to be established. The assessment process will identify the resources required for start-up and initial expenses, as well as the resources necessary for the program's ongoing activities. Since it is unlikely all the identified needs can be funded and initiated immediately, a time-line with milestones and budgetary expectations over several fiscal years can be developed and integrated into the organization's long-term planning. Acknowledging that people's time is one of an organization's most constrained and costly resources, a realistic estimate of employees' and managers' time for their participation in the safety and health program (time for meetings, training, and inspections) must be accounted for in the planning process.

EMPLOYEE PARTICIPATION

While the leadership of an organization can direct a safety and health program to be initiated, employee participation in all aspects of the program is required for the program's success. (In our context, students and faculty in an academic department are included in the definition of employee.) Employees must be notified of the program's development, and be encouraged to be involved in its evolution at its early stages. The initial stages of employee involvement are a way for management to signal to their employees that they value safety and health; that employee input is important and welcomed as part of the process from the beginning. Setting aside time during the workday when employees can contribute to the process also establishes the importance of their contribution, and emphasizes the value the organization places on safety and health.

It should be made clear that worker involvement is regarded as the key condition for achieving a better match between procedures and practice. Worker involvement provides four main benefits that are crucial in building acceptance and adherence to safety procedures:

1. When workers are consulted in the development of procedures it is likely to increase their ownership of them.
2. Worker involvement in developing procedures provides safety managers with an opportunity to communicate the intentions underlying the procedures.
3. Establishing a dialogue between the makers and the users of procedures can also be instrumental in diffusing knowledge about their contents, role and logic.
4. Beyond their mere prescriptive function, procedures are part of an inventory of tools or resources which workers use and this transcends mere compliance and violation.[9]

An open reporting process for workplace hazards, unsafe conditions, safety concerns, near-misses, and unplanned incidents provides another means for employee participation. Establishing a transparent conduit for such information is important to the program's growth and development; employees are best situated in the organization's structure and daily activities to bring this information to management. The program must have a well-defined process for such reporting. Managers and supervisors encourage this by being willing to listen, and document reports and suggestions. Equally essential is direct and timely follow-up with employees about progress, and resolutions related to their ideas and concerns. A visible and strong indicator of support for employee involvement is empowering all employees to be able to stop or shut down a process or activity they deem to be unsafe or hazardous. This could be a scenic carpenter preventing visitors from entering the scene shop until they are wearing the required PPE, or a stagehand stopping the loading of counterweight on the loading rail until the "All Clear" signal is given by the crew onstage and received by the stage crew working above, or an assistant stage manager calling "Hold" during a fight call to make sure the appropriate safety precautions are in place before continuing.

Right-to-Know[10] provides a valuable form of employee participation. In the context of OSHA's Hazard Communication Standard (HCS),[11] Right-to-Know is making sure employees know about the safety and health hazards of the chemical products with which they work.

> 1910.1200—Hazard Communication. (b)(1) This section requires . . . all employers to provide information to their employees about the hazardous chemical to which they are exposed, by means of a hazard communication program, labels, and other forms of warning, safety data sheets, and information and trainings.[12]

We can expand this concept to include all types of workplace hazards (ergonomic, electrical, working-at-heights, etc.). Doing so provides a comprehensive way to include employees in all aspects of the safety and health program's activities. While working on a task, employees regularly make decisions that affect their safety or health. Lacking the information about the hazards associated with the materials, equipment, or the task itself, employees are less able to protect themselves and those around them. A safety and health program with a comprehensive Right-to-Know policy will allow employees to know the hazards related to their work. This includes aspects beyond the chemical make-up of a product, such as job hazard analysis (JHA)[13] of complex tasks, workplace inspection reports that have noted hazards in particular work areas, and ready access to safety and health information for all aspects of the workplace.

In the creative environment of a theatre organization, you can involve employees in your safety and health program in many ways. OSHA provides us with a short list of activities to involve employees in its *Recommended Practices*[14] document. You could translate some of these into your production activities as:

- Provide opportunities for all staff and students to assist in the development of the safety and health program.

- Establish a means to set safety and health goals related to each show produced.

- Encourage staff and students to report hazards in production shops, to develop ways to control the hazard, and to assist with their implementation.
- Require staff and students to develop JHA for specific production elements (scenery, costumes, props).
- Develop and document standard operating procedures (SOPs) for stage equipment and production-related work practices.
- Assist with the training of coworkers on new equipment and new-hires on work practices.
- Participate in the post-production evaluation of safety and health successes and challenges for each show.

Even with a work environment that actively encourages employee participation in the safety and health program, there may be barriers that discourage participation. Among a generational and culturally diverse workforce, there may be employees for whom participation may be challenging. New employees or students may be reticent to raise concerns for fear of retaliation. Cultural backgrounds may not be supportive of speaking up and questioning supervisors or faculty. Language limitations could influence employees' ability to articulate their concerns. Your safety and health program must welcome as well as encourage near-miss, incident, and injury reporting. Follow-up investigations should focus on workplace hazards and underlying conditions rather than blaming individual actions. The program can reinforce such reporting by referencing the whistle-blower protection included in OSHA's injury and illness recordkeeping rule.[15]

Sample Whistleblower Protection Policy

Whistleblower policies are critical tools for protecting individuals who report activities believed to be illegal, dishonest, unethical, or otherwise improper.

1. The organization will not retaliate against a whistleblower. This includes, but is not limited to, protection from retaliation in the form of an adverse employment action such as termination, compensation decreases, or poor work assignments and threats of physical harm. Any whistleblower who believes he/she is being retaliated against must contact the Human Resources Director [or Human Resources representative] immediately. The right of a whistleblower for protection against retaliation does not include immunity for any personal wrongdoing that is alleged and investigated.[16]

HAZARD IDENTIFICATION AND ASSESSMENT

A hazard is anything that has the potential to cause harm. The identification of hazards and the assessment of their risks ground your safety and health program into a proactive process. Start with what you already know, using input from people in all aspects of the workplace. Much may already be documented that will assist with the identification of workplace hazards. Equipment manuals, safety data sheets (SDS), operating procedures, work practices, and documentation of policies can be collected and reviewed by each department. A review of records related to incidents and injuries can provide data on work and work areas on which to focus attention. Delegating portions of the review process related to the identification of hazards is another way for employees and students to participate in the development of the safety and health program.

Inspection of work areas is necessary to identify hazards related to facilities and permanent equipment. These inspections can be done by each department, and include those who regularly work in a particular facility. A team made up of people from several departments to conduct the facilities hazard inspections spreads the workload of the inspections to others in the organization. Inspections can benefit from the insight of individuals who may not be familiar with a particular work area (trap room, costume shop, concessions area, etc.), since they bring fresh attention to potential hazards which might be overlooked by those who routinely work in these areas.

> Similar to olfactory fatigue, regular exposure to workplace hazards can lead to habituation—the lessening of your awareness to a hazard due to routine exposure to the hazard.[17]
>
> Habituation is a decrease in response to a stimulus after repeated presentations. For example, a new sound in your environment, such as a new ringtone, may initially draw your attention or even become distracting. Over time, as you become accustomed to this sound, you pay less attention to the noise and your response to the sound will diminish. This diminished response is habituation.[18]

Individuals or team members who conduct these inspections will benefit from training in hazard identification. This training can be completed in a group setting with many of the tools available online,[19] or from resources noted in the Appendix. For instance, OSHA has a downloadable online hazard identification training tool the inspection team could use as a group learning activity. From the OSHA training tool's website:

> OSHA's Hazard Identification Training Tool is an interactive, online, game-based training tool for small business owners, workers and others interested in learning the core concepts of hazard identification. After using this tool, users will better understand the process to identify hazards in their own workplace.[20]

The examples in this OSHA training tool are related to manufacturing and construction industries, and are not theatre-specific. The value of the training lies in the examples of analysis and the thought processes related to hazard identification. For instance, using this online training tool in a group setting could initiate discussion on how you might apply the principles in your theatre's workplace.

Before initiating a facilities hazard inspection, you need a process to record and assess identified hazards. A form such as the one shown in Figure 3.3 along with photos and related commentary provide a means to capture the necessary information.

Hazards can be identified from existing conditions, such as exposed electrical wires or tripping hazards on walking and working surfaces. Hazards can also be from something missing (a misplaced removable barrier), or the lack of a procedure

Facilities Hazards Inspection Report

To: _____ Department: _____

Location/Building: _____

Date of inspection: _____ Inspected by: _____

The above facility was inspected on the date indicated. The inspection revealed that the conditions listed below present unsafe or hazardous conditions to the users of this facility. Suggested corrections are noted next to each item. Each item is prioritized to indicate the approximate risk level of the condition.

Priority codes are as follows:

	Terminology	Explanation
1	Imminent Danger	Abate hazard immediately (shut down equipment)
2	Serious	Initiate action for correction immediately
3	Non-serious	Initiate action for correction ASAP
4	De minimus	Initiate action when convenient

Room number or Location:

Item #	Equipment or Condition	Solutions or Comments	Priority Code

FIGURE 3.3 Facilities Hazards Inspection Form

(emergency evacuation routes or fire emergency procedures not posted). Identifying health hazards requires an inventory of chemicals and products used in the fabrication shops, as well as in other work areas such as custodial or concessions. If OSHA's Hazard Communication Standard has been implemented in the organization, chemical inventories should have already been completed. If not, the inspection can note a chemical inventory is lacking, and then list this lack as a hazard to be addressed. Due to the potentially severe consequences from exposure to many of the chemicals and products commonly used in theatre production, the need to complete a workplace chemical inventory must be placed high on the priority list.

The hazard identification process described may seem to be focused solely on fixed hazards of the type described in the previous chapter. To some extent this is true because an inspection will investigate and capture hazard data at a point in time in a specific location, such as the trap room during mid-morning on a non-performance day. The fluid hazards related to a production may not be in evidence, or their presence will be fleeting (expected to be removed at the next strike call) and possibly not identified during the inspection. In addition, some hazards identified from the inspection may be due to the lack of a policy, or the need for training. Appropriate PPE may be available but is not being worn by the staff in the costume shop while dyeing fabrics, or barriers to protect the fall hazard at the front edge of the stage exist but may not be installed during a load-in onstage. The inspection process must provide a means to differentiate among these three causes of identified hazards:

1. Fixed hazards related to facilities and equipment conditions.
2. Fluid hazards present as a result of a specific production design or staging requirements.
3. Hazards caused by a lack of education or training.

The three types of identified hazards require different approaches to their prevention and control. Addressing the fixed hazards will be included in the discussion of hazard prevention and control later in this chapter, while the means and methods for the mitigation and control of the other two hazard types will be covered in Chapters 6 and 7.

An assessment of the identified hazards is the next step. The assessment of each hazard must include consideration of the severity of the consequences (level of injury and/or number of people affected) and the likelihood of occurrence, based on frequency of exposure. (You might recognize this as a common process related to risk assessment, which we'll cover in more detail in Chapter 7.) Results from the assessment process provide you with a means to prioritize the allocation of resources. This helps address the "Where do I start?" roadblock by moving from being overwhelmed by all that needs to be done to a planned sequence of tasks and activities to be completed over a projected period of time. Hazards with the highest risk score (most severe consequences and/or most likely to occur) must receive immediate attention and be allocated the most resources. The plan must include some level of response to virtually all identified hazards. Interim responses to some of the hazards might include tagging a piece of stage equipment as "Do Not Use," limiting access to a catwalk area to authorized staff only, or posting warning notices related to PPE use. Completing the identification and assessment of workplace hazards allows you to shift to the next step in the development of your safety and health program.

HAZARD PREVENTION AND CONTROL

The assessment of workplace hazards will develop into an action plan for the safety and health program. Using the prioritized list of workplace hazards, specific plans can be developed to accomplish their prevention and control. A range of options are available, each with its own set of requirements and relative effectiveness. This step provides me with the opportunity to introduce the concept of a "Hierarchy of Controls" and discuss its application in the context of hazard prevention and control. A Hierarchy of Controls is used by safety professionals and risk managers to mitigate hazards in the context of time and resources. "Traditionally, a hierarchy of controls has been used as a means of determining how to implement feasible and effective control solutions."[21] Figure 3.4 illustrates the Hierarchy of Controls graphically.

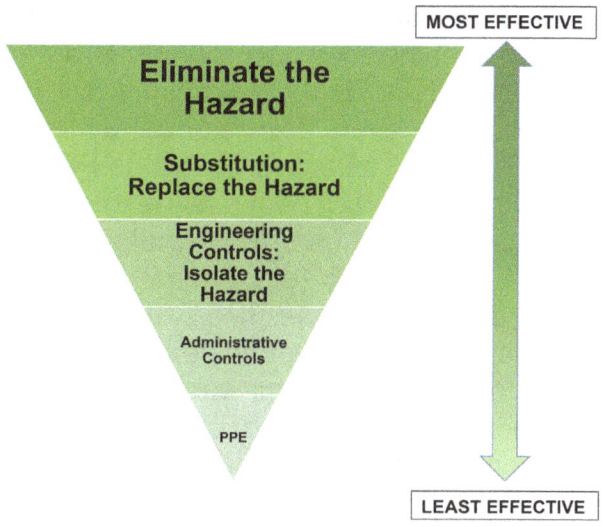

FIGURE 3.4 Hierarchy of Controls

The order of controlling identified hazards, ranked from most effective to least effective is: Elimination; Substitution; Engineering Controls; Administrative Controls; Personal Protective Equipment (PPE). As shown graphically, elimination and then substitution are the most effective means to control hazards. Taking the hazard out of the workplace, such as not allowing the use of the cleaning agent carbon tetrachloride in the costume shop eliminates the specific hazard of exposure to a carcinogen. Substituting liquid scene paint for powdered pigment removes the specific hazard related to the inhalation of particles in the air, but may introduce a new hazard (some liquid paint products contain chemicals that are sensitizers). When substitution is used as a control measure, a new hazard assessment must be done for the new product or process. Elimination and substitution are also effective because they remove reliance on people's behavior from the hazard control equation.

The next three levels in the Hierarchy of Controls (engineering controls, administrative controls, personal protective equipment) rely to varying degrees on the worker taking specific actions for the control to be effective. An engineering control such as a spray booth or machine guard requires the person to use the control in order for it to be effective. Some engineering controls can be interlocked with equipment so the machine will not operate unless the guard is in place, but human ingenuity may discover ways to override such protection. Posted warning signs are examples of administrative controls, as is a lock-out/tag-out system for the control of hazardous energy, or a safety-taped "Keep Clear Area" marked on the floor around a machine tool. Job rotation is an administrative control which reduces an individual's exposure to a hazard (particulates in the air, or noise levels, for instance) by limiting the duration of exposure. The least effective control is PPE, not because PPE is inherently ineffective, but because the effectiveness of PPE is reliant on the actions of the user. The employee must select the correct type of PPE for the task (e.g. chemical splash goggles for exposure to liquid chemicals), use PPE with the required level of protection (heavy-duty nitrile gloves instead of single-use disposable nitrile gloves, for example), and wear the PPE as required in order to achieve the necessary level of protection. "PPE is the least effective way to control hazards because of the high potential for equipment to become ineffective owing to damage, or for it not to be worn appropriately."[22]

Taking into account both the prioritization of identified workplace hazards and the Hierarchy of Controls discussed above, a hazard control plan can be developed and implemented. Such a plan adopts a cyclical and interactive process as illustrated in Figure 3.5. The cycle is similar to any management plan: identify the risks and specify the hazards; assess the risks and rank various controls and mitigations; assign responsibilities, develop deadlines, and allocate resources; implement the hazard controls and risk mitigations; review and evaluate the effectiveness of the hazard control plan.

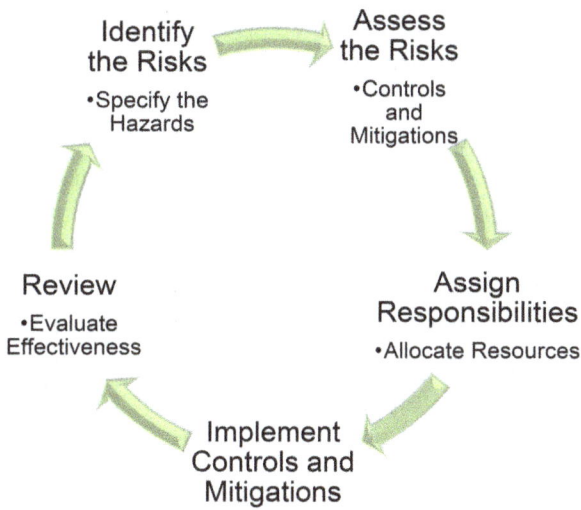

FIGURE 3.5   Hazard Control Plan Management Cycle

The review process can include inspecting work areas or equipment where hazard control measures have been completed. These inspections might represent the beginning of an ongoing inspection process that becomes an integral part of the safety and health program.

The implementation process can function on several levels. The hazards with the greatest risk level must be addressed on a worst-first basis. At the same time, some control measures may be relatively simple and inexpensive to accomplish (euphemistically referred to as low-hanging fruit). Doing the latter, such as purchasing everyone protective eyewear or replacing misplaced machine guards, has the added benefit of completing visible control measures quickly. At the Yale School of Drama, in the early 1980s, we implemented as a first step in our safety and health program a comprehensive hardhat policy for all work done onstage and in adjacent work areas during work calls (load-ins, strikes, and all construction-type work). Doing so reinforced the message of the organization's commitment to the safety and health program. Implementing this policy was visible evidence of the organization's concern for the well-being of its members: students, staff, and faculty.

Not all control measures can be implemented quickly, or at little cost. Dust collection systems, emergency E-stop systems, and spray booths require specialized engineering, infrastructure alterations or extensive installations, and large financial expenditures. Such control measures must have the support of upper management to be funded and implemented. This is where management leadership is critical to success. A safety and health program that is aligned with the organization's core values provides the managers of the safety and health program a means to guide senior leadership through a cost-benefit analysis of costly control measures. While you may not be able to directly relate the safety and health program's expenses to increased productivity in the production shops, costs related to the impact on human capital, risks to reputation due to an accident or injury, and citations for violations of code requirements can seriously impact an organization's bottom-line.

EDUCATION AND TRAINING

The embrace of a safety and health program by a theatre organization triggers the need for a range of education and training programs. From the original inception of the ideas related to a safety and health program to the integration of the program into people's daily work activities, each step requires careful consideration of learning and understanding to assure success. Effectively communicating the goals, mission, and structure of the nascent safety and health program will provide a basis for employees to support the changes a program will bring. Doing so may reduce some of the fears or concerns employees might have about how the program will affect their work life. To quote from an interview with Phil Davis, an experienced management consultant, posted by the Yale School of Management's online newsletter *Yale Insights*,

> Change is hard. . . . For an organizational change effort to succeed, leaders must understand motivation, context, receptivity, sequencing,

and pace. They must communicate effectively and pull the right levers at the right moment in a dynamic situation. Things rarely go according to plan, in no small part because humans are more at ease with the status quo.[23]

For a theatre company or academic department with little structure to their current safety and health practices, anyone who will be potentially affected by the safety and health program can be engaged in early conversations and group meetings to create an awareness of the program, and its anticipated structure and implementation. Input from participants at all levels can help to diffuse perceptions of a top-down or leadership-driven program. Resistance to a safety and health program may evolve through the lack of active participation from all levels within an organization in the program's development, planning, and implementation. On the other hand, clear messages of support for the program from senior leadership (directors, heads of department, department chairs, and artistic and managing directors) are essential to reinforce the alignment of the safety and health program with the organization's mission and goals. An organization with existing safety and health policies and procedures that are to become key elements of a comprehensive safety and health program will also benefit from planned outreach and communication to its members. While change may be more readily accepted as an expected growth of ongoing activities, having input and support is equally important to a program's success.

Employers (managers and supervisors) have legal responsibility for the safety and well-being of their employees; for an academic institution, this reads as faculty and staff having responsibility for the safety and well-being of their students and interns. This responsibility is codified in the United States by Section 5 of the Occupational Safety and Health Act, usually referred to as the General Duty Clause of the OSH Act:

(a) Each employer—

(1) shall furnish to each of his employees employment and a place of employment which are free from recognized hazards that are causing or are likely to cause death or serious physical harm to his employees;
(2) shall comply with occupational safety and health standards promulgated under this Act.

(b) Each employee shall comply with occupational safety and health standards and all rules, regulations, and orders issued pursuant to this Act which are applicable to his own actions and conduct.[24]

Education and training provides a means to define roles and responsibilities for those impacted by the safety and health program. Everyone is expected to fully participate in and support the safety and health program, but there will be varying levels of responsibility for the program from those in different levels of the organization. Because of differing responsibilities, board members and senior leadership (executive director, artistic director, managing director, and academic department chair) need specific training. Managers who implement your safety and health program can do much to educate senior leadership. Activities can include training experiences such as inviting senior leaders to meetings with safety committees, taking them to tour critical high-hazard workplaces (backstage, grids, catwalks, costume and props craft rooms), and conversations among senior leadership and technical managers to discuss hazards, risks, and related safety and health concerns. For other managers (middle management, supervisors, faculty or staff), their oversight and supervision of the workplace requires skills and knowledge related to fundamental concepts of hazard recognition, accident investigation, and responding to employee or student reports of injuries, illnesses, and work-related incidents (accidents and near-misses). As partners with leadership in the safety and health program, employees and students must also be trained in their roles and responsibilities that support these areas: how to recognize and report hazards; procedures required for the reporting and the investigation of accidents and injuries; how to implement policies and procedures in their work; and methods for providing feedback and suggestions related to the safety and health program. The latter aspect is particularly important to the growth and continued effectiveness of the program.

Work activities specific to theatre production are varied and specialized. Each task (rigging, stage construction, costume fabrication, stage combat, rehearsals, crowd management, to name just a very few) requires focused safety and health training as well as hazard recognition integrated into the skillset of those performing these tasks. Whether loading counterweight onto a stage arbor to fly a piece of scenery, or distressing costume fabric to achieve a designed look of age and wear, developing and documenting standard operating procedures (SOPs) for routine production-related tasks is an inevitable evolution of a safety and health program. Including safety and health as part of these procedures provides a means to fully integrate education and training into your safety and health program.

COORDINATION AND COMMUNICATION AMONG ALL EMPLOYEES ON A MULTI-EMPLOYER WORKSITE

The penultimate element in the development of a safety and health program requires consistency in the application of all aspects of the program to anyone present or working in your theatre or performance venues. The discussion related to this element by OSHA is specific to a multi-employer worksite such as a large building construction site, where a host employer (general contractor or construction management company) has overall control of the worksite, while many contractors, subcontractors, and temporary workers perform the work. This idea readily translates into the operations of many theatre organizations when personnel from multiple agencies and temporary workers may assist with the fabrication of production elements, perform as cast members, or work on load-ins and strikes. Academic theatre department faculty and staff are probably familiar with a wide range of non-departmental people (campus facilities staff or custodians) who might be on their stages, or in their shops and rehearsal halls. Whatever the extent of multi-employer or interdepartmental activity in your theatre and production facilities, your safety and health program must have clearly defined processes for assuring the consistent, and well-communicated application of safety and health policies and procedures to all.

A mission statement that indicates the extent of coverage and the inclusiveness of the program provides a means to ensure enforcement of the program's requirements (such as hardhats required to be worn onstage during all production load-in work) by authorizing all staff to interact with anyone who is not complying:

> The Yale School of Drama/Yale Repertory Theatre's commitment to safety, health and personal security is inclusive and pervasive. All

YSD/YRT students, faculty and staff are included in its safety, health and security programs and policies, which are integrated to the fullest extent possible into all aspects of YSD/YRT education, training and production activities. The YSD/YRT safety, health and security programs and policies are intended to provide a safe, healthy and secure environment for all students, staff and faculty.[25]

In a multi-employer work environment, the safety and health program document must detail how each worker is covered by the program. For example, a program's requirement for the training of cast and crew in emergency and evacuation procedures the first time they are onstage, or in the rehearsal hall, must apply to the theatre's own productions as well as to a rental, or any other production company using the theatre's facilities. As such, the process for on-boarding a visiting theatre company or initiating the work of a subcontractor to refurbish a theatre's lighting control system must include:

- hazards present in the worksite;
- procedures for reporting accidents and injuries;
- whom to contact with safety or health concerns;
- specific safety, health, or life safety policies or procedures to be followed that are appropriate to the live event produced or the work being done;
- emergency contact information for key people within the organization;
- contact information and protocols for local emergency responders such as medical and fire services.

Coordination and communication with the visiting company or subcontractor is essential. The scheduling of work, which areas of the facility will be affected by the work, and access control to the worksite must be discussed and agreed upon. For facilities work, knowing well in advance what materials will be brought onsite and the potential safety or health effects of the type of work being done is critical to informing employees, staff, and students who might be affected. A production company coming into your theatre may bring equipment that does not comply with your safety and health program's defined policies (e.g. haze machines that utilize mineral oil), or use stage effects that are not in compliance with local life safety requirements.

PROGRAM EVALUATION AND IMPROVEMENT

Your safety and health program's success requires an initial assessment of its start-up implementation. This evaluation is followed by periodic review of the program's performance and progress to complete the cyclical and iterative process. Gaps and shortcomings identified from these evaluations provide you with opportunities for improvement, and the integration of new ideas or evolving technologies into the safety and health program. Goals and targets related to the safety and health program evolve over time, but data points need to be established from the beginning. Evaluation of safety and health programs is typically based on metrics that are quantifiable and recordable: numbers of injuries; workers' compensation data; reported hazards or near-misses; number and frequency of inspections. These metrics can be either lagging or leading indicators of your program's performance and progress.

> Both *lagging* and *leading* indicators should be used. Lagging indicators generally track worker exposures and injuries that have already occurred. Leading indicators track how well various aspects of the program have been implemented and reflect steps taken to prevent injuries or illnesses before they occur.[26]

Lagging Indicators
- Number and severity of injuries.
- Workers' compensation data.
- Number of accident investigations.
- Citations and violations.
- Results of exposure monitoring indicating hazardous exposures.

Leading Indicators
- Number of employee suggestions.
- Response time related to reported incidents.
- Number of employees or students trained.
- Number and frequency of inspections.
- Number and severity of hazards identified during inspections.
- Near-miss reporting records.

FIGURE 3.6 Lagging and Leading Indicators

Recording and tracking the data needed to assess and monitor your safety and health program's activities requires well-defined and implemented reporting and documentation processes. We noted above the importance of employee participation in the identification and reporting of hazards and reporting of near-misses and injuries. Responsibilities for documenting and maintaining records of these aspects of the program must be clearly defined. OSHA requirements for recordkeeping, notification, and reporting of accident and injury data may well apply to your theatre organization.

In addition to such data, a self-assessment of key aspects of your safety and health program provides benchmarking to gauge your program's progress in relation to your program's goals as well in the context of generally accepted measures of success for safety and health programs. Both OSHA[27] and the National Institute for Occupational Safety and Health (NIOSH)[28] provide links on their websites to several types of assessment tools. One example of a safety and health assessment was developed by the Harvard Center for Work, Health, and Well-Being:

> The Workplace Integrated Safety and Health (WISH) Assessment measures workplace policies, programs, and practices that focus on working conditions and organizational facilitators of worker safety, health, and well-being. The tool can be used by employers and researchers to assess the extent of implementation of an integrated approach.[29]

The initial and subsequent evaluations of your safety and health program will utilize metrics, self-assessments, and other data along with feedback from employees and managers (students, staff, and faculty) to gauge the effectiveness of the program. Progress toward achieving the goals of the safety and health program will be noted by such aspects as:

- Identified hazards are controlled.
- Inspections and investigations proceed as planned.
- Evaluation of collected metrics indicates progress.

- The core elements of the program have been fully implemented.
- Comparing self-assessments to previous assessments shows growth.
- Benchmarks from similar organizations are used as part of self-audits.

Opportunities for improvement to your program will be revealed from the comparison of metrics (data, self-assessments, and feedback) to the goals and expectations defined in the safety and health program's documentation. The evaluation process results in plans to correct shortcomings related to the prevention and control of known hazards. Improvements will be identified that can assist in developing programmatic approaches to hazards resulting from new technologies or changes in operating procedures. The evaluation is not complete until the findings and action plans are made available to all affected by your safety and health program (leadership, managers, employees, faculty, staff, students). Participation and engagement are key elements to the success of your program. Communicating and discussing the results of each annual assessment provide a valuable opportunity for interaction among all the stakeholders in the process.

To assist you with resources for the development of your theatre or academic department's safety and health program, links to safety and health program documents for several theatre organizations are in the Appendix, and on this book's website. OSHA's Safe + Sound campaign provides resources to guide safety and health programs including assessment and employee survey tools.[30] The mission of Safe + Sound emphasizes the importance of these and other core elements: "Every workplace should have a safety and health program that includes management leadership, worker participation, and a systematic approach to finding and fixing hazards."[31]

The OSHA Safe + Sound campaign acknowledges what you might be thinking at this point, "We're not ready and we don't have the money or time to implement a complete safety and health program right now." The Safe + Sound campaign document, *10 Ways to Get Your Program Started*, highlights initial steps you can take as you evolve the more structured parts of a comprehensive program:

> If you are not quite ready to implement a complete safety and health program, here are some simple steps you can take to get started. Completing these steps will give you a solid base from which to take on some of the more structured actions you may want to include in your program.
>
> 1. Establish safety and health as a core value.
> 2. Lead by example.
> 3. Implement a reporting system.
> 4. Provide training.
> 5. Conduct inspections.
> 6. Collect hazard control ideas.
> 7. Implement hazard controls.
> 8. Address emergencies.
> 9. Seek input on workplace changes [from employees, staff, interns, students, and faculty].
> 10. Make improvements to the program.[32]

Taking these ten steps will assist you is establishing your safety and health program. The next several chapters will provide details related to compliance with codes, and an examination of specific policies, procedures, and recommended practices you must include in the work and production activities covered by your safety and health program. Each of the core elements described in this chapter, combined with industry-specific policies and procedures, are essential parts of your program. However, an overarching goal of your program must be compliance:

> The goals of the YSD/YRT Safety and Occupational Health Program are . . . to develop and implement policies and procedures that are in compliance with all applicable codes.[33]

In the next chapter, we will move toward a position of compliance through an examination of the legal codes applicable to your work in theatre production and live events.

NOTES

1 WorksafeNB, "Guide to Workplace Safety & Health Programs," accessed April 9, 2019, https://www.worksafenb.ca/media/1226/worksafenbhsprogramsguidee-1.pdf, 4.
2 Anna Glover, Director of Theatre Safety and Occupational Health, Yale School of Drama, Yale Repertory Theatre, in conversation on July 31, 2018.
3 Occupational Safety and Health Administration (OSHA), "Recommended Practices for Safety and Health Programs," OSHA 3885, accessed November 26, 2018, www.OSHA.gov/shpguidelines; I (my emphasis).
4 OSHA, "Recommended Practices" webpage, accessed November 26, 2018, https://www.osha.gov/shpguidelines/.
5 Richard Byrne, *Be the Best: How to Become a World-Class Safety Professional* (Wigston, Leicestershire, England: IOSH Services Ltd, 2009), 72.
6 Yale School of Drama/Yale Repertory Theatre, "Our Core Values," accessed February 21, 2019, https://www.drama.yale.edu/.
7 Dr. Tim Marsh, *Talking Safety: A User's Guide to World Class Safety Conversation*, 2nd edition (Burlington, VT: Gower Publishing Company, 2013), 57.
8 Goodman Theatre, *Health and Safety Program, 1.1 Policy Statement—The Health and Safety Program*, used with permission.
9 Stian Antonsen, *Safety Culture: Theory, Method and Improvement* (Burlington, VT: Ashgate Publishing Company, 2009), 126.
10 OSHA's Hazard Communication Standard, 29 CFR 1910.1200, is commonly referred to as the Right-to-Know Standard.
11 OSHA, Hazard Communication Standard, accessed November 26, 2018, https://www.osha.gov/dsg/hazcom/index.html.
12 OSHA. Regulations (Standards—29 CFR 1910.1200(b)(1)), accessed February 28, 2019, https://www.osha.gov/laws-regs/regulations/standardnumber/1910/1910.1200.

13 OSHA 3071 *Job Hazard Analysis,* accessed February 15, 2009, https://www.osha.gov/Publications/osha3071.pdf.
14 OSHA, *Recommended Practices*, accessed November 26, 2018, https://www.osha.gov/shpguidelines/docs/OSHA_SHP_Recommended_Practices.pdf, 13.
15 OSHA, *OSH Act of 1970, Judicial Review, Section 11(c),* accessed November 26, 2018, https://www.osha.gov/laws-regs/oshact/section_11
16 National Center for Education Statistics, "The Forum Guide to Data Ethics," Appendix B: Sample Whistle Blower Protection Policy, accessed April 26, 2019, https://nces.ed.gov/pubs2010/dataethics/appendix_b.asp.
17 Nathan Braymen, "Habituation: Implications on Safety," accessed November 26, 2018, https://www.linkedin.com/pulse/habituation-implications-safety-nathan-braymen/.
18 Verywell: Mind, "When and Why Does Habituation Occur?," accessed February 28, 2019, https://www.verywellmind.com/what-is-habituation-2795233.
19 Oregon OSHA, "Hazard Identification and Control," accessed November 26, 2018, https://osha.oregon.gov/Pages/topics/hazard-identification.aspx.
20 OSHA, *Hazard Identification Training Tool,* accessed November 26, 2018, https://www.osha.gov/hazfinder/index.html.
21 National Institute for Occupational Safety and Health (NIOSH), "Workplace Safety & Health Topics," *Hierarchy of Controls*, accessed November 26, 2018, https://www.cdc.gov/niosh/topics/hierarchy/default.html.
22 Dr. Tim Marsh, *Total Safety Culture; Organizational Risk Literacy* (Manchester, UK: Ryder Marsh Safety Limited, 2014), 62.
23 Yale Insights, Yale School of Management, "What Makes an Organization Change?", accessed November 26, 2018, http://insights.som.yale.edu/insights/what-makes-an-organization-change.
24 OSHA, OSH Act of 1970, Duties, Section 5, accessed November 26, 2018, https://www.osha.gov/laws-regs/oshact/section_5.
25 *Yale University School of Drama Safety Handbook 8.20.2018 ed.*, 5, used with permission.
26 OSHA, *Recommended Practices*, accessed November 26, 2018, https://www.osha.gov/shpguidelines/docs/OSHA_SHP_Recommended_Practices.pdf, 27 (emphasis in original).

27 OSHA, "Explore Tools [for safety and health programs]," accessed November 26, 2018, https://www.osha.gov/shpguidelines/explore-tools.html.
28 NIOSH, "Total Worker Health: Planning, Assessment and Evaluation Resources," accessed November 26, 2018, https://www.cdc.gov/niosh/twh/tools.html.
29 Harvard Center for Work, Health, and Well-Being, "Workplace Integrated Safety and Health (WISH) Assessment," accessed November 26, 2018, http://centerforworkhealth.sph.harvard.edu/resources/workplace-integrated-safety-and-health-wish-assessment.
30 OSHA, Safe+Sound, "Safety and Health Programs," accessed November 26, 2018, https://www.osha.gov/safeandsound/safety-and-health-programs.html.
31 OSHA, Safe+Sound, accessed November 26, 2018, https://www.osha.gov/safeandsound/.
32 OSHA, Safe+Sound, "Safety and Health Programs: Resources," accessed December 14, 2018, https://www.osha.gov/safeandsound/safety-and-health-programs.html.
33 *Yale University School of Drama Safety Handbook 8.20.2018 ed.*, 5, used with permission.

BIBLIOGRAPHY

Antonsen, Stian. *Safety Culture: Theory, Method and Improvement.* Burlington, VT: Ashgate Publishing Company, 2009.

Byrne, Richard. *Be the Best: How to Become a World-Class Health and Safety Professional.* Wigston, Leicestershire, England: IOSH Services Ltd, 2009.

Marsh, Tim. *Talking Safety: A User's Guide to World Class Safety Conversation.* Burlington, VT: Gower Publishing Company, 2013.

Marsh, Tim. *Total Safety Culture: Organisational Risk Literacy.* Manchester, England: Ryder Marsh Safety Limited, 2014.

CHAPTER 4

Compliance

William J. Reynolds

In this chapter I will cover legal requirements (codes) related to theatre safety and health that apply to your theatre organization or academic department. Legally enforceable requirements such as those related to fire protection or the structural integrity of buildings are by definition codes. Common usage, however, often refers to legally enforceable requirements as either codes or standards. For instance, the Occupational Safety and Health Administration's (OSHA) legal requirements are known as OSHA standards,[1] while the National Fire Protection Association's (NFPA) fire protection requirements for various types of occupancies are titled the NFPA Life Safety Code. For consistency, the terminology commonly noted in reference to these legal requirements will be used in this text. In the next chapter, we will identify and discuss safety and health standards developed by and used in the theatre industry which, because they have not been "enacted into law by a local, regional or national authority"[2] cannot by strict definition be considered codes. Codes are standards with legal enforceability.

> A code is a standard that has been enacted into law by a local, regional, or national authority having jurisdiction [AHJ] so that the engineer or contractor is legally obligated to comply with the code. Noncompliance can result in being prosecuted. The code may be an industry, government, or voluntary consensus-based standard. A code can include references to standards, which means the standards are incorporated by reference and therefore are part of the code and legally enforceable.[3]

Terminology referring to codes and standards can be confusing because of the definition above. Since a code may have started out as a standard, there is some flexibility in the use of these two terms when referring to a directive or practice that informs a legal course of action or a legal requirement. An example of this is OSHA. When OSHA was established in 1971, existing standards (from the above definition: "an industry, government, or voluntary consensus-based standard") were adopted by a legislative authority, the U.S. Department of Labor, to become the OSHA codes. However, these directives have continued to be referred to as OSHA standards. As noted on the OSHA website under the tab "Law and Regulations":

> OSHA's mission is to ensure that employees work in a safe and healthful environment by setting and enforcing standards, and by providing training, outreach, education and assistance. *Employers must comply with all applicable OSHA standards.* They must also comply with the General Duty Clause of the OSH Act, which requires employers to keep their workplace free of serious recognized hazards.[4]

The language used in codes is intended to create precise meanings, and provide clear understanding of obligation, prohibition, and discretionary action. Previous to 2010, "shall" had been the word used in code documents intended to create an obligation or required action. In the United States, the Federal Plain Writing Act of 2010 and the Federal Plain Language Guidelines "compel the FAA and every federal department to use 'must,' not 'shall' to indicate requirements."[5] You will continue to read many codes using "shall" to indicate an obligation, but over time new or revised code documents will use the word "must." According to the Federal Plain Language Guidelines, the word to use in codes instead of "shall" is:

- "Must" for an obligation, plus,
- "Must not" for a prohibition,
- "May" for a discretionary action, and,
- "Should" for a recommendation.[6]

Examples of the use of all these words, plus "shall" and "can," appear in the text of OSHA standards, as well as other codes. You must read any section of a code carefully to discern which actions you are obliged (legally required) to follow or implement, to know what you cannot do, and to understand which actions are discretionary or simply recommended.

Knowing which codes are applicable to theatre production is essential to complying with their legal requirements. Compliance assures achieving a minimum level of safety and health in the theatre production process. In a fashion similar to the Hierarchy of Controls, we can imagine the relationship of codes, standards, recommended practices, and policies and procedures as depicted in Figure 4.1:

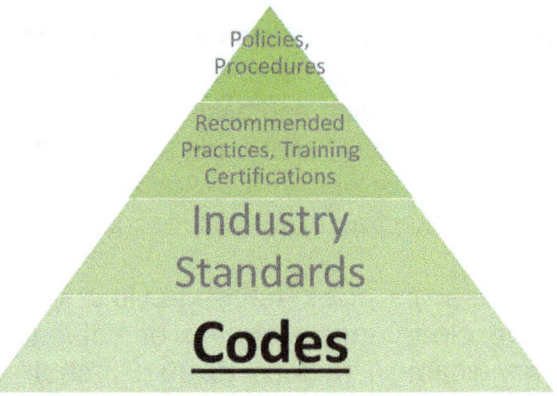

FIGURE 4.1 Hierarchy of Safety Controls: Codes

Compliance with applicable codes forms a baseline on which the other elements related to your theatre safety and health program will be founded. OSHA standards are national in the United States of America, and therefore applicable to virtually all places of employment in the United States. Other codes are regional, state-wide, or local in their adoption by legislative bodies. Building, fire and life safety codes provide examples of the latter:

> As the U.S. developed and expanded in territory over its initial century, local, regional and state-wide legal requirements evolved into a patchwork of building and fire codes. By the 1900s, three regional building codes (National Building Code, Standard Building Code, and Uniform Building Code) plus fire codes from National Fire Protection Association had developed and were in use across the country. Today, all fifty U.S. states, the District of Columbia, and every U.S. Territory has adopted International Code Council[7] model codes at the state or jurisdictional level in whole or as a basis for their building or fire codes. Thirty-Nine states have also adopted the NFPA 101®, Life Safety Code®.[8]

At the end of this chapter, I will note some of the safety codes enforced in other countries, such as Canada, Chile, India, Taiwan, and the United Kingdom, among others. A critical part of your responsibility for safety and health in your organization or academic department is to know which codes apply to your situation.

Compliance with the safety, health, and fire codes enforced in your area is not optional. Compliance is required, but doing so is just the starting point for your safety and health program. Limiting your safety and health program's focus to compliance may result in missed opportunities to establish a program that moves well beyond a minimal level of safety:[9]

> OSHA standards set minimum safety and health requirements; they do not prohibit employers from adopting more stringent requirements.[10]

This text will use as reference points the codes from OSHA (for national safety and health requirements) and NFPA (for regional or local fire and life safety requirements). Depending on your region or local jurisdiction, other fire and life safety codes similar to the NFPA codes might apply, such as the International Building Code (IBC) and the International Fire Code (IFC). To stay succinct, I will include examples of applicable codes from OSHA and NFPA; for brevity I will only scratch the surface of the many codes applicable nationally, regionally, and locally to your theatre's operations. You must investigate these codes to ascertain what is applicable to your organization.

Compliance with codes alone does not guarantee that your theatre safety and health program will function at an appropriate level, nor that the program will effectively be integrated into your theatre production process. Because of this, your safety and health program must clearly identify code compliance as one of several aspects integral to achieving its goals. For instance:

> The goals of the YSD/YRT Theater Safety and Occupational Health Program are to assure the identification and reduction of the risks associated with theater production and training; to reduce or eliminate related health exposures; and to develop and implement policies and procedures that are in compliance with all applicable codes.[11]

Or,

Goodman Theatre Health & Safety Program

1.1 Policy Statement—The Health & Safety Program
The Health & Safety Program has been written to comply with the Occupational Safety and Health Act of 1970, the Right to Know Laws of the State of Illinois, and combines written programs concerning: 1.) emergency procedures, 2.) accident and illness prevention, 3.) personal protective equipment, 4.) the hazard communication standards, and, 5.) respiratory protection and other programs.[12]

OCCUPATIONAL SAFETY AND HEALTH ADMINISTRATION (OSHA)

We'll start with the OSHA standards since they are applicable to virtually all places of employment in the U.S. The Occupational Safety and Health Act of 1970 is self-described as:

An Act to assure safe and healthful working conditions for working men and women; by authorizing enforcement of the standards developed under the Act; by assisting and encouraging the States in their efforts to assure safe and healthful working conditions; by providing for research, information, education, and training in the field of occupational safety and health; and for other purposes.[13]

The applicability of OSHA standards requires an employer–employee relationship for the standards to be enforceable. The General Duty Clause of Section 5 in the OSH Act further clarifies roles and responsibilities for employers and employees. The employees of any theatre organization or academic department will be covered by either the Federal OSHA standards or by a State OSHA plan such as CalOSHA in California or ConnOSHA in Connecticut.[14] State occupational safety and health plans are allowed under Section 18 State Jurisdiction and State Plans of the OSH Act. Approved State Plans must enforce safety and health standards that are at least as protective as the Federal OSHA standards.[15] Students and volunteers (people working in your theatre or department but not being paid) are not technically employees so OSHA does not technically have jurisdiction over their safety or health. But to be consistent and comprehensive, your safety and health program must be inclusive of all people (employees, staff, faculty, students, and volunteers) included in your operations.

The OSH Act defines the term "standard" as follows:

> Standard means a standard which requires conditions, or the adoption or use of one or more practices, means, methods, operations, or processes, reasonably necessary or appropriate to safe or healthful employment and places of employment.[16]

OSHA standards apply to all workplaces and/or they cover particular workplaces. For instance, the OSHA standard related to noise exposure contained in the 1910—General Industry Standard applies to all places of employment,[17] while Subpart AA—Confined Space in Construction (1926.1201(a)) "protects employees engaged in construction activities."[18] The OSHA standards most applicable to theatre production are the General Industry Standard (29 CFR 1910) and the Construction Standard (29 CFR 1926). The syntax used to identify OSHA standards is, for example, 29 CFR 1910.95(d)(3)(ii)(A):

- 29 refers to the Department of Labor;
- CFR is Congressional Federal Register;
- 1910 is a Part number denoting a General Industry Standard (specifically entitled Occupational Safety and Health Standards in the regulations);
- 1910.95 is the standard number (which in this case is entitled Occupational Noise Exposure);
- (d) denotes a section of the standard (monitoring);
- The rest follows in typical form outlining subsections.

OSHA standards are available online at www.osha.gov. The website is fully searchable and contains useful guidance and recommendations you will find helpful in developing and implementing your safety and health program.

The part number for the Construction Industry Standard is 29 CFR 1926—Safety and Health Standards for Construction. (Other parts of the OSHA regulations cover Shipyard Employment: 29

CFR 1915; Marine Terminals: 29 CFR 1917; Longshoring: 29 CFR 1918; Agriculture: 29 CFR 1928.) Recordkeeping: 29 CFR 1904—Recording and Reporting Occupational Injuries and Illness contains standards which apply to all places of employment, so we will identify aspects of 1904 that must be followed by most theatre producing organizations. Standards within a particular part, such as General Industry, are divided into subparts. These subparts create chapters with headings such as 1910 Subpart D—Walking-Working Surfaces. When a specific standard is referenced by OSHA in a citation or a letter of interpretation, its subpart letter is usually not included. The subpart letter provides a means to search within a standard's Table of Contents for a particular topic.

Theatre production requires work and operations that can reasonably be covered either by 29 CFR 1910—General Industry Standard or by 29 CFR 1926—Construction Standard. OSHA has a succinct definition of General Industry: "OSHA uses the term 'general industry' to refer to all industries not included in agriculture, construction, or maritime."[19] In 1910—Subpart B, construction work is defined as "work for construction, alteration, and/or repair, including painting and decorating."[20] Since it is clear our work is neither maritime nor agriculture, either the general industry or the construction standards are applicable. One of the ways to parse the distinction between these two standards is to consider that the type of work occurring during a load-in or fit-up onstage bears close resemblance to a typical construction site, and almost all other workplaces and tasks, such as the fabrication shops and administrative areas, are similar to a general industry setting. Rather than get too involved in debating which of the standards to consider in a particular instance, I will apply two criteria to our discussion: one, common sense and, two, which standard's requirements provide better protection, or are the most preventative.

I'll begin our overview of OSHA standards applicable to theatre production with the General Industry standards: 29 CFR 1910. Then, I will review sections of 29 CFR 1926—Construction that do not overlap with 29 CFR 1910—General Industry, but provide additional or more protective requirements. Then I will go over requirements related to recordkeeping, and recording and reporting accidents, injury, and illness incidents contained in 29 CFR 1904—Recordkeeping.

29 CFR 1910—General Industry has 20 subparts, lettered from A to Z; there is no Subpart C and Subparts U–Y are reserved. A helpful

way to diminish what appears to be the daunting task of working through all 20 subparts and literally hundreds of pages of standards (the text I used for theatre safety classes, published by Mancomm, Inc.[21] comprised 784 pages) is to sort out those subparts and sections of subparts that do not apply to the work we do, such a Subpart R—Special Industries (textiles, bakery equipment, and sawmills, among others) and Subpart T—Commercial Diving Operations. The titles of other subparts may appear to contain wholly applicable standards, but once we look at subheadings and the details of many subparts, we see large sections of them are not relevant to theatre production.

Subpart F—Powered Platforms, Manlifts, and Vehicle-Mounted Work Platforms	Subpart N—Materials Handling and Storage
§1910.66 Powered platforms for building maintenance §1910.67 Vehicle-mounted elevating and rotating work platforms §1910.68 Manlifts	§1910.176 Handling materials—general §1910.177 Servicing multi-piece and single piece rim wheels §1910.178 Powered industrial trucks §1910.179 Overhead and gantry cranes §1910.180 Crawler locomotive and truck cranes §1910.181 Derricks §1910.183 Helicopters §1910.184 Slings
Subpart H—Hazardous Materials	
§1910.101 Compressed gases (general requirements) §1910.102 Acetylene §1910.103 Hydrogen §1910.104 Oxygen §1910.105 Nitrous oxide §1910.106 Flammable liquids §1910.107 Spray finishing using flammable and combustible materials §1910.108 [Reserved] §1910.109 Explosives and blasting agents §1910.110 Storage and handling of liquefied petroleum gases §1910.111 Storage and handling of anhydrous ammonia §§1910.112–1910.113 [Reserved] §1910.119 Process safety management of highly hazardous chemicals §1910.120 Hazardous waste operations and emergency response §1910.121 [Reserved]	**Subpart O—Machinery and Machine Guarding** §1910.211 Definitions §1910.212 General requirements for all machines §1910.213 Woodworking machinery requirements §1910.214 Cooperage machinery [Reserved] §1910.215 Abrasive wheel machinery §1910.216 Mills and calendars in the rubber and plastics industries §1910.217 Mechanical power presses §1910.218 Forging machines §1910.219 Mechanical power-transmission apparatus

FIGURE 4.2 29 CFR 1910, Subparts F, H, N, O

For example, Figure 4.2 illustrates several different subparts, their titles, and numbered sections for specific standards. You'll see from the headings of the numbered sections which of the standards are not applicable to theatre production.

A final example to help remove concerns that your safety and health program could not possibly function in compliance with OSHA standards due to their number and complexity comes from an assessment of 1910 Subpart Z—Toxic and Hazardous Substances. This subpart contains exposure limits for air contaminants and mineral dusts (OSHA Permissible Exposure Limits or PELs) and the Hazard Communication standard (commonly referred to as Haz Com or Right-to-Know). We must comply with these standards. But of the standards numbered from 1910.1000 to 1910.1450 (a total of 29 sections) only four standards are specifically applicable

---

Subpart Z—TOXIC AND HAZARDOUS SUBSTANCES

§1910.1000 Air contaminants
§1910.1001 Asbestos
§1910.1002 Coal tar pitch volatiles; interpretation of term
§1910.1003 13 Carcinogens (4-Nitrobiphenyl, etc.)
§1910.1004 alpha-Naphthylamine
§1910.1005 [Reserved]
§1910.1006 Methyl chloromethyl ether
§1910.1007 3,'-Dichlorobenzidine (and its salts)
§1910.1008 bis-Chloromethyl ether
§1910.1009 beta-Naphthylamine
§1910.1010 Benzidine
§1910.1011 4-Aminodiphenyl
§1910.1012 Ethyleneimine
§1910.1013 beta-Propiolactone
§1910.1014 2-Acetylaminofluorene
§1910.1015 4-Dimethylaminoazobenzene
§1910.1016 N-Nitrosodimethylamine
§1910.1017 Vinyl chloride
§1910.1018 Inorganic arsenic
§1910.1020 Access to employee exposure and medical records
§1910.1024 Beryllium

§1910.1025 Lead
§1910.1026 Chromium (VI)
§1910.1027 Cadmium
§1910.1028 Benzene
§1910.1029 Coke oven emissions
§1910.1030 Bloodborne pathogens
§1910.1043 Cotton dust
§1910.1044 1,2-dibromo-3-chloropropane
§1910.1045 Acrylonitrile
§1910.1047 Ethylene oxide
§1910.1048 Formaldehyde
§1910.1050 Methylenedianiline.
§1910.1051 1,3-Butadiene.§1910.1052 Methylene chloride
§1910.1053 Respirable crystalline silica
§1910.1096 Ionizing radiation
§1910.1200 Hazard communication
§1910.1201 Retention of DOT markings, placards and labels
§1910.1450 Occupational exposure to hazardous chemicals in laboratories
§§1910.1451—1910.1499 [Reserved]

FIGURE 4.3 29 CFR 1910, Subpart Z—Toxic and Hazardous Substances

to a typical theatre production workplace: 1910.1000, 1910.1020, 1910.1030, and 1910.1200. See Figure 4.3.[22]

Other standards might apply in specific circumstances, such as 1910.1053—Respirable crystalline silica if you are using sand or certain concrete mixtures in a show; 1910.001—Asbestos where asbestos might be present in old stage equipment or fire curtains; or 1910.25—Lead, and the other "heavy metal" standards. Lead or other metals might be in paint on old doors or antique furniture, or released into the air from solder or welding operations. You must know about the operations, processes, and materials used in your theatre's workplaces, identify which OSHA standards apply, and then develop policies that will assure compliance.

Many of the remaining subparts have direct connection to the work and the workplaces in theatre production. Except for 1910.24—Step bolts and manhole steps, all of Subpart D—Walking-Working Surfaces applies to the work we do. In Subpart D are requirements to keep our workplaces "in a clean, orderly and sanitary condition."[23] 1910.23—Ladders contains general requirements that apply to all types of ladders: wood ladders cannot be painted; ladders must be inspected before use; employees must face the ladder when climbing up or down,[24] as well as specific details related to the use of portable ladders (1910.23(c)) and fixed ladders (1910.23(d)). Stairways (standard stairs, spiral stairs, and ship stairs) in our workplaces must comply with section 1910.25. Sections 28, 29, and 30 are directly related to overhead work in virtually every theatre. 1910.28—Duty to have fall protection and falling object protection contains requirements related to each employer's responsibilities for employees working at height and loose objects overhead. To paraphrase the requirements:

- This section requires employers to provide protection for each employee exposed to fall and falling object hazards.

- Employer must ensure each employee on an unprotected edge 4-feet or more above a lower level is protected by a guardrail system, safety net system, or personal fall arrest system.

- The employer must ensure each employee wears head protection when exposed to falling object hazards, in addition to mitigating the hazard by erecting toe boards and screens, or limiting employee access to the area below the falling object hazard.[25]

Subpart D, 1910.29 provides guidance on how to comply with the standard through the use of guardrails (1910.29(b)), covers over floor openings and holes (1910.29(e)), stair railings (1910.29(f)), ladder safety systems (1910.29(i)), and personal fall protection systems (1910.29(j)).

Subpart D provides us with examples of the types of training requirements contained in many OSHA standards. Section 1910.30—Training requirements is worth quoting in total here because the format and content are reflected in most of the training sections of other standards.

1910.30 Training requirements

1910.30(a) *Fall hazards.*

1910.30(a)(1) Before any employee is exposed to a fall hazard, the employer must provide training for each employee who uses personal fall protection systems or who is required to be trained as specified elsewhere in this subpart. Employers must ensure employees are trained in the requirements of this paragraph on or before May 17, 2017.

1910.30(a)(2) The employer must ensure each employee is trained by a qualified person.

1910.30(a)(3) The employer must train each employee in at least the following topics:

1910.30(a)(3)(i) The nature of the fall hazards in the work area and how to recognize them;

1910.30(a)(3)(ii) The procedures to be followed to minimize those hazards;

1910.30(a)(3)(iii) The correct procedures for installing, inspecting, operating, maintaining, and disassembling the personal fall protection systems that the employee uses; and

1910.30(a)(3)(iv) The correct use of personal fall protection systems and equipment specified in paragraph (a)(1) of this section, including, but not limited to, proper hook-up, anchoring, and tie-off techniques, and methods of equipment inspection and storage, as specified by the manufacturer.

1910.30(b) *Equipment hazards.*

1910.30(b)(1) The employer must train each employee on or before May 17, 2017 in the proper care, inspection, storage, and use of equipment covered by this subpart before an employee uses the equipment.

1910.30(b)(2) The employer must train each employee who uses a dockboard to properly place and secure it to prevent unintentional movement.

1910.30(b)(3) The employer must train each employee who uses a rope descent system in proper rigging and use of the equipment in accordance with §1910.27.

1910.30(b)(4) The employer must train each employee who uses a designated area in the proper set-up and use of the area.

1910.30(c) *Retraining.* The employer must retrain an employee when the employer has reason to believe the employee does not have the understanding and skill required by paragraphs (a) and (b) of this section. Situations requiring retraining include, but are not limited to, the following:

1910.30(c)(1) When changes in the workplace render previous training obsolete or inadequate;

1910.30(c)(2) When changes in the types of fall protection systems or equipment to be used render previous training obsolete or inadequate; or

1910.30(c)(3) When inadequacies in an affected employee's knowledge or use of fall protection systems or equipment indicate that the employee no longer has the requisite understanding or skill necessary to use equipment or perform the job safely.

1910.30(d) *Training must be understandable.* The employer must provide information and training to each employee in a manner that the employee understands.

Lest this book becomes something like "Everything You Wanted to Know about OSHA 1910, But were Afraid to Ask" in length, I will list the subparts of 1910 that are generally applicable to theatre and live performance. You must integrate the appropriate requirements into your safety and health program.

- 1910 Subpart E—Exit Routes and Emergency Planning
- 1910 Subpart F—Powered Platforms, Manlifts, and Vehicle-Mounted Work Platforms [read the definition of a manlift to understand why this section does apply to our typical aerial work platform or "Genie" lift]
- 1910 Subpart G—Occupational Health and Environmental Control; particularly 1910.94–Ventilation and 1910.95—Occupational noise exposure
- 1910 Subpart H—Hazardous Materials; specifically 1910.101–Compressed gases and 1910.106—Flammable materials
- 1910 Subpart I—Personal Protective Equipment (PPE)
- 1910 Subpart J—General Environmental Controls [while not apparent from the title, this section deals with several applicable topics, such as: housekeeping, waste disposal, water and sanitary systems, confined space, and the control of hazardous energy (lock-out/tag-out)]
- 1910 Subpart K—Medical and First Aid [the shortest subpart in 1910 at less than half a page long]
- 1910 Subpart L—Fire Protection
- 1910 Subpart M—Compressed Gas and Compressed Air Equipment [read the section on air receivers, which are tanks for compressed air]
- 1910 Subpart N—Materials Handling and Storage; specifically 1910.184—Slings
- 1910 Subpart O—Machinery and Machine Guarding
- 1910 Subpart P—Hand and Portable Powered Tools, and Other Hand-Held Equipment
- 1910 Subpart Q—Welding, Cutting, and Brazing
- 1910 Subpart S—Electrical

- 1910 Subpart Z—Toxic and Hazardous Substances [focus on those sections noted in the text above]

Several sections of 29 CFR 1926—Construction Industry Standard contain protective requirements which can be included in your safety and health program's compliance efforts. You should investigate these in detail as well as any others applicable to your theatre or academic department's operations. 29 CFR 1926—Construction Industry Standard is structured the same as other OSHA standards. There are 28 subparts lettered from A to CC, many with headings similar to those in 29 CFR 1910 which contain requirements relevant to theatre. For instance:

Subpart C—General Safety and Health Provisions

Subpart D—Occupational Health and Environmental Controls

Subpart J—Welding and Cutting

Subpart K—Electrical

Subpart Z—Toxic and Hazardous Substances

Subparts with standards specifically applicable to theatre production with content similar to the General Industry standards include:

Subpart E—Personal Protective and Life Safety Equipment

Subpart F—Fire Protection and Prevention

Subpart L—Scaffolds

Subpart M—Fall Protection

Subpart X—Stairways and Ladders

Several subparts of 29 CFR 1926—Construction Industry Standard are generally not applicable to typical theatre production practices, for instance:

Subpart N—Helicopters, Hoists, Elevators, and Conveyers

Subpart P—Excavations

Subpart Q—Concrete and Masonry Construction

Subpart U—Blasting and the Use of Explosives

29 CFR 1926—Construction Industry Standard Subpart C—General Safety and Health Provisions is worth specific examination. This subpart contains several statements of an employer's responsibilities for safety and health in the workplace, with references to the subsequent subparts covering each element. Section 1926.20 gives us unambiguous guidance on these responsibilities:

> That no contractor or subcontractor for any part of the contract work shall require any laborer or mechanic employed in the performance of the contract to work in surroundings or under working conditions which are unsanitary, hazardous, or dangerous to his [or her] health or safety.[26]

Other employer responsibilities contained in this subpart under (b) Accident prevention responsibilities require that each employer initiate and maintain programs to assure compliance with the standards. This is a direct reference to the types of safety and health programs covered in Chapter 3. Employers are also directed to only allow those employees who are qualified by their training or experience to operate equipment and machinery. Section 1926.21 is about training and education; 1926.21(b)(2) states "The employer shall instruct each employee in the recognition and avoidance of unsafe conditions and regulations applicable to his [or her] work environment to control or eliminate any hazards or other exposure to illness or injury." As with the General Industry standards, your safety and health program must include policies and procedures in compliance with those sections of the Construction Industry standards applicable to your workplace.

29 CFR 1904—Recording and Reporting Occupational Injuries and Illness applies to all employers covered by the OSH Act, with only a few specific exclusions.[27] As noted in the previous chapter, the reporting, recording, documentation, and analysis of work-related accidents and injuries are critical elements in the success of your safety and health program. OSHA's requirements in 29 CFR 1904 are broad, and create recording and reporting requirements to provide a minimum level of data. To implement effective assessment, analysis, and improvement, your program should track other data, such as near-misses. OSHA defines its requirements under the 1904 standard:

The purpose of this rule (part 1904) is to require employers to record and report work-related fatalities, injuries, and illnesses.[28]

As with other OSHA standards, which sections of 29 CFR 1904 apply to your organization depends on several factors. Subparts A, B, C, and D cover recording and recordkeeping requirements. Companies with ten or fewer employees at all times during the last calendar year are not required to keep OSHA injury and illness records. Certain industries are partially exempt from OSHA recordkeeping. Appendix A to Subpart B of 29 CFR 1904 contains a list of these partially exempt industries classified by their North American Industry Classification System (NAICS) codes (see Figure 4.4).[29]

NAICS Code	Industry
5121	Motion Picture and Video Industries
5122	Sound Recording Studios
6111	Elementary and Secondary Schools
6112	Junior Colleges
6113	Colleges, Universities, and Professional Schools
6115	Technical and Trade Schools
7114	Agents and Managers for Artists, Athletes, Entertainers, and Other Public Figures
7115	Independent Artists, Writers, and Performers

FIGURE 4.4 29 CFR 1904, Partially Exempt Industries

Most academic institutions are likely to be exempt from the OSHA recordkeeping requirements based on this list of partially exempt industries. On the other hand, regional theatres and other producing organizations are not exempt and must maintain the required accident and illness records. You should obtain legal advice to determine what recordkeeping is required of your organization.

On January 1, 2015, OSHA updated the recordkeeping rules in 29 CFR 1904. First, the update expanded the reporting required of employers covered by OSHA. All employers must report to OSHA (1-800-321-OSHA[6742]):

- All work-related fatalities within 8-hours.
- All work-related inpatient hospitalizations,[30] all amputations, and all losses of an eye within 24-hours.

Second, and significant to many theatre organizations, the update removed several industries that had been partially exempt from keeping injury and illness records. This change affected theatre companies included in the NAICS Codes 7111 and 7113: Performing Arts Companies, and Promoters of Performing Arts, Sports, and Similar Events. If your organization is included in these NAICS codes, you should review the recording requirements contained in 29 CFR 1904, especially section 1904.29—Forms, which includes this requirement:

> You must use OSHA 300, 300-A, and 301 forms, or equivalent forms, for recordable injuries and illnesses. The OSHA 300 form is called the Log of Work-Related Injuries and Illnesses, the 300-A is the Summary of Work-Related Injuries and Illnesses, and the OSHA 301 form is called the Injury and Illness Incident Report.[31]

Compliance with the OSHA standards applicable to theatre production work can seem daunting. However, compliance must be a baseline goal of your safety and health program. The identification, assessment, prioritization, and implementation processes described in the previous chapter provide you with the means to get started. Prioritizing and setting achievable goals ensures your organization will be working towards compliance as your program evolves.

NATIONAL FIRE PROTECTION ASSOCIATION (NFPA)

Fire and life safety codes have a significant impact on theatre production and live performance events. Due to the historical record of significant loss of life incidents in public assembly spaces (theatres and auditoriums) protecting the public receives much attention from the fire protection community. Even though the United States lacks a national fire or life safety code, you must investigate coverage for your organization by checking with your local fire marshal or building code official. For my discussion related to fire and life safety I will focus on the consensus standards developed by the National Fire Protection Association (NFPA), which when adopted by a legislative authority become codes that can be legally enforced.[32] Codes are enforced in one of three ways. OSHA codes are enforced by federal or state OSH offices through inspections and investigations with resultant citations and fines. Fire, life safety, and most building codes are enforced by the legislative designation of an office or individual (town or city building department, building inspector, fire marshal, or state-level structural engineer, for example) tasked with enforcement. Other codes, such as the Americans with Disabilities Act (ADA), are enforced through the courts via lawsuits and legal action.[33]

Compliance with fire and life safety codes requires you to ascertain not only which codes apply to your theatre organization or academic department, but how and by whom they are enforced. The NFPA refers to this enforcement entity as the authority having jurisdiction or AHJ.[34] The standards developed by the International Code Council, such as the International Building Code, reference enforcement by a "building official" as the enforcing authority.[35]

Several NFPA codes have a direct impact on how our theatres and performance events operate:

- NFPA 10—Standard for Portable Fire Extinguishers
- NFPA 70—National Electrical Code
- NFPA 70E—Standard for Electrical Safety in the Workplace
- NFPA 80—Standard for Fire Doors and Other Opening Protectives [stage fire curtains]
- NFPA 101—Life Safety Code
- NFPA 160—Standard for the Use of Flame Effects Before an Audience
- NFPA 701—Standard Methods of Fire Tests for Flame Propagation of Textiles and Films
- NFPA 705—Recommended Practice for a Field Flame Test for Textiles and Films
- NFPA 1126—Standard for the Use of Pyrotechnics Before a Proximate Audience

Other NFPA codes provide architects, engineers, and building officials with requirements and guidance in life safety features to be incorporated into the built environment, such as sprinkler systems, fire detection systems, emergency notifications systems, smoke control, and smoke evacuation systems. The requirements of these and other building codes are reflected in our theatres, auditoriums, and production support and fabrication facilities by the presence of sprinklers, smoke detectors, and fire alarm systems.

The Life Safety Code (NFPA 101) details fire protection for built structures to provide life safety for people inside these structures. The scope includes minimizing the danger to life from fire, minimum criteria for egress facilities for prompt escape or safe sheltering, and other safeguards that will assure sufficient egress time or protection from fire.

> NFPA 101—Chapter 1, Administration, 1.2 Purpose: The purpose of this *Code* is to provide minimum requirements, with due regard to function, for the design, operation and maintenance of buildings and structures for safety to life from fire. Its provisions will also aid life safety in other emergencies.[36]

Building structures described in NFPA 101 are divided into several types of buildings or parts of buildings commonly found in the built environment. The uses of these structures and related fire and life safety code requirements are determined by the type of occupancy: assembly, educational, business, penal, etc. The Life Safety Code is divided into chapters applicable to all types of structures independent of occupancy type: Chapters 1 through 11 and Chapter 43. Life safety features applicable to specific occupancies are covered in Chapters 12 through 42. The chapters for each type of occupancy are specified for either New or Existing occupancies. Differentiating occupancy chapters between new construction and existing buildings provides a means for the code to exempt existing buildings from immediately complying with updates to the code. Chapter 43, *Building Rehabilitation*, contains provisions under which an existing building, or parts of an existing building, would be required to comply with an appropriate New occupancy chapter. Unless your theatre organization is building a new performing arts facility or having major renovations done to a current theatre building, you can focus your compliance efforts primarily on the first eleven chapters, and Chapter 13, *Existing Assembly Occupancies*.

NFPA 101—Life Safety Code, Chapter 1, *Administration* covers the scope and purpose of the code and contains reference to the authority having jurisdiction's (AHJ) administration and enforcement of the provisions of the Life Safety Code. Chapter 2 includes by reference other codes and standards. The definitions contained in Chapter 3 cover terms and concepts used throughout the code. Many AHJs do not have a theatre background, so the terms defined in Chapter 3 (such as aisle accessway, fly gallery, gridiron, pinrail, stage, and vomitory) will be their only point of reference related to the types of buildings in which we work. Conversely, you will be better able to converse and negotiate with your AHJ knowing the definitions of the terms he or she uses in the code's enforcement: exit, fire watch,[37] means of egress,[38] and situational awareness, among many others. Chapter 4 covers the goals, objectives, and fundamental requirements of the code. Chapter 4 contains the requirements for multiple safeguards and at least two means of egress from every building. The enforcement authority delegated to the AHJ is further defined:

> "The AHJ shall determine whether the provisions of this Code have been met. Any requirements that are essential for the safety of building occupants and are not specifically provided for by this Code shall be determined by the AHJ."[39]

Chapter 5 provides criteria for performance-based compliance in lieu of the prescriptive requirements contained elsewhere in the code. The occupancy classifications in Chapter 6 are essential to knowing which of the subsequent occupancy chapters would be applied to your facilities. Exits, means of egress, and related features such as signage and illumination are detailed in Chapter 7, *Means of Egress*. Chapter 7 also includes specifics related to such concerns as:

- decorations in a means of egress (mirrors cannot be placed on or adjacent to an exit door),
- floor surface in an exit to be level (no changes of elevation on the floor of a means of egress over ½ inch), and,
- reliability: "means of egress shall be continuously maintained free of obstructions or impediments to full instant use in case of fire or other emergency.[40]

Continuing with the mandatory chapters in NFPA 101, in Chapter 8, *Features of Fire Protection* are the requirements for fire barriers (with reference to NFPA 80, in which Chapter 20 contains requirements for stage fire curtains), and smoke barriers within buildings. In Chapter 9, *Building Service and Fire Protection*, requirements for detection, notification, and sprinkler systems are included, along with references to other related NFPA standards containing specifics about the design, installation, and maintenance of such systems. Rating and classification of interior finish, contents, and furnishing are covered in Chapter 10. These ratings and classifications are referenced in subsequent occupancy chapters. For instance, assembly occupancies for over 300 people must have Class A or B interior wall and ceiling finishes.[41] Among the type of structures included in Chapter 11, *Special Structures and High Rise Buildings*, is a section on tents (NFPA 101, Section 11.11), noting:

- fire rating for tent materials;
- location and spacing of tents;
- tents can only be used on a temporary basis; and,
- limitations on flammable and combustible material within and adjacent to a tent.

Other than Chapter 43, *Building Rehabilitation*, only the assembly occupancy chapters (Chapters 12 and 13) are applicable to theatres and theatre production facilities. For our purposes, I will list the seven major headings of Chapter 13, *Existing Assembly Occupancies*, and quote essential sections along with brief notes.

Chapter 13.1 *General Requirements.*

> 13.1.1.4 "An existing building housing an assembly occupancy established prior to the effective date of this Code shall be permitted to be approved for continued use if it conforms to, or is made to conform to, the provisions of this Code to the extent that, in the opinion of the AHJ, reasonable life safety against the hazards of fire, explosion, and panic is provided and maintained."
>
> 13.1.6 Minimum Construction Requirements. [Details types of construction for an assembly occupancy based on the number of occupants, and other building factors.]

13.1.7 Occupant Load. [References previous chapters and other details to provide a means to calculate the capacity of assembly spaces based on area and use.]

Chapter 13.2 *Means of Egress Requirements.*

[Includes factors and other limitations used in calculating the capacity, number, and arrangements of the means of egress serving an assembly occupancy. Covers travel distance and clear-space requirements for exit passageways and aisle widths. Illumination, marking, guards, and railings are specified.]

Chapter 13.3 *Protection.*

13.3.1 Protection of Vertical Openings.
13.3.2 Protection from Hazards.
13.3.3 Interior Finish. [Scenery and stage properties are covered in Chapter 13.4.6.]
13.3.4 Detection, Alarm, and Communications Systems.
   13.3.4.2 Initiation. [Requires both manual and automatic initiation of fire alarm systems.]
   13.3.4.3 Notification. [Requires an audible alarm; allows for a voice communications system for notification of occupants.]
13.3.5 Extinguishing Requirements. [Automatic sprinkler systems required in specific assembly occupancies with an occupant load over 100.]

Chapter 13.4 *Special Provisions.*

13.4.1 Life Safety Evaluation. [Contains details of a performance-based life safety evaluation for assembly occupancies if one is required by the AHJ or other provisions of the code.]
13.4.2 Smoke-Protected Assembly Seating.
13.4.3 Limited Access or Underground Buildings.
13.4.4 High-Rise Buildings.
13.4.5 Alcohol-Based Hand-Rub Dispensers. [Since such dispensers contain a flammable liquid, their use in assembly occupancies is specifically allowed by this section.]

13.4.6 Stages and Platforms. [Covers smoke hatches over stages and smoke control in auditoriums. Proscenium opening protection (fire curtain) is detailed, and also referenced to 12.4.6.7, which references NFPA 80, Chapter 20, for compliance.]

    13.4.6.11 Flame-Retardant Requirements. [Includes stage drops, curtains, and fabrics which must be in compliance with NFPA 701; limits the quantity of foamed plastics in scenery.]

        13.4.6.11.3 "Scenery and stage properties not separated from the audience by proscenium opening protection shall be of non-combustible, limited-combustible materials, or fire-retardant-treated wood."

13.4.7 Projection Rooms.
13.4.8 Special Amusements Buildings.[42]
13.4.9 Grandstands
13.4.10 Folding and Telescopic Seating

13.5 Building Services.
13.6 Reserved.
13.7 Operating Features.

13.7.1 Means of Egress Inspection. [Requires the inspection of the means of egress, which must be free of obstructions prior to each opening of the building to the public.]

13.7.2 Special Provisions for Food Service Operations.

13.7.3 Open Flame Devices and Pyrotechnics. [Requires approval by the AHJ, and compliance with NFPA 160 for flame effects and NFPA 1126 for pyrotechnic effect devices.]

13.7.4 Furnishings, Decorations, and Scenery. [By reference to NFPA 101 Section 10.3.1 requires compliance with NFPA 701 for stage fabrics, draperies, curtains, and similar furnishings.]

    13.7.4.2 "The AHJ shall impose controls on the quantity and arrangement of combustible contents in assembly occupancies to provide an adequate level of safety to life from fire."

13.7.5 Special Provisions for Exposition Facilities.

13.7.6 Crowd Managers. [Describes the responsibilities of crowd managers[43] and requirements related to the number of crowd managers based on occupant load.]

    13.7.6.1 [Requires at least one trained crowd manager for every 250 occupants.]

    13.7.6.2 "The crowd manager and crowd manager supervisor shall receive approved training in crowd management techniques."

13.7.7 Drills

    13.7.7.1 "The employees or attendants of assembly occupancies shall be trained and drilled in the duties they are to perform in case of fire, panic, or other emergency to effect orderly exiting."

    13.7.7.3 "an audible announcement shall be made, or a projected image shall be shown, prior to the start of each program that notifies the occupants of the locations of the exits to be used in case of a fire or other emergency." [Required in: theatres, motion picture theatres, auditoriums, similar assembly occupancies with occupant loads of over 300.]

13.7.8 Smoking

    13.7.8.1 "Smoking in assembly occupancies shall be regulated by the AHJ."

13.7.9 [Addresses secured and unsecured seating, and requirements for the posting of occupant load capacities for an assembly occupancy.]

13.7.10 Maintenance of Outdoor Grandstands.

13.7.11 Maintenance and Operation of Folding and Telescoping Seating.

13.7.12 Clothing. [Prohibits the storage of clothing and personal effects (combustibles) in corridors or lobbies except if stored in metal lockers or in areas protected by sprinklers.]

13.7.13 Emergency Action Plans.

Fire and life safety codes other than NFPA 101 Life Safety Code may apply to your area or locale. You are likely to find that the fire and life provisions in these other codes contain requirements similar to those in NFPA 101.

Unlike OSHA standards, NFPA codes are not free. In fact most non-governmental codes, as well as standards developed by industry organizations, have a cost to either download or to purchase hardcopy. The process an organization or industry group uses to develop, vet, and publish an industry standard can be expensive: "Since the consensus-building process is costly, organizations like ANSI [American National Standards Institute] often try to cover expenses by selling or licensing access to standards documents."[44] NFPA codes are available as read-only online for free,[45] so you can examine the chapters with requirements that apply to theatre production without cost. Theatre industry standards developed by the Entertainment Services and Technology Association (ESTA) are currently free to download (as of February, 2019) due to an alliance with ProSight Specialty Insurance.[46]

INTERNATIONAL CODES

Without using clichés, let's acknowledge that national industries have become globalized and the entertainment industry is no exception. Throughout your professional career, or during your academic training, you are likely to interact with theatre professionals from around the world, or to work internationally. In the United States, theatre productions and entertainment events must be in compliance with federal codes such as OSHA and regional or local codes such as NFPA. When producing theatre or live entertainment events in other countries or international regions, you must investigate the applicable governing laws and seek guidance on which codes to follow for your production or event to be in compliance. This chapter has covered some of the codes applicable in the United States. To provide a starting point for international work, I will note some of the governing laws and codes for several countries in which you might work.

Canada

Federal Canadian Occupational Health and Safety (OHS) legislation covers all of Canada, while each of Canada's ten provinces and three territories has additional OHS legislation. The Canadian Centre for Occupational Health and Safety (CCOHS)[47] provides information to help you determine which Canadian governmental department is responsible for worker health and safety in the jurisdiction in which you are working. Once you determine the jurisdiction, CCOHS has links to guide you to the correct contacts. Safety and health standards for compliance with Canadian OHS regulations are maintained by the Canadian Standards Association (CSA).[48] Several Canadian provinces have provincial legislation and guidance resources for theatre production and live entertainment events. For Alberta province, Theatre Alberta has a guide to safety and health in theatre production titled *Safe Stages*.[49] An organization in British Columbia, Actsafe Safety Association,[50] provides free resources and training for the motion picture and performing arts industries. Theatre production regulations and safety guidance for Ontario province are available from several sources. *Safety Guidelines for the Live Performance Industry*[51] has fact sheets, and recommendations for safeguards and safety procedures covering a wide range of topics, from hand props and pyrotechnics to fall protection and rigging systems. Many aspects of live performance, including load-ins, lighting hangs, and strikes, are covered by Ontario Construction Projects Regulations.[52] Electrical equipment and installations for the entertainment industry in Ontario are covered by *Television, Film, Live Performance and Event Electrical Guidelines (ESA-SPEC-003)*.[53] The province of Quebec provides fact sheets of safety rules for film and video production.[54] Employers in Quebec for theatre production must follow the requirements in *Prevention Guidelines for the Performing Arts* (available online in French only).[55]

Chile

Theatre in Chile has a rich history dating back to the mid-19th century. Initially theatre productions served only the rich and upper classes, but in the early 20th century theatre for middle classes developed, and productions from international companies were presented. The year "1913 saw the formation of the National Drama Company (*Companía Dramática Nacional*) and 1917 the Chile's first theatre company."[56] In the early 1940s, the university theatres were established. The first one, in 1941, was the Teatro Experimental of the Universidad de Chile, and a year later the Teatro Ensayo of the Universidad Catolica. Both companies brought new ways of creating and producing theatre in Chile, ways which are still very present today.[57] The growth and development of theatre and the arts in Chile were repressed during the years of the Pinochet dictatorship from 1973 to 1990 as "culture was seen as an act of terrorism by Pinochet."[58] These years saw the closing of many theatres in Chile. The return of democracy in 1990 brought the cultural arts industry back to life. The theatre community is influenced by the experiences and learning brought by artists returned from exile. The "lost decades" of the Pinochet era are reflected in the sense of a young but modern theatre industry in the country. Safety and health regulations specific to theatre production have developed since the end of the Pinochet regime. A useful overview of laws and codes related to theatre production was produced and written in English by the Film Commission Chile, *Shoot in Chile, A Practical Guide for a Chile Film Friendly*. An edition in English is available at: https://www.cultura.gob.cl/wp-content/uploads/2015/03/shoot-in-chile_en.pdf. The *Guide* contains a section on special effects in filming. Another section titled "Safety During Filming" has guidance on working at heights, fire hazards and fire control, and a range of other risks from vehicles in filming to filming around water to the use of firearms. A law regulating the conditions of workers in the entertainment industry, such as actors, circus artists, choreographers, stage crew, designers, etc. includes limits on hours worked per day, and requires employers to pay for unemployment and accident insurance.[59] Chilean labor law includes a right-to-know provision as well as requiring employers "to take all measures necessary to effectively protect the life and health of their employees."[60] Other theatre production resources are published by the Consejo Nacional de la Cultura y las Artes (Ministry of Culture Arts and Heritage) and Agrupación de Diseñadores, Técnicos y Realizadores Escénicos ADTRES (Association of Performing Arts Designers, Technicians, and Scenic Carpenters). Their documents, which include a manual for risk prevention, fall protection, and related labor legislation,[61] are written for and by performing arts technicians in Chile. Large events for over 3,000 attendees are regulated by *Circular N° 28-Intendencia Metropolitana*, which requires special measures to guarantee public order, the safety of event personnel, and protection for public property. Chilean building codes are similar to the International Building Code (IBC), and structures are designed and constructed with seismic activity in mind. An aspect of producing theatre in Chile therefore requires emergency procedures planning due to the relatively high level of seismic activity in the region. Generally, many safety and health requirements applicable to theatre production in Chile are similar to OSHA standards in the United States, so compliance with OSHA is likely to result in compliance with Chilean codes.

India

Occupational safety and health (OSH) in India for its citizens is enshrined in the principles governing the country, the "Directive Principles for State Policy." These principles are protective of child labor, provide for the health and well-being of workers, both men and women, and dictate the establishment of just and humane conditions of work. From these principles, national OSH legislation has been enacted through 16 laws covering working hours and conditions of service and employment. But, these laws are specific to only four sectors of the Indian economy: mining, factories, ports, and construction. These four sectors, which comprise about 10 percent of India's workforce, are referred to as the organized sectors. The rest of the employed population work in the unorganized sector of the economy. Assessments of the situation in India related to OSH note: "Occupational Health and Safety cover for the unorganized sector can well be said as nonexistent."[62] Because no government agency or department deals exclusively with OSH matters,[63] theatre and the entertainment industry have adopted applicable regulations from existing legislation for organized sectors. Aspects of laws covering OSH in the organized sectors addressing working conditions in factories, confined space in mining, and ergonomics in construction have informed work and OSH practices at the National School of Drama, New Delhi, and among the increasingly aware theatre technical supervisors at other theatres. A comprehensive approach to OSH in India which would include theatre and the entertainment industry is evolving. In 2009, the government approved the National Policy on Safety, Health and Environment at Workplace. This policy commits the government to "regulate all economic activities for management of safety and health risks at workplaces and to provide measures so as to ensure safe and healthy working conditions for every working man and woman in the nation."[64] Actions specified to achieve the goals and objectives of the policy are: enforcement via inspections and support for effective implementation; developing national OSH standards; promoting and encouraging compliance through assistance and cooperation; increase awareness of safety and health in the workplace with consultation and training; provisions for research and development of OSH practices; and expand OSH skills through training and academic programs.[65] Progress on these and other actions to integrate the goals of the National Policy into all aspects of work in India has been slow but steady. International guidelines for theatre safety as well the efforts of academic theatre programs may be more influential in the near-term on the level of safety and health in theatre production in India.

The Philippines

As is typical globally, theatre and live entertainment are covered under national safety and health codes, which in the Philippines are contained in Occupational Safety and Health Standards (OSHS).[66] These national occupational safety and health standards were originally "formulated in 1978 in compliance with the constitutional mandate to safeguard the worker's social and economic well-being as well as his [or her] physical safety and health."[67] In 1987, the Occupational Safety and Health Center (OSHC) was created to provide research and training to assist stakeholders (employers, employees, and industry organizations) with implementing the national safety standards. The OSHS covers all places of employment: "Section 1001, *Purpose and Scope*, (2) This Standard shall apply to all places of employment except as otherwise provided in this Standard." The Philippine OSHS (Section Rule 1030 *Training of Personnel in Occupational Safety and Health*) requires at least one "safety man" (safety supervisor or safety manager) in every workplace, as well as a workplace health and safety committee. Section Rule 1060 *Premises of Establishments* includes requirements related to walking-working surfaces and ladders. Other sections of the OSHS cover PPE, hazardous chemicals, electrical safety, and fire protection and control. The latter section contains a provision requiring fire exit drills at least twice a year for every workplace (OSHS, Rule 1940, Section 1948.03). This section also requires fire exit training, "In buildings where the population is of a changing character [such as in theatres], the fire-exit training of the regular employees shall include the proper procedure to direct other occupants to safety." A 2016 Labor Advisory, *Working Conditions in the Movie and Television Industry*, addresses labor issues for this industry not covered by the OSHS, such as hours of work, waiting time, and accommodations while on location.[68] The Philippine occupational safety and health standards are similar to the OSHA standards (general industry and construction) in the United States, but a review of the Philippine Occupational Safety and Health Standards is necessary to assure compliance.

Republic of Korea (South Korea)

The Korean Occupational Safety and Health Act (KOSH Act) in 1987 established, under the Ministry of Employment and Labor (MOEL), the Korean Occupational Safety and Health Agency (KOSHA) to provide oversight and enforcement of the KOSH Act. The Act applies to all businesses in Korea and places responsibility for safety and health in the workplace on employers. KOSHA implements its responsibilities by providing technical support, education, and training, with a focus on "establishment of autonomous safety and health management systems by workplaces," and "promotion of safety culture."[69] Under the Act, employers are required to "provide workers with information on safety and health in the workplace, prevent workers' health problems caused by physical fatigue, mental stress, etc., protect the lives of workers, maintain and promote the safety and health of workers by creating a proper work environment."[70] Chapter II of the Act, *Safety and Health Management Systems*, requires employers to assign a safety and health manager for their workplace(s), who is responsible for overall management and control of virtually all aspects of safety and health. In addition, employers must designate a safety manager to assist the employer and/or the safety and health manager.[71] In contrast to OSHA in the United States, KOSHA places more emphasis on safety and health programs in the workplace, and the assessment and management of risks, with less emphasis on enforcement of specific standards. The use of such terms as "safety assessment," "safety and health management systems," and "safety culture" in the KOSH

Act illustrates this focus. KOSHA promotes local (employer and employee) responsibilities for safety and health by posting on its website articles and guidance about Harm and Hazard Prevention Plans,[72] and safety culture. Korea enacted legislation supporting a national focus on safety and health, not just in the workplace, by designating the 4th day of each month as Safety Check Day: "To enhance people's safety awareness and make safety a habit . . . to spread safety culture on a national level . . . to encourage the participation of everyone on safety-related activities."[73] Implementation of safety and health in the workplace in Korea is similar to the United Kingdom (see below), and other countries where legislation requires safety programs and risk assessments. Recommended practices related to theatre and live entertainment are developing in Korea and regionally in Asia through industry organizations such as China Entertainment Technology Association (CETA),[74] and Taiwan Association of Theatre Technology (TATT).[75]

Singapore

Theatre and the entertainment industry in Singapore are not treated as a separate industry section, so codes and standards for construction and other industries are referenced for theatre productions. The Workplace Safety and Health (WSH) Act enacted in 2003 "covers the safety, health and welfare of persons at work in a workplace. It requires stakeholders to take reasonably practicable steps for the safety and health of workers and others affected by work."[76] To assist employers with compliance, in 2008 the Workplace Safety and Health Council (WSHC) was established. "The [WSH] Council's main functions are to build industry capabilities to better manage WSH; promote safety and health at work; recognise companies with good WSH records; and set acceptable WSH practices."[77] The Workplace Safety and Health Council website[78] clarifies employers' requirements for complying with the WSH Act, and provides guidance documents and self-assessments to assist with doing so. Safety and health management programs are required of many employers,[79] and all employers are required to conduct risk assessments of work activities.[80] The WSHC website has links to many safety and health related documents such as: *Working at Height Toolkit*; *Safety and Health at Work*; *Code of Practice on WSH Risk Management*; *Workplace Safety and Health*

Guidelines [WSHG]: Event Management; WSHG: Safeguarding Against Falling Objects; and WSHG: Tent-related Works.[81] (Links to other codes of practice and technical advisories for working in Singapore are included in the Appendix.) Fire codes for Singapore are under the Singapore Civil Defense Force (SCDF). Fire codes for the built environment are contained in the *Code of Practice for Fire Precautions in Buildings 2018*. The code provides general fire and life safety requirements for all buildings, as well as specific requirements for assembly occupancies. Chapter 9.7.3 *Assembly Occupancy* has charts for the minimum number of exits, clearances between rows of seats, maximum number of seats per row, and illuminations requirements for exit paths.[82] The fire and life safety definitions and code requirements in the Singapore fire code are similar to those in NFPA 101 Life Safety Code. Scenic construction and installation of scenery and production equipment in venues would be covered by both the SCDF Fire Precautions requirements for the flammability of materials, and the Singapore Building Construction Authority (BCA)[83] for structural integrity. Pyrotechnics and similar special effects for live entertainment are achieved through licensed pyrotechnics companies, the activities of which are overseen by the Singapore Police Force (SPF). NFPA 1126—Standard for the Use of Pyrotechnics Before a Proximate Audience inform many of the details that Singapore pyrotechnic companies follow. In general, compliance with codes in theatre production and live entertainment is achieved with the assistance of a Qualified Person: a registered and licensed professional architect or engineer, who provides advice and guidance on relevant submission of plans for approvals.

Taiwan (R.O.C.)

Oversight and enforcement of safety and health regulations in Taiwan (R.O.C.) are under the jurisdiction of "OSHA Taiwan; Occupational Safety and Health Administration, under the Ministry of Labor." OSHA Taiwan has parallels with U.S. OSHA, especially after Taiwan's 2014 Occupational Safety and Health (OSH) Act. The OSH Act expanded coverage of OSHA Taiwan to all workers, including the self-employed. The 2014 Taiwan OSH Act amendments apply OSHA Taiwan regulations to all employers in all industries, and stipulate that "host employers and contractors are jointly liable for occupational injuries due to violations of safety and health regulations."[84] As of 2015 when the Act was fully implemented, machinery, equipment, and appliances not certified as meeting safety standards are prohibited from use. The conceptual framework for safety and health in Taiwan focuses on an employer's responsibilities for a safety and health program, and the management of risk in the workplace. "Required by OSHA [Taiwan], business entities should evaluate workplace risk, implement OSH self-management, enhance OSH communication and management of contractors, and promote safety culture."[85] In addition to compliance with the regulations of OSHA Taiwan, guidance on theatre-specific requirements and recommended practices can be obtained from the Taiwan Association of Theatre Technology (TATT), the Taiwan headquarters of OSISAT (International Organisation of Scenographers, Theatre Architects and Technicians). TATT's mission is "to promote the advancement of the knowledge and skills of theatre artists and technicians, and boost the creativity of theatre design and theatre architecture in Taiwan by conducting and encouraging communication of experience domestically and internationally."[86]

United Kingdom

The United Kingdom (UK) is comprised of England, Scotland, Wales, and Northern Ireland. While the roots of workplace safety and health in the UK go back to 1838, currently safety and health for all employments in the UK is covered by the Health and Safety at Work etc. Act 1974 (HSWA).[87] The HSWA established a new framework for the regulation of safety and health, departing from prescribed and detailed regulations in place up to that time. "The Act introduced a new system based on less-prescriptive and more goal-based regulations, supported by guidance and codes of practice. For the first time employers and employees were to be consulted and engaged in the process of designing a modern health and safety system."[88] The Health and Safety Executive (HSE) was formed under the HSWA to enforce health and safety legislation in all workplaces. "The Health and Safety Executive, with local authorities [LAs] (and other enforcing authorities) is responsible for enforcing the Act and a number of other Acts and Statutory Instruments [SIs, often referred to as regulations] relevant to the working environment."[89] These Acts and SIs create responsibilities which require employers to provide specific safety and health protections in the workplace. Similar to the OSHA General Duty Clause, the HSWA places a general duty for safety and health in the workplace on employers: "It shall be the duty of every employer to ensure, so far as is reasonably practicable, the health, safety and welfare at work of all his [or her] employees."[90] Unlike OSHA's typically prescribed and detailed standards, as noted above, the Acts and regulations established under the HSWA and enforced by the HSE contain performance and goal-based requirements to be implemented by employers in order to be compliant with the Act. The HSWA and related safety and health regulations are enacted through a series of employer responsibilities which, when implemented by the employer in a workplace, will assure compliance with the Act.

These responsibilities are detailed in regulations that have been enacted over the years. Of the many regulations, six are core to safety and health in the workplace in the UK (others are listed in the Appendix):

- Health and Safety (Display Screen Equipment) Regulations 1992
- Personal Protective Equipment at Work Regulations 1992
- Workplace (Health, Safety and Welfare) Regulations 1992
- Manual Handling Operations Regulations 1992
- Provision and Use of Work Equipment Regulations 1998
- Management of Health and Safety at Work Regulations 1999 (the Management Regulations).[91]

The last regulation requires employers to have a policy for managing health and safety in the workplace. This requires a theatre production company to have a safety and health program. Another specific aspect requires employers to assess and control risk in the workplace. This is accomplished through the use of documented risk assessments for all hazards associated with your productions and venues.[92] Other employer responsibilities include: communication with employees about the hazards and risks in the workplace; what means are available for employees' protection; and training and instruction on how to deal with the risks. The enabling regulations also require employers to consult with their employees about safety and health issues.

Another regulation that has had significant impact on theatres and production elements since its update in 2015 is the Construction (Design and Management) Regulations.[93] Among other requirements of these regulations, referred to as CDM, is very specific paperwork to be completed for every production. Other specifics related to the application of the Health and Safety at Work etc. Act can be found in the Health and Safety in the Film, Theatre and Broadcasting Industries section on the HSE website.[94]

In order for your safety and health program to have a foundation built on compliance, you must research the codes applicable to your organization, coordinate program activities with your AHJ or other authorities, and implement policies and procedures to assure code compliance in your production activities and daily operations. Since most codes are written to be enforced across a wide range of industries, businesses, and occupancies, compliance with codes can sometimes seem challenging. Few codes in the United States explicitly apply to the theatre industry and live performance events. In the next chapter I will examine theatre industry-specific consensus standards and training certifications developed by and for the entertainment industry. Compliance with these standards aligns more readily with existing production processes and provides a more familiar framework within which to build your safety and health program, and evolve your theatre safety culture.

NOTES

1. "The [OSH] Act also requires that employers comply with occupational safety and health standards promulgated under the Act, and that employees comply with standards . . . issued under the Act." Occupational Safety and Health Administration (OSHA), Regulations (Standards—29 CFR 1903.1-Purpose and Scope), accessed February 21, 2019, https://www.osha.gov/laws-regs/regulations/standardnumber/1903/1903.1.
2. Michael Heinsdorf, "Code or Standard: What Is the Difference between a Code and a Standard?", Consulting-Specifying Engineer

online, July 1, 2015, accessed February 21, 2019, https://www.csemag.com/articles/code-or-standard/.
3 Ibid.
4 Occupational Safety and Health Administration (OSHA), "Law and Regulations," accessed February 21, 2019, https://www.osha.gov/law-regs.html (emphasis in original).
5 Federal Aviation Administration, "What's the Only Word that Means Mandatory?", accessed May 16, 2019, https://www.faa.gov/about/initiatives/plain_language/articles/mandatory/.
6 Plainlanguage.gov, "Federal Plain Language Guidelines," accessed May 16, 2019, https://plainlanguage.gov/guidelines/.
7 International Code Council (ICC), "About, Who We Are," accessed October 29, 2019, https://www.iccsafe.org/about/who-we-are/.
8 The Exit Light Co., "United States Fire & Building Codes," accessed April 1, 2019, https://www.exitlightco.com/Fire-Codes-Regulations.html.
9 Monona Rossol, *The Health & Safety Guide for Film, TV & Theater* (New York: Allworth Press, Inc.), page xvii.
10 OSHA, "Standards Interpretations," accessed February 21, 2019, https://www.osha.gov/laws-regs/standardinterpretations/2003-04-09.
11 *Yale University School of Drama Safety Handbook 8.20.2018 ed.*, 5; used with permission.
12 Goodman Theatre, Chicago, IL, *Health and Safety Program,* page i; [Permission Pending: to be used with permission.]
13 OSHA, OSH Act, accessed February 21, 2019, https://www.osha.gov/laws-regs/oshact/completeoshact.
14 OSHA Directory, "OSHA Offices by State," accessed February 25, 2019, https://www.osha.gov/html/RAmap.html.
15 OSHA, OSH Act of 1970, Section 18 State Jurisdiction and State Plans, accessed February 21, 2019, https://www.osha.gov/laws-regs/oshact/section_18
16 OSHA, Regulations (Standards—29 CFR 1910.2(f)), accessed February 19, 2019, https://www.osha.gov/laws-regs/regulations/standardnumber/1910/1910.2.
17 "On the other hand, any standard shall apply according to its terms to any employment and place of employment in any industry, even though particular standards are also prescribed for the industry, as in subpart B or subpart R of this part, to the extent that none of such particular standards applies. To illustrate, the general standard

regarding noise exposure in 1910.95 applies to employments and places of employment in pulp, paper, and paperboard mills covered by 1910.261." Occupational Safety and Health Administration (OSHA), Regulations (Standards—29 CFR 1910.5(c)(2)), accessed February 21, 2019, https://www.osha.gov/laws-regs/regulations/standardnumber/1910/1910.5.

18 OSHA, Regulations (Standards—29 CFR 1926.1201(a)), accessed February 18, 2019, https://www.osha.gov/laws-regs/regulations/standardnumber/1926/1926.1201.

19 OSHA, "Safety and Health Topics, General Industry," accessed February 21, 2019, https://www.osha.gov/SLTC/generalindustry/

20 OSHA, Regulations (Standards—29 CFR 1910.12(b)), accessed February 21, 2019, https://www.osha.gov/laws-regs/regulations/standardnumber/1910/1910.12.

21 Mancomm, Inc. *OSHA General Industry Regulations, 29 CFR Parts 1903. 1904, and 1910*. Updated through January 19, 2017 (Iowa: Mancomm, Inc., 2017).

22 Note: It appears that several section numbers are missing from this listing of the section of 29 CFR Subpart Z. These section numbers are omitted from the standard.

23 OSHA, Regulations (Standards—29 CFR 1910.22(a)(1)), accessed February 21, 2019, https://www.osha.gov/laws-regs/regulations/standardnumber/1910/1910.22.

24 OSHA, Regulations (Standards—29 CFR 1910.23(b)), accessed February 21, 2019, https://www.osha.gov/laws-regs/regulations/standardnumber/1910/1910.23.

25 OSHA, Regulations (Standards—29 CFR 1910.28), accessed February 21, 2019, https://www.osha.gov/laws-regs/regulations/standardnumber/1910/1910.28.

26 OSHA, Regulations (Standards—29 CFR 1926.20(a)(1)), accessed February 21, 2019, https://www.osha.gov/laws-regs/regulations/standardnumber/1926/1926.20.

27 OSHA, Regulations (Standards—29 CFR 1904.1), accessed February 21, 2019, https://www.osha.gov/laws-regs/regulations/standardnumber/1904/1904.1.

28 OSHA, Regulations (Standards—29 CFR 1904.0 - Purpose)), accessed February 21, 2019, https://www.osha.gov/laws-regs/regulations/standardnumber/1904/1904.0.

29 "The North American Industry Classification System (NAICS) is the standard used by Federal statistical agencies in classifying business

establishments for the purpose of collecting, analyzing, and publishing statistical data related to the U.S. business economy." "Introduction to NAICS," United States Census Bureau, accessed February 21, 2019, https://www.census.gov/eos/www/naics/.

30 "OSHA defines in-patient hospitalization as a formal admission to the in-patient service of a hospital or clinic for care or treatment." Occupational Safety and Health Administration (OSHA), Regulations (Standards—29 CFR 1904.39(b)(9)), accessed February 21, 2019, https://www.osha.gov/laws-regs/regulations/standardnumber/1904/1904.39.

31 OSHA, Regulations (Standards—29 CFR 1904.29(a)), accessed February 21, 2019, https://www.osha.gov/laws-regs/regulations/standardnumber/1904/1904.29.

32 Access to standards developed and published by the National Fire Protection Association are available free in read-only format online at: https://www.nfpa.org/Codes-and-Standards/All-Codes-and-Standards/Free-access

33 American with Disabilities Act of 1990 as Amended (Title 42, Chapter 126, Section 12101 (b) Purpose), accessed February 21, 2019, https://www.ada.gov/pubs/adastatute08.htm.

34 Ron Cote and Gregory E. Harrington, editors, *Life Safety Code Handbook, 2015 edition* (Quincy, MA: National Fire Protection Association [NFPA], 2014), Section 1.6 (hereafter cited as *NFPA 101*).

35 International Code Council, International Building Code, accessed February 21, 2019, https://www.iccsafe.org/.

36 *NFPA 101, Life Safety Code*, 2018 ed., Chapter 1, Section 1.2, Purpose.

37 *NFPA 101,* Section 3.3.109 "Fire Watch. The assignment of a person or persons to an area for the express purpose of notifying the fire department, the building occupants, or both of an emergency; preventing a fire from occurring; extinguishing small fire; or protecting the public from fire or life safety dangers."

38 *NFPA 101,* Section 3.3.172 "Means of Egress. A continuous and unobstructed way of travel from any point in a building or structure to a public way consisting of three separate and distinct parts: (1) the exit access, (2) the exit, and (3) the exit discharge."

39 *NFPA 101,* Sections 4.6.1.1 and 4.6.1.2.

40 *NFPA 101,* Section 7.1.10.1

41 *NFPA 101,* Section 13.3.3.3.

42 *NFPA 101,* Section 13.3.33.10 "Special Amusement Building. A building that is temporary, permanent, or mobile and contains a device

or system that conveys passengers or provides a walkway along, around, or over a course in any direction as a form of amusement arranged so that the egress path is not readily apparent due to visual or audio distraction or an intentionally confounded egress path, or is not readily available due to the mode of conveyance through the building or structure."

43 Reference links to crowd manager training websites, and online crowd management resources are in the Appendix.

44 Andrew Rusell and Lee Vinsel, "The Joy of Standards," *The New York Times*, February 17, 2019, SR 9. Also online, accessed February 18, 2019, https://www.nytimes.com/2019/02/16/opinion/sunday/standardization.html.

45 NFPA. Main webpage with link to codes and standards, accessed February 21, 2019, http://www.nfpa.org/.

46 Entertainment Services and Technology Association (ESTA), "About TSP [Technical Standards Program]," accessed February 18, 2019, https://tsp.esta.org/tsp/about/about.html.

47 Canadian Centre for Occupational Health and Safety, accessed May 3, 2019, https://www.ccohs.ca/.

48 Canadian Standards Association, accessed May 3, 2019, https://www.csagroup.org/.

49 Theatre Alberta, *Safe Stages,* accessed May 3, 2019, https://www.theatrealberta.com/safe-stages/.

50 Actsafe, accessed May 3, 2019, https://www.actsafe.ca/.

51 Ontario Ministry of Labour, Health and Safety, "Performance Industry," accessed May 3, 2019, https://www.labour.gov.on.ca/english/hs/topics/performance.php.

52 Ontario Ministry of Labour, Health and Safety, "Application of Industrial and Construction Regulations Safety Guidelines for the Live Performance Industry in Ontario," accessed May 3, 2019, https://www.labour.gov.on.ca/english/hs/pubs/liveperformance/gl_live_application.php.

53 *Television, Film, Live Performance and Event Electrical Guidelines, ESA Spec-003 R7 2013,* accessed May 3, 2019, https://www.esasafe.com/assets/files/esasafe/pdf/Bulletins/ESA_Spec-003_R7.pdf.

54 Commission des normes, de l'équité, de la santé et de la sécurité du travail, "Workers: Safety Rules for the Québec Film and Video Industry," accessed May 3, 2019, https://www.csst.qc.ca/en/Pages/safety_rules_film_video_industry.aspx.

55 Commission des normes, de l'équité, de la santé et de la sécurité du travail, *Guide de prévention en milieu de travail à l'intention de la petite et moyenne entreprise, 2e edition*, accessed May 3, 2019, https://www.cnesst.gouv.qc.ca/publications/200/Pages/dc_200_16082.aspx.
56 What Latin America, "Chile Theatre," accessed May 23, 2019, https://www.whatlatinamerica.com/latin-theatre/chile-theatre.html.
57 For more information on the history of the performing arts in Chile, see also Chile Actúa, "Modernización Integral," accessed May 23, 2019, http://www.chileescena.cl/index.php?seccion=modernizacion-integral.
58 Michael Billington, "On with the Show," *The Guardian*, September 7, 2004, accessed May 23, 2019, https://www.theguardian.com/stage/2004/sep/07/theatre.chile.
59 Film Commission Chile, *Shoot in Chile, A Practical Guide for a Chile Film Friendly*, pages 64–65, accessed May 13, 2019, https://www.cultura.gob.cl/wp-content/uploads/2015/03/shoot-in-chile_en.pdf.
60 Ibid, page 64.
61 *Prevención de Riesgos, Legislación Laboral y Seguridad* (Prevention of Risks, Labor Inspection and Security), accessed May 26, 2016, https://www.cultura.gob.cl/wp-content/uploads/2013/11/prevencion_riesgos_vol2.pdf.
62 Government of India, Ministry of Labour and Employment, *Report of the Working Group on Occupational Safety and Health for the Twelfth Five Year Plan (2012 to 2017)*, August 2011, page 139.
63 Shyam Pingle, "Occupational Safety and Health in India: Now and the Future," *Industrial Health 2012,* vol. 50, 169.
64 Government of India, Ministry of Labour and Employment, National Policy on Safety, Health and Environment at Work Place, Section 1.3, accessed May 10, 2019, http://dgfasli.nic.in/info1.htm.
65 Ibid, Section 4.
66 Philippines, Department of Labor and Employment (DLE), Occupational Safety and Health Council (OSHC) website, accessed May 22, 2019, http://oshc.dole.gov.ph/.
67 Philippines, DLE, OSHC, Occupational Safety and Health Standards, as Amended 1989 (Manila, Philippines), Foreword.
68 Philippines, OSHC, Labor Advisory No. 04, Working Conditions in the Movie and Television Industry, accessed May 22, 2019, http://oshc.dole.gov.ph/resource/issuances/labor-advisory.
69 Korean Occupational Safety and Health Act (Enforcement Date 26. Jan. 2012), Article 4 (Duty of the Government), accessed May 21. 2019,

http://english.kosha.or.kr/english/legislation/occupationalSafetyAndHealth.do.
70 Ibid, Article 5 (Duties of Employer).
71 Ibid, Article 13 (Safety and Health Manager), and, Article 15 (Safety Manager, etc.).
72 KOSHA, Sector-Based Activities, 02.Construction, Harm and Hazard Prevention Plan, accessed May 21, 2019, http://english.kosha.or.kr/english/business/harmAndHazardPreventionPlan2.do.
73 KOSHA, "Activities to Promote the Culture of Safety and Health at Work, Safety Check Day," accessed May 21, 2019, http://english.kosha.or.kr/english/business/safetyCheckDay.do.
74 China Entertainment Technology Association (CETA), accessed May 21, 2019, http://en.ceta.com.cn/.
75 Taiwan Association of Theatre Technology (TATT), accessed May 21, 2019, https://www.tatt.org.tw/english.
76 Singapore Government, Ministry of Manpower (MOM), "Workplace Safety and Health Act: What It Covers," accessed May 16, 2019, https://www.mom.gov.sg/workplace-safety-and-health/workplace-safety-and-health-act/what-it-covers.
77 Singapore Workplace Safety and Health Council (WSHC), "About WSH Council," accessed May 22, 2019, https://www.wshc.sg/wps/portal/!ut/p/a1/jY89D4IwEIZ_iwMrd3yIxq1xkCjGAVToYsBgwSBt2kr_vsjkIOht7-V5cvcChRRom3c1y3XN27x5ZxpcooPvuyTG3SZMHCTuHsNk4Tlx4PdANg6sT95_Po4MwV_-GegUMnwwABMntkBZw4uhbkbawlsyoLK8IbKU9IP260proVYWWmiMsY2qrrZifRDKQsGl_q5WXGllPwwQj2OK93nTRWT2AgTnMHU!/dl5/d5/L2dBISEvZ0FBIS9nQSEh/?action=cmsPublicView&cmsId=C-2014080600797.
78 Singapore Workplace Safety and Health Council website, accessed May 16, 2019, https://www.wshc.sg/wps/portal/!ut/p/a1/jY89D4IwEIZ_iwMrd3yIxq0xRqIYB1ChiwGDBYO0aSv9-yKTg6K3vZfnyd0LFFKgbd7VLNc1b_PmIWlwjva-75IYt-swcZC4OwyTmefEq6AHsu_A8uj95-OXIfjLPwEdQ4YPBmDkxAYoa3gx1M1IW3hzBlSW11KW0n7lfl1pLdTCQguNMbZR1cVWrA9CWSi41J_ViisN6ZsB4n5I8TZtuohMnt1CTtU!/dl5/d5/L2dBISEvZ0FBIS9nQSEh/.
79 Singapore Government, Ministry of Manpower, Safety and Health Management Systems, accessed May 16, 2019, https://www.mom.gov.sg/workplace-safety-and-health/safety-and-health-management-systems.
80 Singapore Government, Ministry of Manpower, "Risk Management," accessed May 16, 2019, https://www.mom.gov.sg/work

place-safety-and-health/safety-and-health-management-systems/risk-management.
81 Singapore, WSHC, "Publications," accessed May 22, 2019, https://www.wshc.sg/wps/portal/!ut/p/a1/jY_LDoIwEEW_xQVbOjwE465xISpoDKjQjQGDgEHatJX-vsgKE3zM7k7OycxFBMWINGIbFamsaJPWr0ycs7-zbROHsIF9YABe2dgJty7AzOyAZAgsvagDzAC8yLWMxdH6z4cPg-GXf0LkHRn5oAe-nFgjUtQ06-smuMmsWYEIz685z7n-4N26IJKJuQYaKKV0JcqLLoouMKEBo1yOqyUVEsUDA7H7IYbbtG59PHkCCx0z5Q!!/dl5/d5/L2dBISEvZ0FBIS9nQSEh/?action=publicSearchResource.
82 Singapore Civil Defense Force, Code of Practice for Fire Precautions in Buildings 2018, Section 9.7.3, pages 343–347.
83 Singapore Government, Building and Construction Authority, accessed May 21, 2019, https://www.bca.gov.sg/index.html.
84 SHRM, Risk Management, "Taiwan's New Workplace Safety Law Expands Scope, Regulates 'Overwork'," accessed May 8, 2019, https://www.shrm.org/ResourcesAndTools/hr-topics/risk-management/Pages/Taiwan-Workplace-Safety-Law.aspx.
85 Occupational Safety and Health Administration, Ministry of Labor, Republic of China (Taiwan), *National Occupational Safety and Health Profile of Taiwan, 2014*, accessed May 8, 2019, http://she.mcu.edu.tw/sites/default/files/MCU/National%20Occupational%20Safety%20and%20Health%20Profile%20of%20Taiwan.pdf.
86 Taiwan Association of Theatre Technology (TATT), accessed May 8, 2019, https://www.tatt.org.tw/english. N.B. TATT's website is partially in English, but probably best to communicate for information via email at tatt@tatt.org.tw.
87 Health and Safety Executive (HSE), Health and Safety at Work etc. Act 1974, accessed May 3, 2019, http://www.hse.gov.uk/legislation/hswa.htm.
88 HSE, "The History of HSE," accessed June 26, 2019, http://www.hse.gov.uk/aboutus/timeline/index.htm.
89 HSE, Health and Safety at Work etc. Act 1974, accessed June 26, 2019, http://www.hse.gov.uk/legislation/hswa.htm.
90 HSE, Health and Safety at Work etc. Act 1974, Section 2 (1), accessed May 3, 2019, http://www.legislation.gov.uk/ukpga/1974/37/section/2.
91 Legislation.gov.uk, The Management of Health and Safety at Work Regulations 1999, accessed May 3, 2019, http://www.legislation.gov.uk/uksi/1999/3242/contents/made.

92 Legislation.gov.uk, The Management of Health and Safety at Work Regulations 1999, Section 3. Risk Assessments, accessed May 3, 2019, http://www.legislation.gov.uk/uksi/1999/3242/contents/made.
93 Legislation.gov.uk, The Construction (Design and Management) Regulations 2015, accessed July 2, 2019, http://www.legislation.gov.uk/uksi/2015/51/contents/made.
94 HSE, Guidance, Health and Safety in the Film, Theatre and Broadcasting Industries, accessed May 3, 2019, http://www.hse.gov.uk/entertainment/theatre-tv/index.htm.

BIBLIOGRAPHY

Cote, Ron, and Harrington, Gregory E., editors, *Life Safety Code Handbook, NFPA 101, 2015 edition*. Quincy, MA: National Fire Protection Association, 2014.

Mancomm, Inc. *OSHA General Industry Regulations, 29 CFR Parts 1903. 1904, and 1910*. Davenport, IA: Mancomm, Inc., 2017.

Rossol, Monona. *The Health and Safety Guide for Film, TV, and Theater*, 2nd edition. New York: Allworth Press, 2011.

CHAPTER 5

Industry Standards, Recommended Practices, Training, and Certifications

William J. Reynolds

In the previous chapter, codes are defined as standards with legal enforceability. Industry standards can be defined as recommended practices which have become accepted work practices within an industry. Industry standards are communicated among members of an industry via several methods: documentation of recommended work practices; union or other employment contracts; or by industry-specific Standards Developing Organizations (SDOs). The latter organizations may follow the voluntary guidelines of the American National Standards Institute (ANSI) in the development and documentation of an industry standard. An industry standard developed in compliance with ANSI guidelines is commonly referred to as an ANSI standard.

> ANSI does not develop or approve standards. An industry recommended practice can only be accredited as an ANSI standard if the process for its development and adoption follows the ANSI requirements.
>
> > ANSI facilitates the development of American National Standards (ANS) by accrediting the procedures of standards developing organizations (SDOs). These groups work cooperatively to develop voluntary national consensus standards. Accreditation by ANSI signifies that the procedures used by the standards body in connection with the development of American National Standards meet the Institute's essential requirements for openness, balance, consensus and due process.[1]

The ANSI procedures require a collaborative process similar to the process used in the development of a typical theatre production. An idea or a concept for a standard is proposed. An ANSI-accredited SDO drafts language that codifies the draft standard, which is circulated within the industry. A time-period is announced for public comment. "A panel of interested parties, [subject-matter experts or SMEs], review comments and resolve points of friction. Eventually this process, which often takes years, results in a final published standard."[2]

In this chapter I will discuss industry standards developed by ANSI-accredited SDOs to incorporate into your organization's work practices, although doing so is voluntary unless those standards have been adopted into law in a jurisdiction. Industry standards provide the next foundational level upon which your safety and health programs, and organization's safety culture, will depend for success, (see Figure 5.1).

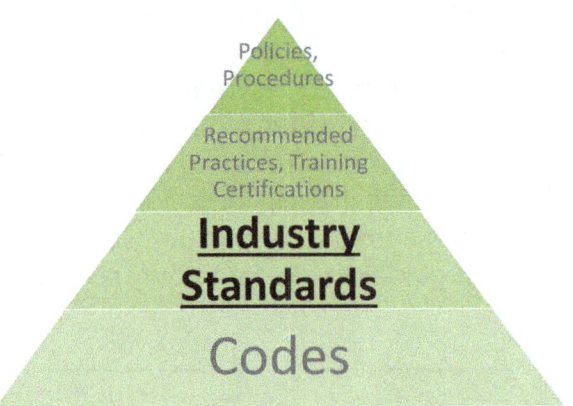

FIGURE 5.1 Hierarchy of Safety Controls: Industry Standards

Also in this chapter I will identify some of the recommended practices, training, and certifications developed and implemented by the live entertainment industry. The integration of industry recommended practices into your organization's work environment may require specific training for some of your employees. The verification of the successful completion of such training is asserted through vetted examination and certification. Examples are the Essential Skills for Entertainment Technicians (eSET), and the Entertainment Technician Certification Program (ETCP). These industry-developed training, and the certifications provided upon completion, can be required elements in your safety and health program. The acceptance of these certifications within the industry assures a base-level of skills and knowledge for your production staff, and signifies your organization's commitment to safety and health. Your employees (and students) benefit from obtaining these industry-recognized training and transferable certifications. As employees they are more likely to be hired, and as students they are more attractive to future employers. Recommended practices, training, and certifications form the next level of our Hierarchy of Safety Controls and provide a strong basis from which to develop related policies and procedures for your safety and health program, (See Figure 5.2).

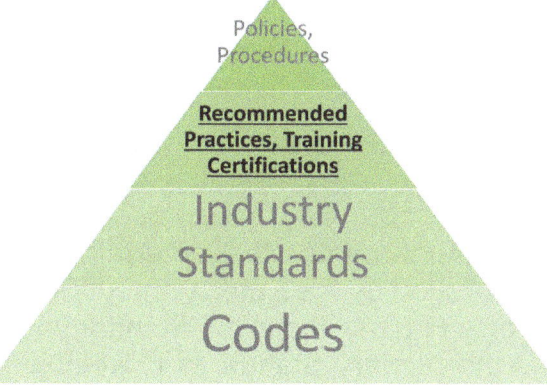

FIGURE 5.2 Hierarchy of Safety Controls: Recommended Practices, Training, and Certifications

Are industry standards and recommended practices legally enforceable? Some circumstances could result in an industry standard or recommended practice being enforced similar to a code. An example would be OSHA in its application of the General Duty Clause of the OSH Act. The General Duty Clause is applicable in the enforcement of OSHA standards through citations and fines resulting from an OSHA inspection. In the absence of a specific OSHA standard against which to cite an employer for a safety violation, an OSHA inspector can cite the General Duty Cause, specifically Section 5(a)(1):

> Each employer shall furnish to each of his [or her] employees employment and a place of employment which are free from *recognized hazards* that are causing or are likely to cause death or serious physical harm to his [or her] employees. [my emphasis]

The existence of a theatre industry safety standard or recommended practice known by an employer but not followed would be evidence of an employer not providing work and a workplace free of recognized hazards, which could result in citations and fines by OSHA. Similarly, in the event of civil litigation related to an accident, injury, or death in a theatre workplace, the existence of an industry standard or recommended practice neither acknowledged nor implemented might be used to implicate the employer as negligent in their legal responsibilities toward their employees or the public. While an industry standard or recommended practice may not be enforceable like a code, the prudent path is to implement industry standards and recommended practices the same as codes. As succinctly stated by Jay Glerum, a noted entertainment industry rigging and safety professional, "Now that we have the standards, we need to use them."[3]

INDUSTRY STANDARDS

ANSI-accredited standards for the entertainment industry are developed and published by the Entertainment Services and Technology Association's (ESTA) Technical Standards Program (TSP). ESTA serves as the primary Standards Developing Organization (SDO) for the entertainment industry in the United States. Initiated in 1994 in the absence of industry-specific consensus standards, the ESTA Technical Standards Program's mission is to create and distribute ANSI standards by and for the entertainment industry.[4] These entertainment industry standards cover a range of technical and procedural aspects of the work and technology of the industry. Examples include:

- ANSI E1.1—Entertainment Technology—Construction and Use of Wire Rope Ladders;
- ANSI E1.3—Entertainment Technology—Lighting Control Systems—0 to 10 Volt Analog Specification;
- ANSI E1.4–1—Entertainment Technology—Manual Counterweight Rigging Systems;
- ANSI E1.55—Standard for Theatrical Makeup Mirror Lighting;

- ANSI E1.50–1—Requirements for the Structural Support of Temporary LED, Video & Display Systems;

- ANSI E1.46—Standard for the Prevention of Falls from Theatrical Stages and Raised Performance Platforms;

- ANSI E1.60—Guidelines for the Use of Raked Stages in Live Performance Environments.

These and other approved and published standards are available from the ESTA Technical Standards Programs Published Documents website: tsp.esta.org.[5]

An ANSI-accredited standard follows a prescribed process for its development, evolution, approval, and publication. The consensus process required by ANSI includes public review and public input on draft versions of a proposed standard. Once a standard is approved via the ANSI-required process, it must be reviewed and updated within five years of its approval. (ANSI refers to the revision process as "periodic maintenance of a standard."[6]) At any time, several ANSI E-standards are in public review either as a proposed standard or an existing standard being updated. Standards in the public review and comment process are posted on the ESTA TSP website, along with instructions and forms for the submission of comments. Anyone can submit comments on standards open for public review. Membership in ESTA or any other organization is not required.[7]

These ANSI E-standards are developed and written by members of each of the nine TSP Working Groups:

> The actual work of creating standards, recommended practices and informational pieces is carried out in the working groups. When a request to develop a standard is made, the TSC [Technical Standards Council] determines whether it belongs under an existing working group or a new group should be created. A working group may create a task group to do the initial writing of the standard then bring it to the full working group for further discussion, refinement, and a vote.[8]

As with submitting comments, anyone with an interest and knowledge in the technology or topics covered by a TSP Working Group can apply for membership as either a voting or non-voting member.

As of 2019, over 60 ANSI E-standards are posted on the ESTA TSP website; typically several standards are posted for public review. The scope of these standards varies. Some contain technically detailed specifications, such as ANSI E1.3—Entertainment Technology—Lighting Control Systems—0 to 10 Volt Analog Control Specification, or ANSI E1.9—Reporting Photometric Performance Data for Luminaires Used in Entertainment Lighting. Other ANSI E-standards have more generalized or less technical data but contain procedural requirements: e.g. ANSI E1.46—Standard for the Prevention of Falls from Theatrical Stages and Raised Performance Platforms. Many of this latter type of standard contain the words "recommended" in their titles, but they are an ANSI E-standard because the recommended industry practices have been vetted via the ANSI-approved consensus process.

As with sections of the OSHA standards, several of the ANSI E-standards are directly applicable to the theatre safety and health policies and procedures of your organization. Your responsibility for safety and health in the workplace, or related to the education of your students, requires a review of all the current ANSI E-standards to determine the extent to which each standard's requirements apply to your organization's safety and health program. By way of example, I will examine some of these E-standards in more detail. For the following ANSI E-standards I will excerpt sections, and quote or describe pertinent content to illustrate their scope and applicability.

ANSI E1.2–2012, Entertainment Technology—Design, Manufacture and Use of Aluminum Trusses and Towers.

"**Section 1—Scope**: This document describes the design, manufacture and use of aluminum trusses, towers and associated aluminum structural components such as head blocks, sleeve blocks, bases, and corner blocks in the entertainment industry. It does not cover individual, separate rigging hardware such as 1/2 couplers and shackles."[9]

Section 5 Use and Care covers loading conditions, handling, and the erection of trusses and towers. **Section 6 User Inspections** has required inspection intervals and frequency of inspections. Procedures for inspection are detailed along with guidance on what items to inspect and what aspects to inspect for each item. These sections provide specifics that could be included in your policies related to the use of trusses and towers in your venues.

ANSI E1.4–1–2016, Entertainment Technology—Manual Counterweight Rigging Systems.

"**Section 1 Scope 1.1 General** This standard applies to permanently installed, manually operated systems of stage rigging hardware for the raising, lowering, and suspension of scenery, lighting, and similar loads. The systems illustrated in the Figures section describe common arrangements of systems used over performance areas.

1.1.1 System Variations This standard applies to variations of manual counterweight rigging, including rope and sandbag systems.

1.4 Intent The purpose of this standard is to establish minimum performance requirements for manual counterweight rigging systems. This standard establishes a basis for reasonable standards of care, for safety and for general welfare with the intent to minimize hazards associated with Manual Counterweight Rigging Systems."[10]

Section 3 Load Suspension Systems Requirements has design details, structural loads, and deflection specifications related to parts of the counterweight system: component assemblies, connections, battens, lift lines, blocks, counterweight arbors, counterweights, sandbags, trim clamps and pinrails. **Section 4** covers operating systems (operating line, tension adjustments, and rope lock). Guide systems for counterbalance technologies are specified in **Section 5**. Documentation, labeling, and the posting of operating instructions and the capacity of the system's components are included in **Section 6**. Inspection and recordkeeping requirements are noted in **Section 7**, for instance,

"**7.2.2 Regular Inspections** Installed rigging systems shall be inspected annually, or more frequently as determined by a qualified person.

7.2.2.1 Manufacturer's Recommendations Inspections shall be performed in accordance with the manufacturer's recommendations and any applicable local code requirements.

7.2.2.2 Inspection Documentation Inspection procedures and results shall be fully documented and the inspection documentation shall be retained by the owner."[11]

Section 8 has design and load factors for system components; this section is referenced by several parts of the previous sections. **Section 9 Basic Functional and Safety Requirements** is clear about compliance with OSHA in reference to guardrails, edge protection, and other OSHA standards related to fall protection.

ANSI E1.47–2017, Entertainment Technology—Recommended Guidelines for Entertainment Rigging System Inspections.

This is a guidance document containing practices and procedures which have been reviewed and approved by entertainment industry practitioners; hence its designation as an ANSI standard. The **Introduction Section** describes the need for the standard and provides an overview of its contents:

"Routine inspection of entertainment rigging systems is required in order to provide a safe working environment and to comply with ANSI rigging standards. This document offers guidance to inform owners, users and inspectors about the process of inspecting entertainment rigging systems."[12]

The defined scope of the standard points to the importance of its contents as you craft the stage rigging inspection requirements to be included in your safety and health program: "These guidelines include recommended inspector qualifications and responsibilities, scope and frequency of inspections, content of the rigging inspection report, and related information concerning the inspection process."[13]

ANSI E1.53–2016, Overhead Mounting of Luminaires, Lighting Accessories, and Other Portable Devices: Specification and Practice.

This standard is structured with sections labeled as informative or normative. The informative sections, such as **Section 1 Introduction (Informative)**, are written with background information, reasons the standard is needed, and other non-mandatory aspects of the standard. The normative sections are written as directives (the word "shall" is consistently used), and must be followed to be in compliance with the standard. The **Introduction** explains that the standard is written in response to reports of luminaires and associated equipment (gel frames, barn doors, etc.) falling, and concerns from members of the Actors' Equity Association about this overhead hazard. (I know of an unsecured barn door falling from an overhead stage light, which fortunately landed in an empty seat next to a patron.) The standard was written to address the then-absence of specific instructions, and documentation of procedures related to installing and securing stage lighting, and similar production equipment, including provisions for secondary support, such as a safety cable.

ANSI E1.32–2012 (R2017), Guide for the Inspection of Entertainment Industry Incandescent Lamp Luminaires.

The recommendations in this guidance standard include the steps for inspections of luminaires (lighting equipment) to be completed before each use and routinely (or periodically), as well as a comprehensive inspection process for such equipment. The frequency is not defined for the routine and comprehensive inspections; your safety and health program's requirement for the frequency of such inspections would depend on environment and usage. To assist in implementing these inspections, Appendix A of the standard contains sample inspection checklists.

Combining the requirements of this standard with those of ANSI E1.53 noted above provides your safety and health program with comprehensive procedures for the care, use, and secure installation of portable stage lighting and other similar equipment.

ANSI E1.46–2016, Standard for the Prevention of Falls from Theatrical Stages and Raised Performance Platforms.

Similar to ANSI E1.53, this standard contains mandatory and informative (or non-mandatory) sections. The standard's scope is defined in a mandatory section:

> **1 Scope (mandatory)** This Standard offers guidance to people working in the entertainment industry on preventing falls by performers, technicians, and members of the public from theatrical stages and raised performance platforms into orchestra pits, into audience areas, into stage traps, and from raised surfaces to surfaces that are lower. Its guidance is intended to be applied to stages and raised platforms used for performance of a show or an event to an audience."[14]

The mandatory requirements of the standard are contained in Section 3.4:

> **"3.4.1 Stages and raised performance platforms shall have a fall protection plan**
>
> **3.4.1.1** The management of performance venues or of theater production companies shall ensure that a fall protection plan be developed, documented, implemented and evaluated for theatrical stages and raised performance platforms that are under their jurisdiction or control."[15]

The fall protection plan is required to provide reasonable measures to protect everyone (staff, crew, performers, and members of the public) who might be exposed to a fall hazard from an elevated level in all areas of the stage and auditorium. The plan must cover all modes of operation and be effective at all times. Complying with this latter requirement prompted one theatre to install signs warning of a fall hazard on the doors which access their stages so custodial and facilities staff are aware of the hazard. Other parts of **Section 3** cover key aspects of the directive related to the fall protection plan's implementation, documentation, evaluation, and revision.

The guidance provided in **Section 4** is non-mandatory and focuses on the use of a risk assessment process to identify fall hazards based on the metrics of likelihood of occurrence and severity of consequences. (I will cover risk assessments in Chapter 7.) The importance of prioritizing fall hazards is discussed, in addition to how to apply the Hierarchy of Controls to such hazards. This section also emphasizes the importance of integrating "reasonable" mitigation measures into your fall protection plan.

Specific guidance with examples of specific mitigations is contained in **Section 5**. This section is indicative of the critical importance of standards developed by and for the entertainment industry. Fall protection measures range from elimination or substitution (not having elevated platforms, covering openings, orchestra pit nets), to engineering controls (guardrails, barriers such as the fire curtain, guarding by distance), to administrative procedures and work practices (rehearsal of performer blocking, edge marking, training, safety monitor, escorts for the public). Compliance with this standard requires using a risk assessment process to determine the risk level of a fall hazard, and then implementing a reasonable industry-specific fall protection measure to mitigate the risk to an acceptable level. This industry standard provides you with a means to address both fixed (i.e. venue-specific) and fluid (i.e. show-specific) hazards with protective measures which, because the mitigations are recommended practices in the entertainment industry, are supportive of the production. I'll address the importance of this in Chapter 8 when we explore how your safety and health program supports the creative process in collaboration with the other artists and practitioners.

RECOMMENDED PRACTICES

We've covered just a few of the ANSI E-standards developed by the ESTA Technical Standards Program to be integrated into your safety and health program. ESTA and other entertainment industry organizations also create recommended practices, which define many of the means and methods for how theatre and live entertainment are created and produced, as well as guiding the education and training for those working (or hoping to work) in the industry. These recommended practices do not follow the consensus and vetting requirements of ANSI, so they are not technically standards.

Industry recommended practices do provide informally vetted and documented practices and procedures you can integrate into your organization's operations without having to develop them. For instance, the Event Safety Alliance (ESA) developed and distributes *The Event Safety Guide* in support of its mission:

> A major goal of the ESA is to transform the culture of the industry (i.e., the way we do things) by deeply integrating safety into all activities so that both individual and group behaviors are affected.[16]

The Event Safety Guide was conceived and first published in 2014 in response to several significant high-profile incidents in the live theatre and entertainment industry, including stage collapses, injuries during audience evacuations, and scaffolding failures.[17] The *Guide* is not currently written as a standard per se; it provides "operational best practices" for those who plan and manage live performance events.

Based on the UK's *Purple Guide to Health, Safety and Welfare in Music and Other Events*,[18] the ESA *Event Safety Guide* covers virtually all aspects of live events. Generally applicable topics include issues of concern for all types of events (e.g. fire safety and weather preparedness), and managing patrons and patron facilities, as well as protecting workers and the worksite. Details related to specific types of live events are included, covering large and small events, electronic and classical music events, and conventions and trade shows, among others. In 2016 ESA and ESTA collaborated to create the Event Safety Working Group within the TSP. The goal of this Working Group is to rewrite sections of *The Event Safety Guide* to become a suite of American National Standards. As of this writing, one section is complete, ANSI ES1.19–2018, Safety Requirements for Special Event Structures,[19] and 13 other sections of the *Guide* are designated and being developed by subgroups of the Working Group.

The ESA also sponsors an annual Event Safety Summit and a Severe Weather Summit in accordance with its mission to provide industry-specific safety training:

> Safe events are built on a foundation of assessment, training, documentation, hazard control, and response-related activities. Understanding

these tasks and how they complement each other is essential to developing a safety plan that is effective in protecting your guests, team, and infrastructure.[20]

Recommended practices in rigging for the industry are defined in the International Code of Practice for Entertainment Rigging (ICOPER), developed and maintained by ESTA. As described, this Code of Practice is intended to be foundational, and to encourage the standardization of policies and training related to entertainment rigging:

> The practices described in the Code are intended to provide a universal foundation for those engaged in planning, managing and executing entertainment rigging. ICOPER also provides guidelines for those who wish to develop policy, design training content or help establish certification criteria.[21]

TRAINING AND CERTIFICATIONS

Entertainment recommended practices are also established through industry-specific training, certifications related to completing training, and credentialing that verifies learned skills and knowledge through exams. Several organizations provide such training and certifications for the entertainment industry. The United States Institute for Theater Technology (USITT) maintains access to a range of training opportunities in such areas as rigging, costuming, welding, and scenic construction. Online courses are available via the USITT website: http://www.usitt.org/. INNOVA—Online Learning for Professionals in Entertainment Design and Technology[22] was created through a collaboration by USITT and Entertainment Services and Technology Association (ESTA). Some courses offered through INNOVA provide continuing education (CE) credit to assist entertainment industry practitioners maintain their certifications. Other courses afford an opportunity to increase knowledge or explore entertainment industry ANSI standards. Quick Fire Sessions on ESTA's American National Standards are free; more in-depth online training is available for a fee. Hands-on classroom training is provided several times a year at various locations in the United States and at the annual USITT Conference & Stage Expo.[23] The USITT Essential Skills for Entertainment Technicians (eSET) is a certificate program designed to verify via examination a baseline of knowledge and skills vetted by professionals and educators in the industry:

> The vision of the Essential Skills for Entertainment Technicians [eSET] tests is to provide a uniform set of criteria, basic knowledge, and skills across all fields in the technical arts to promote higher quality for more productive and safe environments for the entertainment industry.[24]

ESTA manages and administers the Entertainment Technician Certification Program (ETCP):

> An industry-wide program that has brought together an unprecedented group of industry organizations, businesses and individuals to create a program of rigorous assessments for professional technicians. ETCP focuses on disciplines that directly affect the health and safety of crews, performers, and audiences. You may become certified through ETCP in the following areas: Rigger—Arena, Rigger—Theatre, Entertainment Electrician and Portable Power Distribution Technician.[25]

ETCP certification requires a combination of education, work experience, and passing an exam offered at testing centers across the United States.[26] The value of an ETCP certification to those working is frequently highlighted in the "ETCP News" section of *Protocol*, an industry publication of ESTA. In the Spring 2018 issue, Tracy Nunnally notes: "I feel that ETCP certifications add legitimacy to my professional opinions . . . Having years of experience means that I probably know what I'm doing, but combining the experience with an ETCP certification means that a body of other professionals *also* think I know what I am doing."[27]

The ETCP certification programs, as well as the eSET exams, influence the curricular requirements of academic programs across the United States. In an article entitled "ETCP Rigging Certification in an Educational Setting," Andrew Young, an educator and ETCP-certified rigger, notes:

> ETCP has fundamentally changed rigging instruction and how universities are preparing aspiring technicians.[28]

Aligning theatre production academic curricula with industry standards and recommended practices has multiple benefits for a theatre department's safety and health program, as well as for the education of students in the department. Graduates with such academic credentials are more prepared to be successful in their employment, and they are more likely to be readily hired, because employers are increasingly requiring these and other credentials for their employees.[29]

The International Alliance of Theatrical Stage Employees (IATSE) has a long history of developing, providing, and encouraging training for its members. Such training is facilitated through the IATSE Training Trust Fund (TTF):

> The IATSE Entertainment and Exhibition Industries Training Trust Fund is the result of a partnership between the IATSE and Signatory Employers. The IATSE Training Trust Fund facilitates training opportunities for IATSE workers to achieve and maintain the skills, ability, and knowledge necessary to meet the ever changing technologies in the entertainment and exhibition industries.[30]

Training in industry recommended practices and theatre safety available through the TTF covers such topics as safety for motion picture/television (MPTV) workers, and audio/visual (AV) essentials. Through an OSHA Alliance partnership among OSHA, USITT, and IATSE,[31] an OSHA-10/General Entertainment Safety course was developed; attendees who complete this course receive an OSHA-10 General Industry card.

National and local fire codes require those responsible for the safety and health of patrons in assembly occupancies to have training in crowd management and emergency procedures. For instance, the National Fire Protection Association (NFPA) Life Safety Code, NFPA 101, contains the following requirements:

> 13.7.6.1 Assembly occupancies shall be provided with a minimum of one trained crowd manager or crowd manager supervisor. Where the occupant load exceeds 250, additional trained crowd managers or crowd manager supervisors shall be provided at a ratio of one crowd manager or crowd manager supervisor for every 250 occupants.[32]

Crowd manager training can comprise a wide range and depth of topics. Theatre managers must assess their organizational and venue requirements for such training, and then seek the appropriate training for their house management and front-of-house staff. Many factors will influence the extent of crowd management training appropriate for your situation. Among these factors are the size and complexity of your venue(s), the types of patrons typically in attendance (young or older; frequent or infrequent attendees; or differing levels of mobility or special needs, for instance), and the potential risks associated with an event's contents (i.e. political or controversial).

Crowd manager training and certification courses are available from several sources. Fire Marshal Support Services provides a two-hour online training which might be appropriate for smaller venues or included as part of an academic program's theatre management course requirements.[33] After the 2003 Station nightclub fire in West Warwick, RI, the State of Rhode Island required all assembly occupancies in the state to have at least one trained crowd manager on duty. The Office of the RI State Fire Marshal offers a four-hour crowd manager training course each month at locations around the state. The Rhode Island Trained Crowd Manager license must be renewed every five years.[34] The Commonwealth of Massachusetts also updated its fire safety requirements after the Station nightclub fire. To assist with compliance, the Massachusetts Department of Fire Services provides online crowd manager training.[35] More comprehensive crowd manager training is offered through the International Association of Venue Managers (IAVM). Training available via IAVM's website provides general online and venue-specific training. IAVM offers a trained crowd manager course (TCM; approximately eight total hours), and a crowd manager supervisor course (CMS; approximately 14 total hours). The IAVM also hosts the Academy for Venue Safety & Security (AVSS). AVSS week-long classes are scheduled on specific weeks over two years to accommodate the schedules of working professionals.

> AVSS is a dynamic, two-year school built to train venue and event managers, security professionals, and other key personnel involved in every aspect of venue safety and security. The curriculum, developed

and taught by a diverse team of experts, is designed to equip each and every attendee with the recommended practices, resources, and tools needed to face the evolving challenge of providing a safe venue for everyone.[36]

The policies and procedures you implement in your theatre organization's safety and health program, or theatre department's academic curricula, are likely to represent a combination of many industry-specific practices:

- following specific industry standards;
- the implementation of industry recommended practices; and,
- requiring appropriate safety and health training and certifications for employees or students.

Related to the last point, theatre production organizations can include a requirement for specific training and certifications in their job descriptions when hiring staff, such as the ETCP Entertainment Electrician certification for a master electrician. Resources of time and money can be allocated to enable existing staff to obtain these required training and certifications during their employment. Academic theatre and performing arts departments are uniquely positioned to impact safety and health practices in theatre and live entertainment through the academic requirements for their students. The integration of industry standards and recommended practices into academic curricula creates consistency of knowledge and skills among their graduates. This establishes expectations for a high level of safety and health in their work across the industry.

In the next chapter I will investigate examples of policies and procedures related to specific hazards typical of theatre productions and live performance events. These include hazards such as stage fog, live flame, and stage weapons. These policies and procedures are often based on industry standards and recommended practices, but can be adapted as part of your safety and health program to meet the requirements of your theatre organization or academic department.

NOTES

1 American National Standards Institute (ANSI), "Introduction to ANSI," accessed March 28, 2019, https://www.ansi.org/about_ansi/introduction/introduction?menuid=1.
2 Andrew Rusell and Lee Vinsel, "The Joy of Standards," *The New York Times*, February 17, 2019, SR 9. Also online, accessed February 18, 2019, https://www.nytimes.com/2019/02/16/opinion/sunday/standardization.html.
3 Jay O. Glerum, "Using Standards," draft of an article submitted to *Protocol, The Journal of the Entertainment Technology Industry*, 2014.
4 Entertainment Services and Technology Association (ESTA), Technical Standards Program, "About the Technical Standards Program," accessed November 26, 2018, http://tsp.esta.org/tsp/about/about.html.
5 ESTA, Technical Standards Program, "Published Documents," accessed February 28, 2019, https://tsp.esta.org/tsp/documents/published_docs.php.
6 ANSI, "Introduction to ANSI, ANSI Essential Requirements," accessed March 28, 2019, https://www.ansi.org/about_ansi/introduction/introduction?menuid=1.
7 ESTA, Technical Standards Program, "Public Review Documents," accessed November 26, 2018, http://tsp.esta.org/tsp/documents/public_review_docs.php.
8 ESTA, Technical Standards Program, "TSP Working Groups," accessed April 29, 2019, http://tsp.esta.org/tsp/working_groups/index.html.
9 ESTA, ANSI E1.2–2012, accessed November 26, 2018, http://tsp.esta.org/tsp/documents/published_docs.php.
10 ESTA, ANSI E1.4–1–2016, accessed November 26, 2018, http://tsp.esta.org/tsp/documents/published_docs.php.
11 Ibid.
12 ESTA, ANSI E1.47–2017, accessed November 26, 2018, http://tsp.esta.org/tsp/documents/published_docs.php.
13 Ibid.
14 ESTA, ANSI E1.46–2016, accessed November 26, 2018, http://tsp.esta.org/tsp/documents/published_docs.php.
15 Ibid.
16 Event Safety Alliance (ESA), accessed February 22, 2019, http://eventsafetyalliance.org/.
17 Donald C. Cooper, editor, *The Event Safety Guide*, created by the Event Safety Alliance (New York: Skyhorse Publishing, 2014), 5.

18 Events Industry Forum, *The Purple Guide to Health, Safety and Welfare at Music and Other Events*, accessed February 22, 2019, https://www.thepurpleguide.co.uk/.
19 ESTA, ANSI ES1.19–2018, accessed May 10, 2019, https://tsp.esta.org/tsp/documents/published_docs.php.
20 ESA, "Event Safety Summit," accessed November 26, 2018, http://eventsafetyalliance.org/.
21 ESTA, International Code of Practice for Entertainment Rigging, accessed November 26, 2018, http://www.esta.org/.
22 USITT, INNOVA—On Demand Learning, accessed May 11, 2019, https://www.usitt.org/education-training.
23 USITT, Symposia & Master Classes, accessed November 26, 2018, https://www.usitt.org/master/.
24 USITT, Essential Skills for the Entertainment Technician (eSET), accessed November 26, 2018, https://www.usitt.org/education-training.
25 ESTA, Entertainment Technician Certification Program (ETCP), accessed November 26, 2018, https://etcp.esta.org/.
26 ESTA, "ETCP General Testing Information," accessed November 26, 2018, http://etcp.esta.org/certify/certify.html.
27 Tracy Nunnally, "ETCP Certification Makes a Difference," *Protocol, The Journal of the Entertainment Technology Industry*, Vol. 23, No.2, Spring 2018, 82.
28 Andrew Young, "ETCP Rigging in an Educational Setting," *Protocol, The Journal of the Entertainment Technology Industry*, Vol. 23, No. 1, Winter 2018, 80.
29 Ibid, page 82.
30 International Alliance of Theatrical Stage Employees (IASTE), "Training Trust Fund (TTF)," accessed April 29, 2019, https://www.iatsetrainingtrust.org/about.
31 Occupational Safety and Health Administration, "USITT, IASTE Alliance Renewal, 2018," accessed November 26, 2018, https://www.osha.gov/dcsp/alliances/usitt_iatse/usitt-iatse_renewal2017.html.
32 Ron Cote and Gregory E. Harrington, editors, *Life Safety Code Handbook, 2015 edition* (Quincy, MA: National Fire Protection Association [NFPA], 2014),
33 Fire Marshall Support Services, LLC, Crowd Manager Training, accessed November 26, 2018, https://www.crowdmanagers.com/training.

34 State of Rhode Island, Office of the State Fire Marshal, Crowd Management, accessed April 29, 2019, http://fire-marshal.ri.gov/fireacademy/crowdmanagement.php.
35 Commonwealth of Massachusetts Department of Fire Services, DFS-Crowd Manager 2017, accessed November 26, 2018, http://public.eopsselearning.com/course/index.php?categoryid=3.
36 International Association of Venue Managers (IAVM), Academy for Venue Safety and Security, accessed November 26, 2018, http://iavm.org/avss/avss-home.

BIBLIOGRAPHY

Cooper, Donald C., editor. *The Event Safety Guide*, created by the Event Safety Alliance, New York: Skyhorse Publishing, 2014.

Cote, Ron, and Harrington, Gregory E., editors. *Life Safety Code Handbook, NFPA 101, 2015 edition*. Quincy, MA: National Fire Protection Association, 2014.

CHAPTER 6

Policies and Procedures
Specific Hazards

William J. Reynolds

The codes, industry standards, and recommended practices described in the previous chapters provide guidance on how to achieve compliance with their requirements, but not necessarily the means and methods to successfully do so. Policies developed as part of your theatre safety and health program will contain the details necessary to direct specific actions for compliance. In this chapter I identify several theatre production–related hazards, and provide examples of policies to assess and mitigate them. The examples are gleaned from policies and procedures I developed and implemented for the Yale School of Drama/Yale Repertory Theatre (YSD/YRT), as well as from policies and procedures provided by other theatres and academic theatre departments. Policies related to these and many other theatre production hazards must be included in your safety and health program. Some policies will be specific to your organization or academic department; others can be borrowed and adapted from standardized policies available from OSHA[1] and other safety and health resources.[2]

Policies and procedures form the final piece to complete the Hierarchy of Safety Controls, (see Figure 6.1).

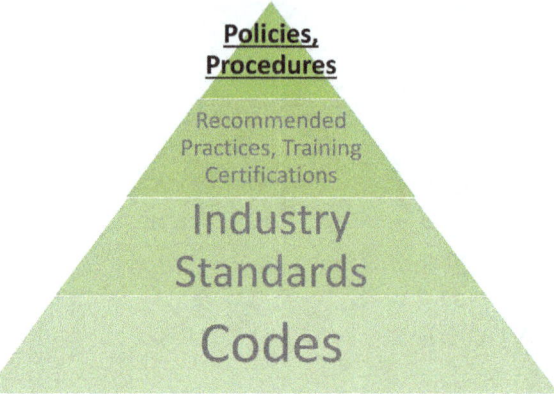

FIGURE 6.1 Hierarchy of Safety Controls: Policies and Procedures

To provide a range of examples applicable to theatre production, I will discuss safety and health policies related to the following:

- personal protective equipment;
- fall prevention and fall protection;
- stage fog and haze;
- stage weapons;
- live flame onstage;
- fire and life safety.

Other aspects of your safety and health program, though not directly related to fabrication and performance, also require specific policies, such as:

- patron alerts and notifications;
- incident reporting and recording.

Samples of these and other policies are included as links to e-documents in the Appendix.

PERSONAL PROTECTIVE EQUIPMENT

The Hierarchy of Control of Hazards (see Figure 3.4) places personal protective equipment (PPE) as the last piece in the protective structure for the control of hazards in the workplace.

Using personal protective equipment is often essential, but it is generally the last line of defense after engineering controls, work practices, and administrative controls.[3]

With this caveat, the availability and use of PPE in your workplace or as part of the activities of your academic program are integral to providing total worker/student protection. A PPE policy integrated into your curriculum provides training for students in preparation for their future employment.

Compliance with exposure limits may require the use of PPE in many aspects of fabrication in theatre production shops. Engineering controls can reduce exposures below an OSHA Permissible Exposure Limit (PEL), but PPE use may provide employees and students with an addition level of protection. For instance, a scenic carpenter may choose to wear an N95 respirator while cutting wood in the scene shop due to the irritant dust in the air even though the exposure level does not exceed an OSHA PEL. Whether for code compliance, or for implementation of industry recommended practices, many theatre production work activities require the use of PPE in such circumstances as:

- work gloves worn to protect from splinters or abrasion when handling raw lumber or newly cut steel;
- steel-toe boots worn while moving heavy scenic materials: platforms, stage weights, etc.;
- protective eyewear donned in dusty environments or around fabrication tools that generate particles in the air in spite of effective machine guarding;
- hardhats worn during load-in or strike activities to protect from head-bump hazards or loose objects overhead.

And finally, exposures not effectively eliminated or reliably limited through the use of other hazard control measures will require the use of PPE at all times. For instance, adequate eye protection is worn at all times in a carpentry shop even with proper machine guards and dust collection systems due to the likelihood of dust particles in the air.

A personal protective equipment policy is necessary and must be established and implemented as part of your safety and health program. The OSHA standard for PPE in General Industry, 29 CFR 1910 Subpart I, Sections 1910.132 through 1910.140 defines an employer's requirements for PPE in the workplace and serves as an outline for the steps necessary for an effective and compliant PPE policy. Your PPE policy must include details of how your organization or academic theatre department will address at least the following:

- The assessment of those hazards which necessitate the use of PPE.
- The selection of appropriate PPE to provide protection from identified hazards.
- Providing the required PPE to those affected by or exposed to the hazards.
- Training required for the use, maintenance, and storage of the PPE.
- Assuring the correct fit of the PPE by providing PPE in appropriate size and design.
- Procedures for assuring the adequacy of employee or student-owned PPE.
- The periodic reviewing of the PPE program to evaluate its effectiveness and to update it as necessary.[4]

The effective integration of a PPE policy into your workplace or academic safety and health program depends on clarity, consistency, and financial support. OSHA requires employers to provide or pay for most PPE required in the workplace:

> With few exceptions, OSHA requires employers to pay for personal protective equipment when it is used to comply with OSHA standards. These typically include: hard hats, gloves, goggles, safety shoes, safety glasses, welding helmets and goggles, face shields, chemical protective equipment and fall protection equipment.[5]

Providing PPE to non-employees (students, unpaid interns, or volunteers) must be addressed by your PPE policy. For consistency, and to further implement a positive safety culture, treating employees and non-employees (students) the same in your policy is the best course of action. The cost of providing PPE to all who are required to use it implies a financial commitment. Such an expenditure reinforces the verbal and written commitments to safety and health through the allocation of money in support of the program. Your PPE policy can include providing more than the minimum required by OSHA. For instance, among the exceptions referenced above, OSHA does not require employers to pay for non-specialty safety toe protective footwear (such as steel-toe boots).[6] Even though not required by OSHA, providing funds as part of your PPE policy to offset the cost of steel-toe boots required by your policy is a clear sign of the organization's support for safety and health. Success also requires support from your theatre or academic department's leadership. The most obvious indication of support for your PPE program is consistent PPE use by everyone exposed to hazards in the theatre production process, from the show's director wearing eye protection in the fabrication shops while conferring with the production staff to the theatre department chair wearing a hardhat onstage when observing from backstage during a production's load-in or fit-up. Providing hardhats with their names on it, or purchasing specially selected protective eyewear, to members of senior leadership is a proven way to assure visible support for the program.

FALL PREVENTION AND FALL PROTECTION (FP/FP)

Compliance with applicable codes and standards is an overarching requirement for your safety and health program. The duty to have fall protection is clearly defined by OSHA.

> 29 CFR 1910.28(a)(1) This section requires employers to provide protections for each employee exposed to fall and falling object hazards.[7]

To comply with this OSHA standard, your policies related to fall prevention and fall protection (FP/FP), and protection from falling objects, must be detailed and comprehensive.

Incorporating the industry standard ANSI E1.46—2016, Standard for the Prevention of Falls from Theatrical Stages and Raised Performance Platforms into your FP/FP policy is one means for your organization or academic department to comply with OSHA's requirement. ANSI E1.46—2016 primarily addresses fall prevention on stages and stage performance platforms, but the standard requires assessment and the implementation of fall prevention strategies to address all possible uses of stages and stage platforms by all who might be exposed to the hazard, including custodial staff, outside contractors, and visitors.

While the preponderance of exposures to fall hazards occur within the technical production departments (scenic, lighting, and projections, for instance), at times virtually anyone in the theatre organization or academic department might work-at-height, or be exposed to other fall hazards. Because of this, and to comply with ANSI E1.46—2016, your FP/FP policy needs to address all likely fall hazards. Your policy's requirements will be greater for the production department's activities; for other departments, general statements related to the use of ladders, step-stools, rolling stair platforms, and the like will assure your fall protection policy is inclusive of all employees, staff, or students who are exposed to fall hazards. The flexibility of job duties within a theatre's workforce may also require specific training to be completed in advance of working-at-height, or before using ladders or lifts. For instance, a scenic designer may need to use a personnel lift (aerial work platform, AWP, or mobile elevated work platform, MEWP) to reach upper portions of the scenery for set dressing. Your FP/FP policy must address such situations. The policy must describe the steps to be taken to approve the use of AWP/MEWP equipment, what training is required for its use, and who is authorized to provide the training. Related to compliance, your FP/FP program must include the requirements of the ANSI A92 Mobile Elevating Work Platform (MEWP/AWP) Design, Safe-use and Training suite of standards.[8]

Protection from fall hazards can be accomplished using several technologies: guardrail systems, safety net systems, or personal fall protection systems (PFPS).[9] Fall hazards protected by permanent guardrails need not be specifically noted in your fall protection policy. However, for locations protected by removable guardrails, by non-compliant guardrails,[10] or by a removable safety net system, specific precautions, and approvals and training will be required.

Protection from fall hazards using personal fall protection systems (PFPS) requires separate, documented, and detailed policies. Personal fall protection systems include personal fall arrest systems (PFAS), as well as positioning systems, travel restraint systems, and fall rescue systems. A guide is available online from the International Safety Equipment Association (ISEA), which provides an overview of the requirements for a PFPS policy. In their guide, the scope of a PFPS policy contains specific aspects to include:

> Following hazard identification, a written site-specific program should be developed with detailed work procedures to protect employees. The plan should state what fall prevention and protection measures are to be used, how they are to be used, a rescue plan, and who is responsible for overall supervision and training.[11]

Developing policies and procedures related to PFPS may require hiring a rigging consultant or engineer to assure compliance with entertainment industry rigging standards. The International Code of Practice for Entertainment Rigging (ICOPER) states in Section 1.4 *On-site work:*

> Methods of access for work at height, fall protection systems and rescue must be designed by a qualified person and deemed to be adequate for the proposed work.[12]

> Industry-specific resources for fall protection systems are available from entertainment rigging consultants, stage rigging companies, and organizations that specialize in entertainment rigging. The Entertainment Technician Certification Program (ETCP) website has a searchable database of ETCP-recognized contractors, employers, and labor providers.[13] The listings in this database connect the value of ETCP-certified training, in this case entertainment rigging, with assurance that service providers who have obtained such training will be competent and professional:

> The Entertainment Technician Certification Program (ETCP) is an industry-wide program that has brought together an unprecedented group of industry organizations, businesses and individuals to create a program of rigorous assessments for professional technicians.[14]

The ETCP database will assist you in locating and engaging vetted rigging professionals in the planning and implementation of your fall prevention and protection program.

Falling hazard protection, protection from loose objects used in an overhead work area, must be addressed by a policy that is preventative as well as protective. The International Safety Equipment Association (ISEA) along with other safety industry organizations developed an ANSI standard related to reducing falling objects hazards: ANSI/ISEA 121–2018, American National Standard for Dropped Object Prevention Solutions. The standard provides falling hazards protection via four prevention strategies:

- **Anchor Attachments**: Solutions that are applied to anchors being used at height to create secure connection points for tool tethers and which are not integral to that anchor.

- **Tool Attachments**: Solutions that are applied to tools being used at height to create secure connection points for tool tethers and which are not integral to that tool.

- **Tool Tether**: A length of material with at least one connector on each end that will connect a tool to an anchor.

- **Container**: A bucket, tool bag or similar device used to hold or transport tools or other equipment.[15]

The scope of this standard is primarily focused on manufacturers of equipment designed to prevent objects (tools and equipment) used in overhead work from dropping to work areas below. Such equipment provides engineering solutions that are preventative. Protective solutions such as PPE (hardhats, protective footwear, and eyewear), while important, may not be protective enough to prevent an injury from a dropped object. Considering that a 1-pound (0.5 kg) crescent wrench falling from a height of 100 feet (31 m) has an impact force of 250 pounds (113 kg), your policy related to falling hazards (dropped objects) must include prevention as well as protection measures.

STAGE FOG AND HAZE

During the decade from 1990 to 2000, several medical studies were conducted on the possible health hazards from occupational exposure to stage fog and haze typical of theatre productions and live performance events. The National Institute for Occupational

Safety and Health (NIOSH) investigated possible health effects in Broadway productions at the request of the Actors' Equity Association (AEA) and the League of American Theatres and Producers, Inc. (LATP).[16] By the year 2000, as a result of these studies and subsequent investigations conducted by Mount Sinai School of Medicine and the ENVIRON Corp, exposure limits for stage fog and haze were developed and published.[17] To meet these limits, peak exposure for stage fog and haze produced by glycols must be below 40 mg/m^3; for haze created by mineral oil peak exposure must be below 25 mg/m^3.[18]

Exposure limits are enforced on behalf of members of Actors' Equity via AEA contracts.

> Quantifiable limits have been placed on a variety of smoke and haze products containing glycol, glycerol, and mineral oil ("Products"). Consequently, Producers/Theatres may use only those Products tested as part of the Study and, further, must use them only within the limits specified.[19]

In the absence of an applicable standard or contractual requirement, these exposure limits should be adopted and incorporated into your safety and health program. A statement in your policy document such as the one below should note this requirement:

> The use of fog and haze onstage generated by glycol or glycerol must comply with Actors' Equity Association Guidelines for Theatrical Smoke and Haze, and with the XYZ Repertory Theatre Theatrical Fog and Haze policy. Fog and haze onstage generated by dry ice or liquid nitrogen must be in compliance with the Fog Testing Protocols posted by Entertainment Services and Technology Association.[20]

Measuring exposure levels for stage fog and haze may seem complicated. Actors' Equity and ESTA provide guidance on the process used to monitor exposure levels and instructions on the use of the AEA-required aerosol monitoring device for stage fog and haze: a PDR-1000 AN.[21] ESTA has protocols for measuring exposure levels of stage fog or haze generated by dry ice or liquid nitrogen.[22]

Other sources for safety policies related to stage fog and haze in theatre productions include the motion picture industry[23] and Actsafe Safety Association, Canada.[24] Guidance documents from both organizations include a list of chemicals prohibited from use in creating stage fog and haze, and these restrictions should also be included in your policy.

The following substances should not be used:

a) Known human carcinogens including any particulates of combustion [smoke], including tobacco smoke (except where such smoke results from the smoking of tobacco by an actor in a scene);
b) Fumed and hydrolyzed chlorides;
c) Ethylene glycol and Diethylene glycol;
d) Mineral oils;
e) Aliphatic and aromatic hydrocarbons including petroleum distillates;
f) Hexachloroethane and Cyclohexylamine.[25]

In addition to the NIOSH stage fog and haze exposure limits, exposure precautions recommended by the study should be part of your stage fog and haze policy. The NIOSH study and the Mount Sinai/ENVIRON study both conclude exposure to stage fog and haze at the levels recorded in the studies did not cause serious health effects such as occupational asthma.[26] The studies did conclude, however, that exposure to glycol fog and haze had "irritative [irritating] and mucous membrane drying properties"[27] and "elevated exposures to mineral oil haze are associated with increased reporting of throat symptoms."[28] Because of the potential for these health effects, in addition to restricting exposures to below the peak limits in the Equity guidelines, your policy should include ways to limit cast and crew exposure to stage fog and haze in terms of dose and duration: that is, for all stage personnel exposure to the least amount of fog or haze for the shortest possible time. (Notification of patrons who might be exposed to stage fog or haze during performances must also be included in your policy—see Patron Alerts and Notifications below.)

STAGE WEAPONS

The use of stage weapons (blank-firing firearms, swords, knives, and other edged weapons) in theatre productions and live entertainment has a long and storied history. Their use has sadly been paralleled by a history of injuries and deaths from their misuse. Documented accidents involving the use of weapons onstage can be found as far back as 1882.

> 05/07/1882—Actor William Rignold was accidentally stabbed in the chest by fellow actor Mr. J. H. Barnes during a performance of Macbeth at the Theatre Royal, Drury Lane. In the last act of the play, the two gentlemen were engaged in a swordfight in which Rignold's character, Macbeth, is killed. The normal practice was for Mr. Barnes to thrust his sword to the side of his opponent, but on the night in question he mistimed the move and the point of his blade penetrated Rignold's chest. Luckily, the injury was not serious and Rignold was able to continue in the role.[29]

I imagine there have been unreported stage weapons–related accidents in live theatrical productions going back to theatre's early roots in ancient history. Because of the potential severity of an injury from a stage weapon and the relatively high likelihood of occurrence during an intense scene of staged violence, your safety and health policy for the use of stage weapons must be detailed and specific.

Sources for guidance on the content and practices of your policy would include industry recommended practices published by several organizations. Groups already cited in the notes, such as the Industry-Wide Labor Management Safety Committee, Actors' Equity Association, and Actsafe, post guidance documents on their websites. Many university theatre departments have developed stage weapons policies which can provide models for your safety and health program's policy, for instance: University of California and Yale University Undergraduate Production.[30] Regional, national, and international theatre organizations have implemented stage weapons policies in their production activities. The Association of British Theatre Technicians (ABTT) publishes the Code of Practice 06 Weapons in Stage Productions, and the UK Health Safety Executive (HSE) posts an information sheet on the management of stage weapons in productions.[31] Links included in these citations and provided via the website for this book will assist you in locating such documents to help guide the development of your stage weapons policy.

Stage weapons policies have many common elements. One basic concept these policies follow is maintaining strict control of all stage weapons by a designated authorized person at all times through the use of documented chain-of-custody protocols and adequate security devices. Other requirements shared by stage weapons policies include:

- Treat all stage weapons (firearms and edged weapons) as if they are real; capable of causing serious injury or death.

- Use only blank-firing, replica, or dummy firearms. Live-firing guns and live ammunition are prohibited.

- Develop and follow specific and detailed protocols for the management of stage weapons by a designated weapons handler.

- The duties of the weapons handler include the care, cleaning, and maintenance of the stage weapons.

- Only stage combat–worthy edged weapons may be used for staged combat. Replica, decorative, and any edged weapon not designed and constructed for staged combat are prohibited from such use.

- Stage weapons must be kept out-of-sight from the public and others not part of the show's production team except for onstage during public performances.

- Each individual (actor or stage crew) who will handle or use a stage weapon will be trained in its functions and safe use.

- The need for a fight director is assessed for each production, and a qualified person is assigned or hired to serve as fight director based on the assessed risk.

- The use of stage weapons must be in compliance with all local and national legal requirements.

Your stage weapons policy is likely to be one of the longest and most detailed of your safety and health program's policies.

The need for strict oversight of all stage weapons at all times, beginning with their selection and acquisition, and including their storage, transportation, care, and use, requires a high level of training and expertise by the designated staff weapons supervisor. The extent of the stage weapons required for a production such as Stephen Sondheim's *Assassins*, for instance, may require a stage weapons expert or fight director be hired for the production. In any event, provision for adequate resources (time and budget) must be part of your policy.

LIVE FLAME ONSTAGE

The use of live flame onstage in a theatre production can encompass a range of flame effects, from a lighted match or candle to torches, bonfires, and gas-fed flame effects. The basis for your safety and health policy related to live flame onstage is NFPA 101—Life Safety Code, and NFPA 160—Standard for the Use of Flame Effects Before an Audience. (Guidance on the use of live flame onstage is also available from several organizations, including: Contract Services Administration Trust Fund,[32] Actsafe Safety Association,[33] and Safety Ontario.[34]) Your policy must define steps to follow during the production process to ensure compliance with these standards, and with all local requirements applicable to your situation. These steps include providing a clear definition of how a live flame effect will be integrated into the production process. Approval for a live flame effect in a show is required by an authority having jurisdiction (AHJ) before an audience is present. However, your policy could allow for an internal review by a designated member of the production's leadership (production manager or technical director, for instance), who provisionally authorizes the staging and rehearsal of scenes with a candle or a torch with the caveat that final approval by the AHJ will be required before the first public performance. Your policy must require preliminary discussion with the AHJ and provisional approval for any extensive or unusual use of live flame or flame effects in a show. Local governmental or campus restrictions on smoking or live flame (such as candles) in public buildings or campus facilities may limit the ability to rehearse live flame moments in a rehearsal hall, or in any location other than the venue. In this case, your policy should indicate that these live flame moments will be introduced into the show only during technical rehearsals onstage.

Your live flame policy must require documentation of the plan for the use of live flame onstage, the provisions to be taken to limit combustibles onstage, and require flame retardant (FR) treating of flammable materials adjacent to the live flame. The live flame policy must include developing and implementing a fire protection plan (designating a fire watch, locating fire extinguishers, and detailing emergency procedures), as well as noting extinguishing requirements such as a bucket of water to douse burned paper, or an FR gel in an ashtray to put out a lit cigarette. Documents related to each instance of live flame in a production must be provided to the AHJ for their review and approval. Details related to each instance of live flame must include at least: how the flame is being lit, how it is used onstage, how long the flame will be burning, and provisions for extinguishing the flame. The policy must indicate that samples and a demonstration of the live flame effect may be required by the AHJ. Once approved, any alteration in staging or change to the live flame plan must subsequently be reapproved by the AHJ.

FIRE AND LIFE SAFETY

Your Live Flame Onstage policy is but one aspect of the policies related to fire and life safety. The focus of a fire and life safety policy will be compliance with NFPA 101—Life Safety Code, and/or similar local or regional codes. Requirements related to fire and life safety will be referenced in many parts of your safety and health program, for instance, fire and life safety in fabrication shops; in assembly spaces; in performance venues; for patrons. An AHJ's approval for a show to proceed will typically require a life safety fire inspection of the stage, scenery, and auditorium by the AHJ. A clear and well-documented procedure for such inspections must be included in your policy. The scheduling will require coordination with your production calendar to assure inspections by the AHJ occur in advance of the first public performance of each show. The participants in the inspection, and the materials and documents to be provided at the inspections, must be detailed in your policy. Which of your production staff who will participate in the life safety fire inspection may vary depending on the production.

For instance, a scenic design with extensive fabricated foliage may require the properties master to verify the fire-retardant process used on the foliage and to have adequate samples for flame testing during the inspection.[35] The stage manager may be required to document each instance of live flame in the production, describing specifics of the scene and staging, length of time for each flame effect, and fire protection precautions that will be in place for each flame effect. Figure 6.2 is an example of a form for such documentation.

[PRODUCTION TITLE] **Live Flame and Smoking Incidents**
By [Author]
Directed by [Director]

Scene	Flame Source	Characters Smoking	Characters in Scene	Pages of Flame	Time Lit (min:sec)	Location Onstage	Location Ashtrays	Notes	Flammable Materials Onstage
[Example] 2	[Example] Cigar #1	[Example] Solider (Slate H.)	[Example] Soldier (Slate H.), Parlor Maid (Sarah S.)	[Example] 7–10	[Example] 3:30	[Example] All of Circle	[Example] 1 mounted on pedestal	[Example] Lit Offstage Left by lighter Put out on pedestal ashtray	[Example] None (nothing onstage but painted wood pedestal)

FIRE SAFETY PRECAUTIONS
[Example] · Candles will be lit once set onstage and blown out before being moved in scene changes
[Example] · Stage crew fire watch will be stationed backstage with a fire extinguisher and line-of-sight to the stage action

[Stage Manager], SM
[Assistant Stage Manager], ASM

FIGURE 6.2 Sample Live Flame and Smoking Incidents Form

For a flexible seating plan, such as a black box theatre, or proposed alterations to the seating layout in a fixed-seating auditorium, a complete floorplan showing the seating and stage, noting the total audience capacity and exit routes, must be included with the documentation provided to the AHJ. Your campus fire marshal or local fire department may require additional information, such as the dates, times, and number of performances, contact information for key production personnel, and FR certificates for scenic materials (the latter are required to verify compliance with NFPA 701[36]).

Your safety and health program will include many other requirements related to fire and life safety. These are also documented in your safety and health handbook. Specific policies are often cross-referenced in a safety and health handbook, including the fire and life safety requirements applicable to all aspects of an organization's activities and facilities. The scale and scope will vary for each organization or department, but you should include at a minimum some of the following:

- fire reporting procedures;
- evacuation requirements and procedures;
- evacuation assembly locations, and refuge points;
- shelter-in-place procedures and sheltering locations;
- prohibitions related to the use of fire and flame inside buildings;
- smoking restrictions; and,
- means of egress designated and kept clear.

PATRON ALERTS AND NOTIFICATIONS

Theatres routinely post informational signs in their lobbies containing notices or warnings for patrons. These signs might inform patrons that stage fog or haze is used in the show, the staging has moments of nudity, or stage weapons appear onstage. A policy related to patron notification provides an example of how the size of your organization or department can affect the level of detail a policy might require. A single statement in your safety and health handbook might suffice, such as:

> For all productions in XYZ Theatre venues, signs will be posted in the theatre lobby for each show to notify patrons if any of the following are included in the performance: extreme staged violence, stage fog and haze, nudity, adult language or situations, loud sounds or sound cues, strobe lighting effects, or stage weapons.

A more comprehensive Patron Notification policy will include all aspects of patron interactions and customer service. Such a policy would include defined roles and responsibilities, a procedure for the assessment of the need for patron notification by the artistic leadership, specific words or phrases to be used on lobby notices, and training required for house management and front-of-house staff related to the notifications. Additionally, an assessment of the means to communicate a patron notification must be required to assure the effective communication of information via a variety of techniques: written, verbal, pictorial. A scripted message may be necessary for use by box office and telemarketing personnel to inform potential patrons of information related to such notifications.

INCIDENT REPORTING AND RECORDING

Comprehensive knowledge about all incidents (accidents, near-misses,[37] and injuries) is an essential aspect of a safety and health program. In theatre productions, such incidents can occur during any part of the production process: rehearsals, production fabrication, load-ins, performances, or during academic production-related activities and classroom situations. Recordkeeping related to all reported incidents creates useful data. Those who are responsible for the oversight and support of your safety and health program can use this data to assess, evaluate, and update aspects of the program. OSHA has specific recordkeeping and reporting requirements. To achieve your program's goal of compliance, all incidents must be reported and recorded using the required OSHA forms.

Data collected from incident reporting can serve several purposes. Your policy related to incident reporting and recording must clarify the reason(s) for the policy and the intended uses for the collected data. By way of example, consider the content of two recordkeeping documents: one whose purpose is related to compliance with OSHA 29 CFR 1904—Recording and Reporting Occupational Injuries and Illnesses; the other document, which is intended to facilitate incident investigation in order to determine root cause in support of accident prevention. 29 CFR 1904 requires most employers (including theatre producing organizations) to maintain an OSHA 300 log, which documents data for each reportable work-related injury or illness (see Figure 6.3).

Reporting on an OSHA 300 log is numbers driven, and is intended to provide quantitative data for analysis by agencies such as the U.S. Federal Bureau of Labor Statistics. Such statistics are rearward looking and provide for the assessment of overall

OSHA's Form 300 (Rev. 01/2004)
Log of Work-Related Injuries and Illnesses

Year _____

Identify the person

(A) Case no.	(B) Employee's name	(C) Job Title (e.g., Welder)

Describe the case

(D) Date of injury or onset of illness (mo./day)	(E) Where the event occurred (e.g. loading dock north end)	(F) Describe injury or illness, parts of body affected, and object/substance that directly injured or made person ill (e.g. second-degree burns on right forearm from acetylene torch)

Classify the case

CHECK ONLY ONE box for each case based on the most serious outcome for that case:

Death (G)	Days away from work (H)	Remained at work		Enter the number of days the injured or ill worker was:		Check the "injury" column or choose one type of illness: (M)					
		Job transfer or restriction (I)	Other recordable cases (J)	Away from work (days) (K)	On job transfer or restriction (days) (L)	Injury (1)	Skin disorder (2)	Respiratory condition (3)	Poisoning (4)	Hearing loss (5)	All other illnesses (6)

FIGURE 6.3 OSHA 300 Log Required Data Fields

trends. These lagging indicators help identify high-risk industries or occupations. Related to the latter, OSHA uses this data in the identification of high-risk industries to establish National, and Local Emphasis Programs.[38]

> National Emphasis Programs (NEPs) are temporary programs that focus OSHA's resources on particular hazards and high-hazard industries. Existing and potential new emphasis programs are evaluated using inspection data, injury and illness data, National Institute for Occupational Safety and Health (NIOSH) reports, peer-reviewed literature, analysis of inspection findings, and other available information sources.[39]

Accident prevention is better served by qualitative records. Data and lagging indicators help identify and quantify what happened. Root cause analysis using qualitative records provides descriptive assessment of why something happened. OSHA provides an advisory document, *Incident [Accident] Investigations: A Guide for Employers*,[40] which describes root causes as:

> The underlying reasons why unsafe conditions exist, or if a procedure or safety rule was not followed in a workplace. Root causes generally reflect management, design, planning, organizational, or operational failings. (e.g., a guard had not been repaired; failure to use the guard was routinely overlooked by supervisors to ensure the speed of production.)[41]

The *Guide* describes a systematic approach to incident investigation using a focus on root causes. Doing so provides a means to fully understand why an incident occurred, and avoids focusing on blame or fault. Included with this *Guide* is an Incident Investigation Form, tips for effective documentation of incidents using photographs and sketches, and a checklist of questions to help identify root causes. The investigative process described in this *Guide* along with the related forms document data not required on the OSHA 300 log, including assessments and analysis details such as:

- What part of the body was injured, and if a near-miss (no injury), how might the person have been hurt?

- Full description of the incident: What was the person doing prior to the incident; what tools or equipment were involved; the location and time of the incident?
- What were the causes of the incident: workplace conditions; contributing actions by the injured person, or by others?
- Were safety regulations in place and used?
- Was safety equipment or guards in place or used; PPE available and used?
- What could have been done to prevent this incident? How can future incidents be prevented?

Your incident reporting and recording policy must contain elements of both aspects: data collection and accident prevention. Quantitative incident data is required for assessment of your safety and health program's evolution as well as for compliance with OSHA or other regulatory requirements. Qualitative accident investigation details are necessary to determine the root causes of accidents, and to formulate effective corrective actions for a proactive incident and illness prevention program.

The success of your incident reporting and recording policy is dependent on your staff, faculty, and students reporting each incident. Generally, lack of reporting of accidents and injuries by employees is a widespread problem: nearly 10 percent of employees do not report their work-related injuries.[42] According to an article in *The New York Times*, "workers routinely underreport work-related injuries and illnesses . . . workers did not report job-related injuries because they feared being fired or disciplined."[43] Non-reporting of incidents and injuries by employees in the entertainment industry is even more prevalent. A medical study released in 2018 noted among the 67 percent of theatre personnel surveyed who had experienced at least one theatre-related head impact injury, 70 percent had not reported the injury and continued working.[44] The historical legacy of "the Show Must Go On," and other internal cultural influences, are among the reasons for this high rate of non-reporting. Altering the impact of this cultural legacy will require extra effort to guarantee you will have reliable data from which to grow and improve your program.

Without data, you cannot analyze trends, and without analysis you cannot implement accident prevention. There is an interdependent relationship among near-misses and minor injuries (requiring only first aid), intermediate incidents (requiring hospitalization), and major events (amputation or death).[45] In other words, the effective reporting and investigation of near-misses and minor injuries may be preventative of more serious accidents. Because of this relationship, your policy must encourage incident reporting. Any perceived negative consequences of doing so in your theatre organization or academic department will discourage reporting of all incidents, accidents, and injuries. For instance, an employee's improper use of a tool or piece of equipment results in an injury. If the reporting of the incident negatively affects her or his performance evaluation, the employee's motivation to report such incidents will be negatively affected. This is especially true for near-miss and minor injury incidents. The safety culture of your organization or academic department must encourage incident reporting, and your policy should have well-defined and simple reporting processes.

Encouraging consistent reporting of near-misses is often challenging. According to the National Safety Council:

> A near miss is an unplanned event that doesn't result in injury or death, but could have. Often these incidents . . . are not reported. No harm done, right? But by not reporting near misses, employees also are not doing anything to prevent more, potentially serious incidents from occurring in the future. Near misses occur every day in every industry, and most serious, catastrophic and loss-producing incidents are preceded by these warnings.[46]

While the specific relationship among the number of hazardous conditions, near-miss incidents, minor injuries, and more serious consequences (lost workday injuries or deaths) is debated among safety professionals,[47] Figure 6.4 gives a representation of the general idea.

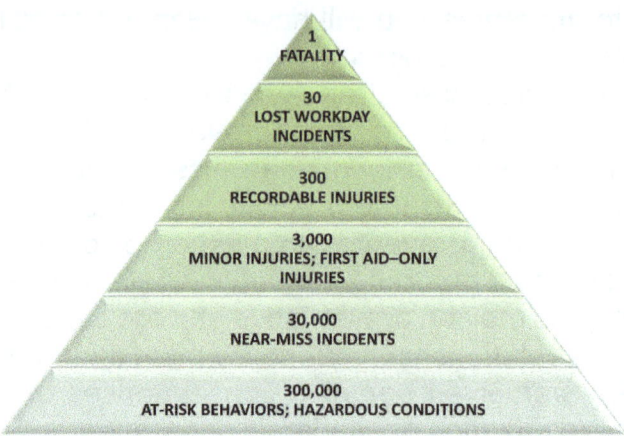

FIGURE 6.4 Relationship of Hazardous Conditions to Injuries and Fatalities (numbers are estimates)

Each theatre organization or academic department should assess how best to encourage the reporting of all incidents, especially hazardous conditions, near-misses, and minor injuries. Active, effective, and timely follow-up on each reported incident is essential to reinforce the messaging that underlies a strong safety culture: each person in your workplace or academic department is valued, and each has a significant role to play in the success of your safety and health program.

Before we explore other ideas that support a culture of safety for your theatre organization or academic department, in the next chapter I will discuss several strategies used by safety professionals in other industries. I will show how you can integrate aspects of these strategies into your safety and health program in support of your theatre's production process. As we often do in the conceptualization, development, and actualization of a live performance event, we can draw ideas and inspiration from a variety of safety sources outside of our industry. Most importantly, we'll learn how various strategies used to build your safety program, which might seem complicated or burdensome, are in fact supportive of your organization's artistic mission or your department's educational goals.

NOTES

1 Occupational Safety and Health Administration (OSHA), "Help for Employers, Sample Programs," accessed March 15, 2019, https://www.osha.gov/dcsp/compliance_assistance/sampleprograms.html, and eTools, eMatrix, Expert Advisors, and V-Tools, accessed March 15, 2019, https://www.osha.gov/dts/osta/oshasoft/
2 Several universities and safety resources businesses post safety and health policy documents. For example: the University of California Riverside posts their Environmental, Health & Safety Forms at https://ehs.ucr.edu/forms/, accessed February 27, 2019. Online safety resources businesses provide forms and documents for purchase. Also, contact your peers in the entertainment industry and theatre academic programs for documents they may be able to share.
3 OSHA, "Personal Protective Equipment Factsheet," accessed March 15, 2019, https://www.osha.gov/SLTC/personalprotectiveequipment/hazards_solutions.html.
4 OSHA, "Personal Protective Equipment; OSHA Publication 3151," accessed March 15, 2019, https://www.osha.gov/SLTC/personalprotectiveequipment/hazards_solutions.html.
5 OSHA, "Personal Protective Equipment, Payment for Personal Protective Equipment," accessed March 15, 2019, https://www.osha.gov/SLTC/personalprotectiveequipment/payment.html.
6 Ibid.
7 OSHA, Regulations (Standards—29 CFR 1910.28(a)(1))), accessed March 17, 2019, https://www.osha.gov/pls/oshaweb/owadisp.show_document?p_id=9720&p_table=STANDARDS.
8 ANSI Webstore, ANSI/SAIA A92 MEWP standards, accessed June 19, 2019, https://webstore.ansi.org/Search/Find?in=1&st=ansi%2Fsaia+A92.
9 OSHA, Regulations (Standards—29 CFR 1910.28(b)(1)(i))), accessed March 15, 2019, https://www.osha.gov/pls/oshaweb/owadisp.show_document?p_id=9720&p_table=STANDARDS.
10 The front of an auditorium balcony is an example of a location with non-compliant guardrails in a work area. NFPA 101 and other codes allow for a lower (26-inches-high) railing at the front of a seating row in a balcony due to sightline restrictions. Since this railing is less than the required height of a guardrail in a work area (42-inches-high), fall protection must be provided when working in this area.

11 International Safety Equipment Association (ISEA), *Fall Protection Equipment Use and Selection Guide*, accessed March 15, 2019, https://safetyequipment.org/wp-content/uploads/2017/05/FPUserGuide2017.pdf, 5.
12 Entertainment Technician Certification Program (ETCP), International Code of Practice for Entertainment Rigging, accessed March 15, 2019, https://www.esta.org/ESTA/icoper.php
13 ETCP, "Find ETCP Recognized Contractors, Employers or Labor Providers," accessed March 15, 2019, https://etcp.esta.org/.
14 ETCP, "Setting the Stage for Safety," accessed March 15, 2019, http://etcp.esta.org/.
15 ANSI/ISEA 121–2018, American National Standard for Dropped Object Prevention Solutions, 1–2.
16 National Institute for Occupational Safety and Health (NIOSH), *Health Hazard Evaluation, HETA 90-0355-2449*, August 1994, accessed February 27, 2019, https://www.cdc.gov/niosh/hhe/reports/pdfs/1990-0355-2449.pdf
17 Jacqueline M. Moline, M.D., M.Sc. et al., and Joseph H. Highland, PhD. et al., *Health Effects Evaluation of Theatrical Smoke, Haze, and Pyrotechnics,* 2000, accessed February 27, 2019, https://www.actorsequity.org/resources/Producers/safe-and-sanitary/smoke-and-haze/.
18 Ibid, page ES-6.
19 Actors' Equity Association (AEA), Theatrical Smoke and Haze Regulations, accessed February 27, 2019, https://www.actorsequity.org/resources/Producers/safe-and-sanitary/smoke-and-haze/.
20 To avoid confusion, omit the word "smoke" from your policy documents and conversations related to such stage effects. The *Merriam-Webster's Dictionary* defines smoke as: "the gaseous products of burning materials especially of organic origin made visible by the presence of small particles of carbon." You do not want your authority having jurisdiction to think you are setting fires on your stage to create your fog or haze effects.
21 For references related to stage fog and haze exposure monitoring, see: Entertainment Services and Technology Association (ESTA), *Introduction to Modern Atmospheric Effects, 5th Edition,* accessed June 19, 2019, https://tsp.esta.org/tsp/documents/published_docs.php, and,
   AEA, Theatrical Smoke and Haze Regulations, accessed June 19, 2019, https://www.actorsequity.org/resources/Producers/safe-and-sanitary/smoke-and-haze/.

22 ESTA, Fog & Smoke Working Group—Fog Testing Protocols, accessed June 19, 2019, https://tsp.esta.org/tsp/working_groups/FS/fogtesting.html.
23 Contract Services Administration Services Trust Fund, Industry-Wide Labor Management Safety Committee, *Safety Bulletin #10*, accessed February 27, 2019, https://www.csatf.org/bulletintro.shtml.
24 Actsafe, *Safety Bulletin #10*, Actsafe Safety Association, Burnaby, B.C., Canada, accessed February 27, 2019, http://www.actsafe.ca/category/resources/safety-bulletins/motion-picture/.
25 Contract Services Administration Services Trust Fund, Industry-Wide Labor Management Safety Committee, *Safety Bulletin #10*, accessed February 27, 2019, https://www.csatf.org/bulletintro.shtml.
26 NIOSH, *Health Hazard Evaluation, HETA 90-0355-2449*, August 1994, accessed March 15, 2019, https://www.cdc.gov/niosh/hhe/reports/pdfs/1990-0355-2449.pdf, 19.
27 Ibid.
28 Jacqueline M. Moline, M.D., M.Sc. et al., and Joseph H. Highland, PhD. et al., *Health Effects Evaluation of Theatrical Smoke, Haze, and Pyrotechnics, June 6, 2000*, accessed March 15, 2019, https://actorsequity.org/resources/Producers/safe-and-sanitary/smoke-and-haze/, page ES-6.
29 Don Gillan, "Weapons on the Stage," accessed June 19, 2019, http://www.stagebeauty.net/th-frames.html?http&&&www.stagebeauty.net/th-weapons.html.
30 Yale University, Yale Undergraduate Production, Prop Weapon and Stage Combat Policy, accessed March 4, 2019, https://up.yalecollege.yale.edu/regulations/prop-weapon-and-stage-combat-policy. Used with permission.
31 Health Safety Executive (HSE), *Management of Firearms and Other Weapons in Productions*, accessed June 19, 2019, https://www.met.police.uk/SysSiteAssets/media/downloads/central/advice/filming/management-of-weapons-and-other-firearms-in-productions.pdf.
32 Contract Services Administration Trust Fund, *Safety Bulletins*, accessed March 5, 2019, https://www.csatf.org/bulletintro.shtml.
33 Actsafe Safety Association, "Open Flames," accessed March 5, 2019, https://www.actsafe.ca/?s=open+flames.
34 Theatre Ontario, Performance Industry Guidelines, accessed March 5, 2019, https://www.labour.gov.on.ca/english/hs/topics/performance.php.

35 Reference NFPA 705 Recommended Practice for a Field Flame Test for Textiles and Films, accessed March 15, 2019, https://www.nfpa.org/Codes-and-Standards/All-Codes-and-Standards/Codes-and-Standards.

36 Reference NFPA 701 Standard Methods of Fire Tests for Flame Propagation of Textiles and Films, accessed March 15, 2019, https://www.nfpa.org/Codes-and-Standards/All-Codes-and-Standards/Codes-and-Standards.

37 "OSHA defines a near miss as an incident in which no property was damaged and no personal injury was sustained, but where, given a slight shift in time or position, damage or injury easily could have occurred," "How Reporting Close Calls Can Prevent Future Incidents," *Safety+Health*, January 1, 2012, accessed March 15, 2019, https://www.safetyandhealthmagazine.com/articles/6843--articles-6843-everybody-gets-to-go-home-in-one-piece.

38 OSHA, "Enforcement," accessed March 15, 2019, https://www.osha.gov/dep/index.html.

39 OSHA, "Enforcement/Directives – NEP," accessed April 14, 2019, https://www.osha.gov/enforcement/directives/nep.

40 OSHA, "Incident [Accident] Investigations: A Guide for Employers," accessed March 15, 2019, https://www.osha.gov/dcsp/products/topics/incidentinvestigation/index.html.

41 Ibid., 2.

42 Brett Snider, Esq., "How Many Workplace Injuries Go Unreported," *FindLaw*, December 20, 2013, accessed March 15, 2019, https://blogs.findlaw.com/injured/2013/12/how-many-workplace-injuries-go-unreported.html.

43 Steven Greenhouse, "Work-Related Injuries Underreported," *The New York Times*, November 16, 2009, accessed March 15, 2019, https://www.nytimes.com/2009/11/17/us/17osha.html.

44 Science Daily: Science News, "High Number of Concussion-Related Symptoms in Performing Arts," accessed March 15, 2019, www.sciencedaily.com/releases/2018/04/180403155031.htm.

45 Risk Engineering "The Heinrich/Bird Safety Pyramid: Pioneering Safety Research Has Become a Safety Myth," accessed March 15, 2019, https://risk-engineering.org/concept/Heinrich-Bird-accident-pyramid.

46 National Safety Council, "Tools and Resources, Near-Miss-Reporting," accessed March 15, 2019, https://www.nsc.org/work-safety/tools-resources/near-miss-reporting.

47 Tim Marsh, *Total Safety Culture: Organisational Risk Literacy* (Manchester, England: Ryder Marsh Safety Limited, 2014), 50.

BIBLIOGRAPHY

International Safety Equipment Association, ANSI/ISEA 121-2018, American National Standard for Dropped Equipment Prevention, Arlington, VA: International Safety Equipment Association, 2018.

Marsh, Tim. *Total Safety Culture: Organisational Risk Literacy*. Manchester, England: Ryder Marsh Safety Limited, 2014.

CHAPTER 7

Borrowing Safety Strategies
William J. Reynolds

Safety and health program elements applied to the fabrication technologies for a theatre production (woodworking, metalworking, sewing, and painting, among others) are similar to those in safety and health programs for general industry. For instance, safety and health policies applicable to the operations of a commercial furniture shop would be implemented with many of the same means and methods as those for a scenic shop or paint shop at a theatre or academic theatre department. In this chapter, I will discuss several standardized safety strategies proven successful in other industries. I will note how these strategies can be used to evolve your safety and health programs toward an emphasis on injury prevention and an effective reduction of risk. These safety strategies are:

- Checklists
- Operational Inspections
- Identification of Hazards
- Alone (Lone) Work Policy
- Prevention through Design (PtD)
- Risk Assessments
- Field Level Hazard Assessments
- Serious Injury and Fatality (SIF) Prevention

My discussion of these injury prevention and risk reduction strategies will assume a typical theatre or live event production process. (I readily acknowledge there is no single production model followed by all theatre organizations or academic departments.) I'll assume the following steps will be involved in a typical production's process; please refer to the texts in the notes for other ideas and examples.[1]

Selection
- Exploration of projects to produce
- Selection of projects
- Conceptualization of projects
- Determination of each project's required resources
- Integration of selected projects into season or other ongoing activities
- Determination of appropriate venue

Development
- Assemble (or assign) a team for each project (director, designers, cast, technical and management staff, etc.)
- Develop artistic concepts and design ideas for each project
- Finalize artistic concepts, and complete the design package (sketches, drawings, floorplans, elevations, etc.)

Implementation
- Assess the resources required by the design concept
- Align design with resources (budgeting)
- Begin technical design for fabrication
- Initiate rehearsal process

Preparation and Fabrication
- Evolution of the project through rehearsal
- Development of the physical production in the technical shops
- Begin integrating performers into the physical production before installation (fittings, rehearsal scenery, etc.)
- Installation of the physical production into the venue and related production support spaces

Finalize the Integration of Performers and Production Elements (technical rehearsals)

Performances

Removal (load-out or strike), Restoration of the Venue

The roles and responsibilities for safety and health will vary among theatre production organizations and academic departments. Few theatre organizations or academic departments are large enough or have sufficient resources to employ a full-time safety and health director. Responsibility for safety and health is often delegated departmentally to department heads (scenic, electrics, stage crew, stage management, etc.) and coordinated through a senior leadership position (general manager or production manager) or possibly a safety and health committee.[2] With such departmental delegation in mind, a typical theatre organizational model will underlie my discussion of the integration of these safety and health strategies in collaboration with the production process. Figure 7.1 provides a simplified organizational example for reference.

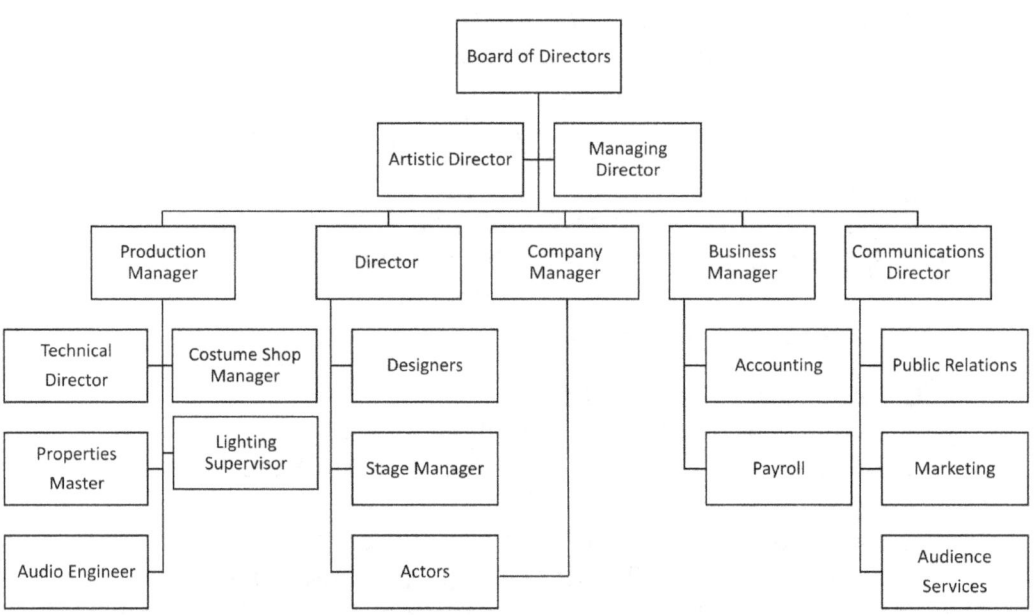

FIGURE 7.1 Typical Theatre Organizational Chart (simplified)

CHECKLISTS

The organization chart (Figure 7.1) is illustrative of the complexity of a typical theatre producing organization. The processes and technologies required for a theatre production further complicate the challenge of keeping all aspects of a production on track. Whether large or small,

> No matter how the project is categorized, any entertainment enterprise is an effort that can become very complicated as the number of participants expands. . . . Performance events require multiple disciplines and the involvement of many individuals to support the performance and enhance the audience experience.[3]

To manage this complexity, we develop personal strategies to keep our daily lives and work requirements on track. We might turn to software solutions or cell phone apps. But as is often the case, the best solution may be the simplest.

In his slim but informative book, *The Checklist Manifesto: How to Get Things Right*, Atul Gawande recommends the simple but compelling strategy of making checklists. He notes that the humble checklist, "almost ridiculous in its simplicity," can keep complicated processes and technologies on track, and avoid operational coordination failures. Checklists help ensure that many aspects of your production process proceed as planned:

- your rehearsal reports have been sent, and to the right people;
- your venue has been cleared, restored, and prepared for the next user;
- you have covered all the required topics for the nightly training of your front-of-house (FOH) staff;
- each connection in a production rigging system has been inspected and verified before each use; or,
- the precise steps for a complex automation cue have been completed in the correct order.

Medicine, aviation, the nuclear industry, investment banking, and military defense systems, among others, have found that checklists used by individuals and organizational teams have increased rates of success, and decreased the likelihood of failures. But as Gawande acknowledges,

> We don't like checklists. They can be painstaking. They're not much fun.[4]

Many of us take pride in our ability to keep track of things in our heads, of being able to juggle many aspects of a complex task without having to resort to cross-checks or back-ups. We may even perceive that much of our value to an organization derives from our knowledge, ability, and determination. But we face challenges of increased complexity, the evolving nature of the creative process, and constrained time for responding to change. We may overlook the possibility of reducing risk by decreasing the likelihood of error through the use of a simple checklist. The effective use of checklists to observe conditions, to cross-check systems, and to complete diverse tasks can help make a complex theatre event safe and successful. "Most accidents are caused by omission rather than by a deliberate act—by someone 'forgetting' to check something, leaving a box or cable in someone else's way."[5]

As Gawande notes, among the reasons we often don't like checklists is they must be carefully developed and tested to be useful and effective. To aid in their success, he provides us with a Checklist for Checklists (see Figure 7.2).

Checklists can either be of a DO–CONFIRM or READ–DO format. A checklist is not a comprehensive how-to guide or standard operating procedure (SOP) to be used by a person who lacks the technical skills or knowledge to understand and complete the task. "Good checklists are precise, practical, and easy to use. Instead of spelling out everything, they provide brief reminders of important steps that are easy to miss."[6] A checklist assumes a level of professional knowledge, experience, and training. In fact, as in medicine, aviation, or aerospace occupations, the user is expected to know what they are doing. The checklist is intended as a check to make sure no steps are overlooked, and actions are completed in the correct order. As Bryan Huneycutt, Disney Parks Safety Program Manager, succinctly noted, "Checklists are fantastic when used properly."[7]

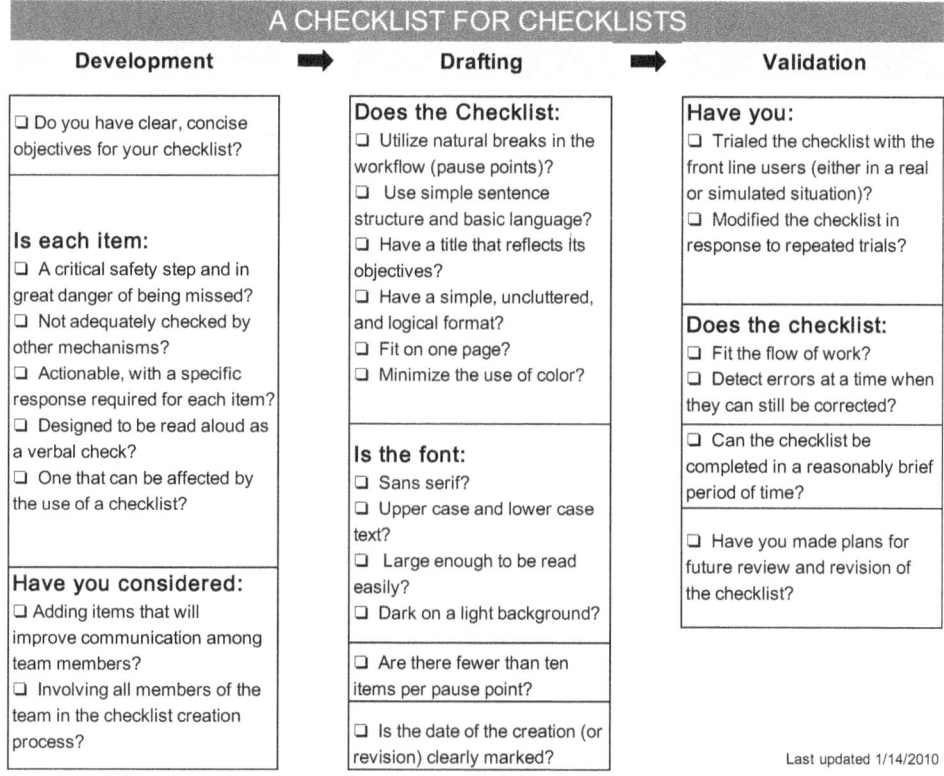

FIGURE 7.2 A Checklist for Checklists

Checklists must be dynamic documents that should be maintained and updated by each department. Like all aspects of your written safety and health program, checklists require regular review to assure the steps are current, accurate, and effective. A checklist intended for more than one-time use must be signed by the person who created the checklist and dated. The checklist might also include note of when the checklist should be reviewed and updated based on its date of origin. To confirm that the checklist steps effectively guide a trained user though the process or action, checklists should be audited and tested by someone other than the person who created the checklist. Gawande notes the needs for testing, modification, and review of checklists under the "Validation" section in his Checklist for Checklists (Figure 7.2 above).

I invite you to exercise your expertise and creativity by making a short list of the tasks for which you might develop checklists. The appropriateness of a particular checklist will vary from organization to organization, and from department to department. Checklists can be useful throughout a theatre organization or academic department, not just in the technical production areas. Consider using a checklist for such non-technical activities as:

- Welcoming and on-boarding members of a new cast:
  ○ fill out all the required in-house forms,
  ○ submit required paperwork,
  ○ comply with AEA requirements.

- Training FOH staff and ushers:
  ○ P.A.S.S. fire extinguisher training,
  ○ specific responsibilities assigned during an evacuation,
  ○ designate the locations of emergency response equipment.

- Reviewing contractual requirements in an application for rental of your venue:
  ○ proof of insurance provided,
  ○ names and contact information of responsible persons listed,
  ○ specifics related to load-in, residency, and strike are documented.

OPERATIONAL INSPECTIONS

The mention of inspections may bring to mind hiring a rigging consultant to inspect and assess the condition of your counterweight rigging system, or engaging an engineer to assess the condition of your orchestra pit lift. Mechanical systems and equipment do require regular inspections to ensure they will operate correctly and reliably. Operational inspections, on the other hand, assure that facilities, production equipment, scenery, public spaces, and many other aspects of a venue or production are in place and ready to use. Many industries utilize operational or visual inspections as part of their routine activities. For instance, OSHA requires a visual inspection (examination) of forklifts before each use:

> Industrial trucks [forklifts] shall be examined before being placed in service, and shall not be placed in service if the examination shows

any condition adversely affecting the safety of the vehicle. Such examination shall be made at least daily.[8]

Agricultural vehicles and farm equipment are given a daily walk-around visual inspection before each use, starting with the work area.[9] The United States Federal Aviation Administration requires pilots to perform a walk-around visual inspection of their aircraft before each flight.

> The visual [operational] preflight assessment is an important step in mitigating airplane flight hazards. The purpose of the preflight assessment is to ensure that the airplane meets regulatory airworthiness standards and is in a safe mechanical condition prior to flight. . . . The visual preflight inspection of the airplane should begin while approaching the airplane on the ramp. The pilot should make note of the general appearance of the airplane, looking for discrepancies such as misalignment of the landing gear and airplane structure.[10]

Common aspects of operational inspections are they are completed before each use, and the inspection is primarily a visual assessment of the work area and equipment. Both of these aspects were evident to me one day as I watched an operational inspection of an aircraft while I was waiting to board. Looking out at the airplane from the windows of the terminal, I watched as the pilot slowly completed a circuit around her plane, visually inspecting each surface and the undercarriage, looking into each end of the jet engines, and checking hatches were closed and handles were removed.

Operational inspections of shops, work areas, rehearsals halls, and backstage are probably already part of your safety and health program, though possibly not specifically required in a program document. Your scene shop foreman probably walks-thru the scene shop at the start of each workday looking to see if the space and equipment are ready for the day's use. An ASM (assistant stage manager) typically arrives early to rehearsal to make sure the rehearsal room is ready for the day's activities. The house carpenter or stage carpenter for a show is likely to arrive early to walk the backstage area before the crew and cast arrive for the evening's performance. To be fully integrated into your safety and health program, though, such operational inspections must be specifically required, and individuals designated to conduct them.

Keeping a record of these inspections is also important. A completed and signed production or FOH checklist can serve to document completion of the inspection.

Another example of an operational inspection is the safety inspection conducted for the stage and scenery before the start of the first technical rehearsal for a show.[11] (Or, before the cast and crew of a production are rehearsing onstage for the first time.) The pre-tech safety inspection is primarily a visual inspection looking for such hazards as:

- uneven surfaces (unprotected cables on the floor, unmarked edges, etc.);
- exposed sharp edges (on railings, door openings, archways, etc.);
- head-injury hazards (equipment at low head height, unpadded low clearance openings, equipment in backstage pathways, etc.); and,
- unprotected pinch-points (structures, cables and drives related to stage lifts, mechanical systems for automation, etc.).

Other aspects of such an inspection can include checking the stability of elevated performance platforms and railings, barriers to limit unauthorized access to hazardous areas backstage, and sufficient backstage lighting (blue-lights) for actor pathways and crew work areas.

A pre-tech safety inspection is just one of many operational inspections to integrate into your safety and health program. Other operational inspections can include:

- Checking dressing rooms before each use by actors; or before each performance event.
- Inspection of the FOH and public areas of a venue before an audience arrives, which can include checking that exit doors are available for use and that egress paths are clear.[12]
- Preparations in advance of the first day of rehearsal in the rehearsal hall, which might include checking exits, availability of first aid supplies, the posting of informational notices, checking for hazards such a loose cables, sharp edges, and uneven surfaces.

IDENTIFICATION OF HAZARDS

Potential hazards must be identified in order to be assessed, and then eliminated or mitigated. Fixed hazards present in venues, rehearsal halls, and fabrication shops will be identified during the facilities inspections which are part of your safety and health program's routine activities. The artistic concepts, creative designs, and evolving staging ideas that develop for each show can present what I call fluid hazards. Some fluid hazards are indeed unique to a particular show, but many fluid hazards are common and repetitive from show to show. The identification of common theatre hazards is often incorporated into each production department's routine activities (fall hazards on offstage escape stairs; combustibles adjacent to live flame onstage; overhead hazards of stage lighting and audio equipment, etc.). Beyond these more common production hazards, each department must develop a process for the identification of hazards unique to a specific show.

What constitutes a hazard? "A hazard is any existing or potential condition that can lead to injury, illness, or death to people; damage to or loss of a system, equipment, or property; or damage to the environment."[13] The identification of hazards can be accomplished using a standard list of hazard types, such as the Hazard Assessment Checklist posted on the CalOSHA website.[14] This type of checklist poses questions to focus attention on hazard recognition and situational awareness: Are walking paths clear? Or, do exit doors open freely and without obstructions?

> Questions encourage thinking and prevent us from operating in the fast brain (habits/non-conscious). Questions will ignite intention and attention in the slow brain [conscious attention and thought] and encourage people to really see, think about and understand what is going on in their situational field at work.[15]

To assist each department with hazard identification for a specific theatre production or live event, a list (checklist) of typical production elements having the potential to cause harm can help guide attention to hazards present in the script, concept, or design. Doing so is particularly important during the Selection, Development, and Implementation phases described above. Samples of such lists for various production departments are included in the e-documents for this book. Figure 7.3 shows a partial section from one example for a Props Department:

Production Hazard Identification Safety Checklist

This checklist is to be completed by the production's Associate Production Manager to identify potential hazards in the production, and submitted at the end of the production's budget period. The Director of Theatre Safety will confer with appropriate production department heads to determine which policies or procedures will be needed in the production plan or technical design to mitigate identified hazards and reduce recognized risks.

Production: _____
Venue: _____
APM: _____
Date: _____

Props	Does the production require the use of:	NO	YES
Props Master	Consumable, food, or other perishable items?	☐	☐
	Break-away furniture?	☐	☐
	Break-away glassware, dishes, or other items?	☐	☐
	Stage blood, or other liquids?	☐	☐
	Stage guns?	☐	☐
	Stage guns that fire?	☐	☐
	Edged weapons: knives, swords, etc.?	☐	☐
	Are there edged weapons used in stage combat?	☐	☐
	Live flame: torches, candles, matches, lighters, etc.?	☐	☐
	Live animals onstage?	☐	☐
	OTHER HAZARDS (list below):	☐	☐

FIGURE 7.3 Production Hazards Identification Checklist—Props

The identification of hazards is a means to focus attention on critical aspects of a production to make the most full and effective use of available resources. In addition, having a well-developed process for the identification of hazards is the first step toward assessing the risks these hazards represent.

ALONE WORKER

An Alone, or Lone Worker Policy has at its core the identification of the hazards and the assessment of the risk to someone working by themselves. Most of the work related to a theatre production requires the efforts of many people working together to complete tasks. In theatre producing organizations as well as academic theatre departments, there are many instances, however, when a staff member or a student is working alone. Examples of lone work might include: a lighting designer inputting light cues in the control booth; a stage manager setting up in a rehearsal room before the cast arrives; a wardrobe supervisor doing post-show laundry in the costume shop; or, a student designer finalizing a scale model in the design studio. Situations of lone work are not unique to theatre productions; virtually every industry and occupation involves activities requiring someone to work alone. OSHA standards address working alone in the context of a hazardous work location, and the requirement to provide appropriate oversight for employees in addition to assuring effective emergency response. For instance, 29 CFR 1926.800(f)(5) requires "any employee working alone underground in a hazardous location, who is both out of the range of natural unassisted voice communication and not under observation by other persons, shall be provided with an effective means of obtaining assistance in an emergency."[16] The Health and Safety Executive (HSE) for the United Kingdom (UK), in its *Working Alone* guidance leaflet, notes a clear context for alone work, and the employer's responsibilities: "Working alone is not in itself against the law and it will often be safe to do so. However, the [UK] law requires employers to consider carefully, and then deal with, any health and safety risks for people working alone."[17] Safety professionals in industry and for college campuses recommend including a working alone policy as part of your safety and health program.[18]

Your Alone Worker Policy starts with the identification of hazardous tasks, for instance working-at-heights or using power machine tools, and the designation of hazardous or isolated work locations, such as storage facilities or machine rooms. You then must determine in which circumstances alone work is allowed, and for what type of work or in which locations alone work is prohibited. Your policy can be encompassed by a single statement like the University of Connecticut's Working Alone Policy: "No student is permitted to Work Alone in an Immediately Hazardous Environment."[19] *The Yale School of Drama's Safety Handbook 2018* notes restrictions to working alone, and an assessment and approval process to allow lone work to occur:

- Working alone is prohibited if the work involves hazards such as dangerous tools or equipment, hazardous chemicals, overhead rigging, and working from ladders or elevated platforms. A "buddy system" can be used to allow such work to be scheduled.

- Working alone in production shops or on stage is not allowed. Exceptions to this policy may be granted by the supervisor of the shop or production after a risk assessment has been made of the proposed work.

- Working alone in classrooms, studios, and rehearsal halls is discouraged. If possible, work with others, or have someone periodically check on your well-being. When you must work alone, make sure that someone knows where you are and when you expect to complete your work.[20]

Your assessments may indicate the need for specific and detailed requirements for alone work in a variety of locations and circumstances, as well as differing levels of assessment and approvals for employees, students, volunteers, or temporary workers. The Washington State Department of Labor & Industries details the following procedures to follow in developing a lone work policy.

- Conduct risk assessments to determine if work may be done safely by lone workers.
- Train lone workers in emergency response.
- Establish a clear action plan in the event of an emergency.
- Set limits for what is permissible during lone work.
- Require supervisors to make periodic visits to observe lone workers.
- Ensure regular contact between lone workers and supervisors via phone or radio.
- Use automatic warning devices to alert others if signals are not received periodically from a lone worker.
- Verify lone workers have returned to fixed base or home after completing a task.[21]

The Appendix contains links to samples of such policies as well as links to guidance documents.

PREVENTION THROUGH DESIGN (PtD)

PtD is a program developed by the National Institute for Occupational Safety and Health (NIOSH; an agency of the Centers for

Disease Control and Prevention), in support of its mission: "To develop new knowledge in the field of occupational safety and health and to transfer that knowledge into practice."[22] As described on the NIOSH PtD website, Prevention through Design is based on a simple concept:

> One of the best ways to prevent occupational injuries, illnesses, and fatalities is to eliminate hazards and minimize risks early in the design or re-design process and incorporate methods of safe design into all phases of hazard and risk mitigation. Although a long history of designing for safety for the general public exists in the U.S., less attention has gone to factoring the safety, health and well-being of workers into the design, re-design and retrofit of new and existing workplaces, tools and equipment, and work processes. The National Institute for Occupational Safety and Health (NIOSH) currently leads a nationwide initiative called Prevention through Design (PtD). PtD addresses occupational safety and health needs by eliminating hazards and minimizing risks to workers throughout the life cycle of work premises, tools, equipment, machinery, substances, and work processes including their construction, manufacture, use, maintenance, and ultimate disposal or re-use.[23]

The implementation of PtD into the production process and life cycle for a theatre production addresses risk reduction at the most effective levels of the Hierarchy of Controls—Elimination and Substitution (see Figure 7.4).

NIOSH's Prevention through Design concept focuses on minimizing risks to workers. However, the scope of your safety and health program must use an inclusive definition of worker: employees, volunteers, students, faculty, as well as patrons and the general public. Considering PtD in the context of this inclusive definition reveals the importance of this concept to the success of your safety and health program. Effective application of PtD can reduce risk to everyone affected by the program. Implementing PtD requires safety and health to be represented at the table from the earliest development of a theatre production or live event process. Integrating safety and health considerations early into the process of a theatre production might seem to impose limitations on the creativity of the artistic vision. The opposite is actually the case. I've seen this illustrated in several productions I worked on over the

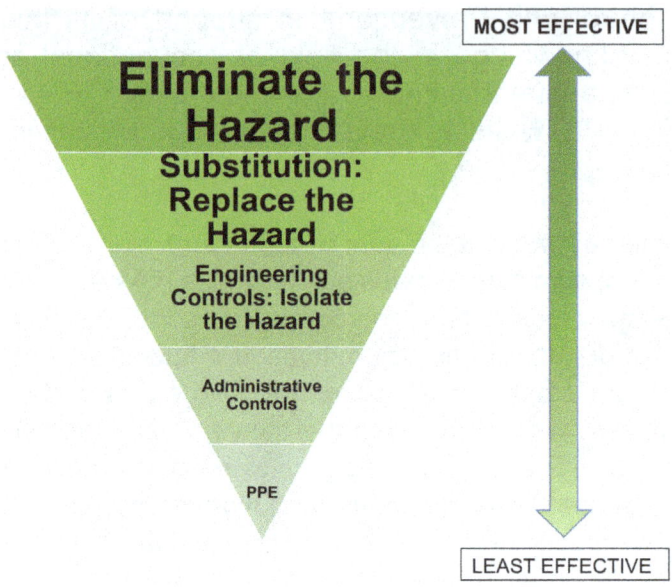

FIGURE 7.4 Hierarchy of Controls—PtD

years where actors' safety concerns over an unprotected exposed edge of an elevated acting platform, a convoluted backstage exiting path, or a glossy and slippery finish on the stage floor limited the types of staging or stage action that could be implemented in the show. Had the concepts of PtD been integrated as part of the production planning process, these hazards could have been identified and addressed during the design phase, allowing for more creative latitude in the staging of the show. The very nature of the theatre production process relies on collaboration, which inherently refers to "a talented mix of individuals coming together for a common goal—to create a successful show or event."[24] It becomes the role of the various departmental collaborators to manage the implementation of PtD in support of this "common goal": the show's artistic vision.

Also inherent in the common goal is the safety and health of all involved in the production. Identifying hazards and assessing risks during the developmental stages of a production require those responsible for safety and health to become engaged in the collaboration. This will provide support for the underlying artistic vision, while contributing means and methods to achieve the production, eliminate hazards, and reduce risk. As long as we think of "design" in the Prevention through Design concept as encompassing all aspects of the production process (not just the design of costumes or scenery), we can imagine ways in which PtD can positively impact the process. Because the theatre industry embraces collaboration as the organizational structure which best supports the creative process, safety and health's role is as essential to success as the contributions of the other collaborators.

PtD brings a key advantage to the production process by providing the most effective use of resources, helping the production organization or academic department get the most bang for its production budget buck. Identifying and mitigating hazards early in the process can reduce costs as the project develops. Mitigating or eliminating a hazard before an element for a show is completed is less expensive than after it is completed. Consider the following examples:

> The director's creative concepts for a large-scale musical require fluid and quick transitions from scene-to-scene during *a vista* scene changes. The large cast and crew will be required to relocate themselves onstage during these transitions. A detailed assessment of traffic patterns onstage was not completed until late in the process after the technical design and budgeting was completed and much of the structure for the deck was built. The assessment revealed many of the paths for the cast and crew would be blocked during the scene transitions by moving scenery and large props. This required a redesign of several scenic elements and parts of the stage deck to provide for actor and crew paths during the changes. Parts of the already built stage deck had to be redesigned and rebuilt. Had a detailed assessment of each scene change been plotted earlier in the process, alterations to the scenic elements and stage deck could have made during the budgeting process.

Or,

> The scenic design of an academic theatre department's production of *Romeo and Juliet* included several tall walls with extensive molding

details and textured finishes. The show would be produced on campus, and then toured to local schools and performance venues by the student cast and crew. In order to reduce the number of set pieces to be handled during the tour, the walls were sized to just fit in a 14-foot box truck. As the show was installed on the stage for the campus performances, most of the molding was securely attached and a heavy texture finish applied. At the strike of the show from the campus theatre, the finished walls were discovered to be excessively heavy to safely move. The initial stop of the local tour had to be delayed while the weight of the scenic walls was reduced by removing and refabricating the molding to be removable. The cost of doing so and the delay in the schedule could have been avoided had the finished weight of the scenic walls been evaluated during the design phase of the production.

RISK ASSESSMENTS

The quantitative analysis and assessment of the hazards associated with a product, machine, activity, or exposure was a process developed by safety professionals in science and industry. Assessing the risk(s) of hazards, initially termed Probability Risk Assessment (PRA), evolved in the 1970s and 1980s as a means to manage the risks of such complex systems as nuclear reactors, military defense systems, and NASA's space exploration programs.[25] While OSHA does not specifically require risk assessments as part of its standards it does include the assessment of risk as one of the core elements of a recommended safety program.[26] In the UK, legislation was enacted in 1992 creating a legal requirement for employers to assess risk in the workplace.[27] Other countries also require risk assessments as part of their safety and health codes including Ireland;[28] Germany;[29] and other member countries of the European Union.[30]

Completing a risk assessment involves a relatively simple process. As Marco van Beek notes, "A risk assessment is a vital part of everyday life. We all assess risks from the moment we get up in the morning. All that changes in our professional lives is that we have to start writing it down."[31] As described in ANSI/ASSE Z590.3-2011 (r2016), a risk assessment is "a process that commences with hazard identification and analysis, through which the probable severity of harm or damage is established, followed by an estimate of the probability of the incident or exposure occurring, and concluding with a statement of risk."[32]

A hazard's risk level can be assessed based on the product of the likelihood of occurrence times the severity of consequences: Risk = Likelihood × Severity. Likelihood and severity are assigned a numerical value, typically 1 to 5 with 1 representing the least likely to occur (rare occurrence), or the least severe consequences (no or only minor injury). A greater likelihood and/or more severe consequences will result in a higher risk score. An online search of risk assessment resources reveals a multitude of methods for this assessment from a variety of organizations and industries, including: Ready.gov,[33] Environmental Protection Agency (EPA),[34] American Society of Safety Professionals (ASSP) Risk Assessment Institute,[35] and the Health Safety Executive (HSE) of the United Kingdom.[36] (The comprehensive details related to the risk assessment process on the HSE website are indicative of the legal requirement for risk assessments in the UK.)

In the United States, the entertainment industry has begun to integrate the concepts of risk assessments into its planning and accident prevention processes. The growth of risk assessment in the industry is best illustrated by the guidance included in ANSI E1.46–2016, Standard for the Prevention of Falls from Theatrical Stages and Raised Performance Platforms.[37] Section 4 General Guidance (informative) of this standard recommends:

4.1 Use Risk Assessment

4.1.1 General

> Start with a risk assessment to determine what fall risks there might be and their severity. The risk assessment will allow you to prioritize which risks are most in need of reduction or elimination.[38]

The quantification of risk required by this standard is based on a matrix that pairs likelihood with severity to establish a risk score. The 5x5 grid in Figure 7.5 is included in Section 4 of the fall prevention standard.

		SEVERITY				
		Insignificant (1)	Minor (2)	Moderate (3)	Major (4)	Extreme (5)
PROBABILITY	Very Unlikely (1)	1	2	3	4	5
	Unlikely (2)	2	4	6	8	10
	Possible (3)	3	6	9	12	15
	Probable (4)	4	8	12	16	20
	Very Likely (5)	5	10	15	20	25

Risk Ranking
- Low Risk 1–3
- Moderate Risk 4–8
- High Risk 9–14
- Extreme Risk 15–25

FIGURE 7.5 Risk Assessment Matrix (adapted from ANSI E1.46—2016)

The risk assessment and resulting risk score aids in the prioritization of hazards. Hazards with a low risk score—risk level 1, 2, or 3—might receive less attention, or have a lower priority to address. Hazards with a high or extreme risk score—risk level 9 and above—must be carefully assessed, and mitigated, or eliminated. An advantage of the color-coded risk assessment matrix is the visibility of higher risk in the color code of the matrix: the red boxes indicate hazards that require the most attention (resources, mitigation, elimination, etc.) due to a higher risk score than those in yellow. Once the initial risk scores are established for hazards, methods for reducing a high risk score are developed and documented. The Hierarchy of Controls discussed in Chapter 3 provides a model to follow to reduce a high risk score. The math is simple. Any change in a process—from elimination of a hazard to substituting a less hazardous process to the use of PPE—will result in a reduction of either the likelihood of occurrence, the severity of consequences, or both. The residual risk score is then assessed to ensure the level of risk has been reduced to an acceptable level.

Safety Risk Assessment Form

This form **must** be distributed to all persons named in the Owner column; where possible both as a hard copy and electronically

Reference:												
Date:		Assessor:					Department/ Area:					
Activity Describe the activity and the ways in which it could pose a risk	**Hazards** e.g. personal injury, electric shock, people or objects falling from height, crushing	**Persons at risk**	**Risk before control measures**			**Controls** Describe controls used to reduce risk to a tolerable or preferably acceptable rating	**Residual Risk after control measures**			**Additional controls** e.g. monitor and review, suggestions for future activities	**Owner** Person responsible for the controls
			Severity	Likeli-hood	S × L		Severity	Likeli-hood	S × L		

Risk Scoring Key	**Severity**		**Likelihood**	
	Fatality	5	Certain or imminent	5
	Major injury, disabling illness, major damage	4	Very likely	4
	Lost time injury, illness, damage	3	May happen	3
	Minor injury, minor damage	2	Unlikely	2
	Delay only	1	Very unlikely	1

Risk Rating Categories	10 to 25	Unacceptable	Do not proceed; seek immediate guidance from the safety team
	6 to 9	Tolerable	Proceed with caution but seek to reduce risk further if possible
	1 to 5	Acceptable	Proceed

Order of Control Measures	**Most effective** ↓ **Least effective**		
		Eliminate	Ask yourself if the activity needs to be carried out
		Substitute	Ask yourself if the same effect can be achieved with something less risky
		Reduce	Ask yourself if you can use less of something, or limit the time etc
		Isolate	Make sure that the risk is contained to the smallest possible area
		Enclose	Make sure that no-one can get to the hazard
		Other Engineering Controls	Emergency stop buttons, automated controls etc
		Safe System of Work	Carry out the work according to a specific step-by-step program with training
		Training/Communication	Safety team can advise
		PPE	Use of ear defenders, hard hat, toetectors etc
		Discipline and Enforcement	Telling people to be careful

FIGURE 7.6 Sample Risk Assessment Documentation Form

You might find the concept of 'an acceptable level of risk' challenging. Two basic assumptions underlie this concept:

1. Safety practitioners should accept that zero risk is not attainable for hazards that cannot be eliminated. Where hazards cannot be eliminated, the goal should be to reduce risks so that the residual risks are acceptable.

2. In general terms, all that can be said is that the residual risk, after determining the severity of outcome of an event and the event probability, and the taking of preventive action, must be acceptable in the particular setting being considered.[39]

Individuals and organizations must determine the level of acceptable risk[40] applied to the evaluation of a risk level related to their production choices and creative activities. "This requires the use of risk assessments and the communication of risk-based information to help decision makers understand the nature of the risk and whether it is considered acceptable."[41] Opinions among senior leadership and the production team may vary, but a mutually defined agreement of acceptable risk is critical for consistency in risk assessments throughout the organization.

Transferring the details and results of the risk assessment to a chart such as shown in Figure 7.6[42] provides documentation of your assessment as well as the mitigations required to reduce the level of risk to an acceptable level. (For further explanation of the risk assessment process, please refer to Section 4 of the fall prevention standard ANSI E1.46–2016, and any of the related resources in the Appendix.)

FIELD LEVEL HAZARD ASSESSMENTS (FLHA)

Risk assessments described above are typically completed well in advance of a project's start as part of the conceptualization, planning, and budgeting phases. A field level hazard assessment (FLHA) is implemented by the people assigned to complete a task before they start working. FLHA is a process requiring the worker to take several specific steps at the start of a job:

- Stop, and think about the work to be done;
- Look around and identify hazards;
- Assess the hazards;
- Control the hazards; and
- Begin or resume work.

A field level hazard assessment combines the concepts and processes of hazard identification, risk assessment, and checklists. A key advantage of FLHA is to bring the safety and health benefits of these strategies to the job site. Integrating FLHA into your theatre production's fabrication and installation tasks also empowers employees and staff (whether paid, students, or volunteers) to be more fully engaged in your safety and health program. Field level hazard assessments provide a means to encourage the routine and deliberate identification and control of workplace hazards.

Consider the following scenario to illustrate how a FLHA might be used.

> The scene shop staff are tasked with the job of constructing and installing a raked deck on the stage floor of a typical proscenium theatre. The technical drawings are reviewed with the shop carpenters, and the necessary raw materials, tools, and equipment are provided. Before their work begins, the team take a few minutes to complete a field level hazard assessment. Their first step is to review their work plan and inspect the work area to identify any hazards. They realize their work area is adjacent to other work onstage and would block access to stage equipment and egress paths. Some of the tools and equipment they will be using generate high noise levels. These hazards are then assessed and measures to control the hazards are implemented. To mitigate these hazards, the staff relocate their tools, equipment, and raw materials, and mark "Keep Clear" paths with cones and safety tape. They also make sure they have hearing protection, verbally warn those working near them about the noise levels, and post signs at the stage entry points to note "Hearing Protection is Required." Once the protective actions, materials, and/or equipment required to control the identified hazards are in place, the job can begin.

The steps described in this example have been incorporated into an FLHA reminder symbol found on many types of assessment forms (see Figure 7.7).

FIGURE 7.7 Field Level Hazard Assessment Symbol

Many examples of FLHA forms and formats can be found on the Internet; the links in the following note are a few samples.[43] Figure 7.8 illustrates how you might adapt the hazard assessment part of an FLHA form to apply to your theatre or production operations.

Field Level Hazard Assessment

Section A: Potential Hazards Checklist

YES	NO	Potential Hazards
☐	☐	Have clear instructions been provided?
☐	☐	Is there adequate PPE?
☐	☐	Are there electrical hazards?
☐	☐	Are there ergonomic hazards: lifting, pulling, overexertion, awkward body position, noise, etc.?
☐	☐	Other workers posing hazards in the work area?
☐	☐	Potential for slip and fall hazards?
☐	☐	Is there risk of overhead falling objects?
☐	☐	Is there adequate work lighting?
☐	☐	Are there open trap or lift areas in the stage floor?
☐	☐	Will the orchestra pit be exposed?

FIGURE 7.8 Sample FLHA Potential Hazards Checklist

Toolbox talks are a safety strategy allied with filed level hazard assessments.

> A Toolbox Talk is an informal safety meeting that focuses on safety topics related to the specific job, such as workplace hazards and safe work practices. Meetings are normally short in duration and are generally conducted at the job site prior to the commencement of a job or work shift. It is one of the very effective methods to refresh workers' knowledge, cover last minute safety checks, and exchange information with the experienced workers. Toolbox Talks are also intended to facilitate health and safety discussions on the job site and promote your organization's safety culture. Toolbox talks/meetings are sometimes referred to as tailgate meetings or safety briefings.[44]

You probably already gather your staff or students together before each work call to discuss the work plan for the day, and to assign tasks. A toolbox talk can be added to this routine. Topics covered can be related to the jobs for the day, to discuss safety policy changes, review near-misses from a previous work call, or provide opportunities for safety concerns to be raised. Toolbox talks provide an opportunity to encourage participation from your staff in promoting a positive safety culture. This can be accomplished by asking or assigning a different member of your staff to lead the toolbox talk each day. If you have a regular work schedule with full-time staff, a rotating schedule for the responsibility of leading the talk allows for some preparation and possibly a small amount of good natured competition among your employees. Once the brief toolbox talk is completed, each work team can then complete an FLHA for their assigned tasks.

SERIOUS INJURY AND FATALITY (SIF) PREVENTION

The strategies and practices used by safety and health professionals described above are effective. The Bureau of Labor Statistics (BLS) illustrates the success of these practices across all industries by the almost 50 percent reduction of the total nonfatal recordable cases (TRC-nonfatal) in the United States from 5.0 incidents per 100 full-time workers in 2003 down to 2.8 TRC-nonfatal in 2017.[45] You might experience a similar reduction in incidents as you develop your safety and health program, and integrate safety and health practices into your production process.

Sadly though, there has not been a similar decline in the number of workplace fatalities across all industries in the United States during the same time period. The total number of fatal workplace injuries recorded in 2003 (5,575 employees), compared to the total number in 2016 (5,190 employees), shows only about a 6 percent reduction in the total number of fatal workplace injuries. Additionally, the total number of workplace fatalities has been virtually flat between 2008 and 2016.[46] The number of employee fatalities recorded in the performing arts (according to BLS Table A-1 for NAICS codes 7111 and 7115) has been similarly flat, with about the same number annually from 2006 to 2011 (ranging from 13 to 16 per year).[47]

The Campbell Institute of the National Safety Council has noted this lack of progress in serious injury and fatality (SIF) prevention:

> While it is encouraging that the nation's overall recordable incident rate is decreasing, the next step in the journey to safety excellence is the elimination of serious injuries and life altering events.[48]

As documented in their research paper "Serious Injury and Fatality Prevention: Perspectives and Practices" the lack of correlation between the statistical decline in nonfatal incidents, and SIFs may indicate a flaw in the long-accepted concept posited by H. W. Heinrich of a causal relationship among near-misses, minor injuries, and serious injuries and fatalities.

The Campbell Institute's re-evaluation of Heinrich's safety triangle[49] (see Figure 7.9), represents a shift away from the conceptualization that the root cause for SIFs is an accretion of near-misses and minor injuries. SIF incidents can and do occur without such precursors. Research data indicates as few as 21 percent of all reported workplace incidents had SIF potential.[50] Because of this, "safety professionals cannot simply reduce minor incidents and expect to reduce serious injuries and fatalities overall."[51] Incidents with SIF potential are often related to hazards or activities with a high risk score, even though these hazards or activities have not caused reported minor injuries. Results from this research and the reassessment of Heinrich's safety triangle provide ample reasons for an eclectic approach to accident and injury prevention in

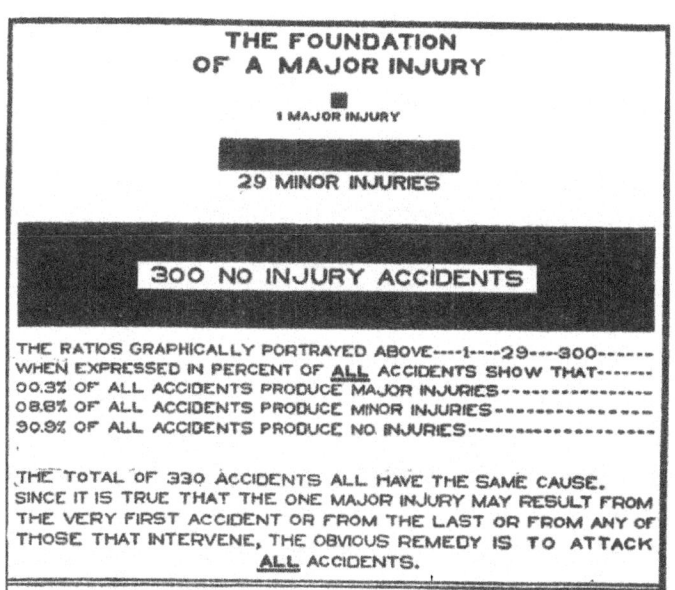

FIGURE 7.9 H. W. Heinrich Safety Triangle, from *Industrial Accident Prevention: A Scientific Approach*, 1931

your safety and health program, using all the tools described in this chapter and elsewhere in this book.

Take for example the SIF incident which occurred during a circus performance that involved a hair-hang act. Eight performers were seriously injured when the elevated rig supporting them failed and they fell over 20 feet to the ground. The root cause of the accident was determined by OSHA to be an incorrectly loaded carabiner.[52] The OSHA assessment did not report any previous near-misses or minor injuries related to this root cause; the potential for a SIF was overlooked due to the lack of such precursors. Applying several of the strategies described above, in particular a risk assessment, the level of risk would have been apparent from a resultant high risk score. A Prevention through Design (PtD) evaluation of the single-point of failure (the connection point of the carabiner to the bridle lines of the hanging-rig structure) is likely to have resulted in a more appropriately engineered rigging system. Once the rigging system was designed and completed, a checklist could have been developed to assure the attachment and alignment of the rigging connections. An operational inspection completed just before the start of each performance of the hair-hang act would have further enhanced the risk reduction by providing a visual cross-check of the rigging system.

Such a comprehensive package of safety practices, combining aspects of the strategies described in this chapter, is both possible and effective to reduce the risks of the high hazard and unique elements we frequently integrate into the activities of our shows and live events.

Safety and health in the performing arts and the entertainment industry can benefit from strategies, ideas, and techniques already in use by safety professionals in other industries. We do not need to invent means and methods to create an effective safety and health program, we just need to do what we do best. Through our collaborations we routinely discover ways to implement creative solutions to challenging artistic concepts and design ideas. We can similarly bring creative solutions to the unique requirements of our safety and health programs by utilizing existing safety and health strategies from other industries. No wheels need to be reinvented; no magic formulae need be applied. Your safety and health program is like all other aspects of what you do in the context of your organization: define mission; set goals; identify and gather resources; and then get the job done. In the next chapter, I will take the requirements and concepts related to safety and health I've discussed so far and pull them together to ensure a positive culture of safety. Doing so will provide you with the tools needed to bring your current safety culture to the same level of excellence as the rest of your organization's activities.

NOTES

1 Mark Shanda and Dennis Dorn, *Technical Management for the Performing Arts: Utilizing Time, Talent, and Money* (New York: Focal Press, 2016), 159–171. Also, Cary Gillett and Jay Sheehan, *The Production Manager's Toolkit: Successful Production Management in Theatre and Performing Arts* (New York: Routledge, 2017), 37–51. And, Zachary Stribling and Richard Girtain, *The Technical Director's*

Toolkit: Process, Forms, and Philosophies for Successful Technical Direction (New York: Focal Press, 2016), 20–26.
2. Gillett and Sheehan, *Production Manager's Toolkit*, 97.
3. Mark Shanda and Dennis Dorn, *Technical Management for the Performing Arts: Utilizing Time, Talent, and Money* (New York: Focal Press, 2016), 3–4.
4. Atul Gawande, *The Checklist Manifesto: How to Get Things Right* (New York: Metropolitan Books, 2009), 173.
5. Marco van Beek, *A Practical Guide to Health and Safety in the Entertainment Industry* (Cambridge, England: Entertainment Technology Press), 13.
6. Gawande, *Summary of the Checklist Manifesto* (San Bernardino, CA: FastReads, 2016), 13.
7. Bryan L. Huneycutt, Safety Program Manager, Disney Parks Live Entertainment, USITT 2019 Conference session presenter, "Hold Please," March 22, 2019.
8. Occupational Safety and Health Administration (OSHA), Regulations (Standards—29 CFR 1910.178(q)(7)), accessed March 17, 2019, https://www.osha.gov/pls/oshaweb/owadisp.show_document?p_table=STANDARDS&p_id=9828.
9. Canadian Agricultural Safety Association, "#8, Pre-operational Inspection of Equipment," accessed March 17, 2019, http://www.agsafetyweek.ca/uploads/1/3/3/4/13345670/casw2014_toolboxtalks8_en.pdf.
10. Federal Aviation Administration (FAA), *Airplane Flying Handbook*, Chapter 2, "Ground Operations," accessed March 17, 2019, https://www.faa.gov/regulations_policies/handbooks_manuals/aviation/airplane_handbook/.
11. Stribling and Girtain, *The Technical Director's Toolkit*, 126.
12. Ron Cote and Gregory E. Harrington, editors, *Life Safety Code Handbook, 2015 edition* (Quincy, MA: National Fire Protection Association [NFPA], 2014), Chapter 13 "Existing Assembly Occupancies, 13.7.1 Means of Egress Inspections."
13. SKYbrary, "Hazard Identification-Definitions," accessed March 17, 2019, https://www.skybrary.aero/index.php/Hazard_Identification.
14. CalOSHA, Safety and Health, Injury and Illness Prevention Program webpage, "Sample Forms and Checklists," accessed March 17, 2019, https://www.dir.ca.gov/dosh/etools/09-031/tools.htm.
15. Rajni Walia, "Seeing Is Suspect: What Am I Missing Here?", *Safety+ Health,* January 2019, 52.

16 OSHA, Regulations (Standards—29 CFR 1926.800(f)(5)), accessed May 6, 2019, https://www.osha.gov/laws-regs/regulations/standard number/1926/1926.800.
17 Health and Safety Executive (HSE), *Working Alone: Health and Safety Guidance on the Risks of Lone Working,* accessed May 6, 2019, http://www.hse.gov.uk/pubns/indg73.pdf.
18 National Safety Council (NSC), "Lone Worker Safety," *Safety+ Health*, July 25, 2015, accessed May 6, 2019, https://www.safetyandhealth magazine.com/articles/12628-lone-worker-safety.
19 University of Connecticut, Policies & Procedures, Working Alone Policy, accessed May 6, 2019, https://policy.uconn.edu/2012/07/30/working-alone-policy/#.
20 *Yale School of Drama Safety Handbook*, As of 8.20.2018, pages 13–14.
21 Washington State Department of Labor and Industries, *Working Alone Safely*, accessed May 6, 2019, http://www.lni.wa.gov/safety/trainingprevention/online/courseinfo.asp?P_ID=160.
22 The National Institute for Occupational Safety and Health (NIOSH), "About NIOSH-Mission," accessed March 17, 2019, https://www.cdc.gov/niosh/about/default.html.
23 NIOSH, Prevention through Design Program, "Program Description," accessed March 17, 2019, https://www.cdc.gov/niosh/programs/ptdesign/description.html.
24 Gillett and Sheehan, *Production Manager's Toolkit*, 17.
25 C. Klüppelberg et al., editors, *Risk—A Multidisciplinary Introduction*, Chapter One (Cham, Switzerland: Springer International Publishing, 2014), 30–31, accessed March 17, 2019, https://pdfs.seman ticscholar.org/988c/d35ae4fb9d1cb157ece5d564e69e660ab709.pdf.
26 OSHA, *Recommended Practices for Safety and Health Programs,* accessed March 17, 2019, https://www.osha.gov/shpguidelines/haz ard-Identification.html.
27 Health Safety Executive (HSE), Risk Management webpage, accessed March 17, 2019, http://www.hse.gov.uk/risk/index.htm.
28 Health and Safety Authority (HSA), Safety Statement and Risk Assessment webpage, accessed March 17, 2019, http://www.hsa.ie/eng/Topics/Managing_Health_and_Safety/Safety_Statement_and_Risk_Assessment/#WhatisaRiskAssessment.
29 Gemeinsame Deutsche Arbiets (GDA), Joint German Occupational Safety and Health Strategy (GDA) Guideline "Risk assessment und

documentation," accessed March 17, 2019, http://www.gda-portal.de/EN/Download/pdf/InfoSheet-GuidelineRiskassessment.pdf?__blob=publicationFile&v=2.
30 European Agency for Safety & Health at Work, Risk Assessments webpage links, accessed March 17, 2019, https://osha.europa.eu/en/search/site?search_block_form=risk+assessment&op=Search.
31 Marco van Beek, *A Practical Guide*, 25.
32 ANSI/ASSE Z590.3–2011 (r2016) "Prevention through Design: Guidelines for Addressing Occupational Hazards and Risks in Design and Redesign Processes," as quoted in *Professional Safety*, November 2017, 35.
33 Ready.gov, Risk Assessment page, accessed April 25, 2018, https://www.ready.gov/risk-assessment.
34 Environmental Protection Agency (EPA), Risk Assessment webpage, accessed April 25, 2018, https://www.epa.gov/risk
35 American Society of Safety Professionals (ASSP), Risk Assessment Institute webpage, accessed on March 17, 2019, http://www.oshrisk.org/.
36 Health Safety Executive, Risk Assessment webpage, accessed March 17, 2019, http://www.hse.gov.uk/risk/index.htm
37 Entertainment Services and Technology Association (ESTA), ANSI E1.46–2016, Standard for the Prevention of Falls from Theatrical Stages and Raised Performance Platforms, accessed March 17, 2019, http://tsp.esta.org/tsp/documents/published_docs.php.
38 Ibid.
39 Fred A. Manuele and Bruce W. Main, "On Acceptable Risk," accessed March 17, 2019, http://www.ehstoday.com/news/ehs_imp_35066.
40 "Acceptable risk refers to the level of human and property loss that can be tolerated by an individual, household, group, organization, community, region, state, or nation. . . . The concept of acceptable risk evolved partly from the understanding that absolute safety is generally an unachievable goal, and that even very low exposures to certain toxic substances may confer some level of risk." Acceptable Risk Law and Legal Definition, US Legal webpage, accessed March 19, 2019, https://definitions.uslegal.com/a/acceptable-risk/.
41 Bruce K. Lyon and Georgi Popov, "Communicating & Managing Risk: The Key Result of Risk Management," *Professional Safety*, November 2017, 38.
42 Anna Glover, Safety Risk Assessment Form, created for Yale School of Drama/Yale Repertory Theatre; used with permission.

43 Examples of Field Level Hazard Assessment forms can be found at: https://www.uregina.ca/hr/hsw/assets/docs/pdf/Procedures/Facilities%20Management%20Field%20Level%20Hazard%20Assessment%20Procedure%20and%20toolbox%20form.pdf.
 Or, https://wssolutions.ca/wp-content/uploads/2016/05/Field-Level-Hazard-Assessment-Form-WSS.pdf.
 Or, http://www.tollestrup.com/images/safety/Field%20Level%20Hazard%20Assessment.pdf.
44 British Columbia, CA, Constructions Safety Alliance, Toolbox Talks, accessed May 2, 2019, https://www.bccsa.ca/Toolbox-Talks-.html
45 United States Department of Labor, Bureau of Labor Statistics (BLS), Injuries, Illnesses, and Fatalities, *2017 Survey of Occupational Injuries & Illnesses Charts Package 2017*, accessed March 17, 2019, https://www.bls.gov/iif/osch0062.pdf.
46 BLS, *Fatal Occupational Injuries Charts*, accessed March 17, 2019, https://www.bls.gov/iif/osch0062.pdf.
47 BLS, Injuries, Illnesses, and Fatalities webpage, accessed March 17, 2019, https://www.bls.gov/iif/.
48 The Campbell Institute: Research, *Serious Injury and Fatality Prevention: Perspectives and Practices*, page 3, accessed March 17, 2019, https://www.thecampbellinstitute.org/research/.
49 W. H. Heinrich, *Industrial Accident Prevention: A Scientific Approach* (New York: McGraw-Hill Book Company. 1931), 91
50 Donald K. Martin and Alison Black, *Preventing Serious Injuries and Fatalities (SIFs): A New Study Reveals Precursors and Paradigms,* accessed May 29, 2019, https://dekra-insight.com/images/white-paper-documents/wp_preventing-sif_us_A4.pdf
51 Ibid, page 6.
52 OSHA, Construction Incidents Investigation Engineering Report, *Incident at the Ringling Bros. and Barnum & Bailey Performance in Providence, RI*, accessed March 17, 2019, https://www.osha.gov/doc/engineering/2014_r_05.html.

BIBLIOGRAPHY

Cote, Ron, and Harrington, Gregory E., editors. *Life Safety Code Handbook, NFPA 101, 2015 edition.* Quincy, MA: National Fire Protection Association, 2014.

Gawande, Atul. *The Checklist Manifesto: How to Get Things Right*. New York: Metropolitan Books, 2009.

Gawande, Atul. *Summary of the Checklist Manifesto*. San Bernardino, CA: FastReads, 2016.

Gillett, Cary, and Sheehan, Jay. *The Production Manager's Toolkit: Successful Production Management in Theatre and Performing Arts*. New York: Routledge, 2017.

Heinrich, H. W. *Industrial Accident Prevention: A Scientific Approach*. New York: McGraw-Hill Book Company, 1931.

Shanda, Mark, and Dorn, Dennis. *Technical Management for the Performing Arts: Utilizing Time, Talent, and Money*. New York: Focal Press, 2016.

Stribling, Zachary, and Girtain, Richard. *The Technical Director's Toolkit: Process, Forms, and Philosophies for Successful Technical Direction*. New York: Focal Press, 2016.

van Beek, Marco. *A Practical Guide to Health and Safety in the Entertainment Industry*. Cambridge, England: Entertainment Technology Press Ltd., 2000.

CHAPTER 8

Putting It All Together
Safety Culture

William J. Reynolds

I introduced the concept of safety culture in Chapter 1. In Chapter 3, I examined the key elements required of an effective safety and health program. Several chapters have focused on compliance with codes and industry standards. The implementation of policies and procedures in your theatre safety and health program provides the means to reduce the risks for many of the hazards specific to our industry. Learning from safety professionals in other industries, there are effective techniques you can successfully integrate into your safety and health programs. Each piece seems simple and straightforward. Yet, has safety taken an active seat at your organization's production table as an essential element of your theatre's or academic department's artistic activities?

The key to making this happen is both easy and hard. Safety as a concept is easy;[1] available resources, texts, training, and examples of success show us what is possible. The difficulty comes in moving from our existing patterns in the use of resources and ways of doing things to the integration of a positive safety culture that will impact every aspect of your production organization's or theatre department's activities. You know what needs to be done; you now need to take the steps to move the culture of safety in your theatre organization and academic department to a level of excellence that is on par with rest of what you do.

COMMUNICATION

Communication is a key element that underlies the success of initiating your safety and health program and integrating it into your organization. Effective communication skills are essential for the success of any collaborative project; such skills are particularly important in the performing arts.[2] It is clichéd to note that volumes have been written about communication skills and organization effectiveness. "Effective communication is essential to successfully managing operational risk, or for that matter, almost any other aspect of an organization."[3] Several communication techniques are especially useful in managing the difficult conversations which arise as concerns related to safety and health develop during the evolution of a production. Many communications skills are applicable. "An effective manager makes use of various methods and modes of communication and, with practice, becomes expert at selecting the appropriate method to achieve specific project goals."[4] I will focus on two of the many communication techniques: listening skills (e.g. active listening, critical listening, or empathetic listening) and how to say "no" by having the "Yes, but . . ." conversation.

FIGURE 8.1 Listening Skills

Renowned theatre artists such as Danny Glover[5] and Meryl Streep[6] tell us successful acting is just listening. Listening skills are also critical to success in a safety and health program's activities. Listening leads to understanding:

> All people want to be listened to. To distinguish between the problem that is expressed (i.e., the set does not do what I thought it would)

versus the underlying problem (i.e., I don't trust the set designer) can sometimes be the key to successfully solving the issue. To get to the root of the issue requires understanding what people need.[7]

The most basic of all human needs is the need to understand and be understood. The best way to understand people is to listen to them.[8]

Each person involved in a collaborative project has a commitment to the overarching goal(s) of the project. In addition, each person has personal goals that are interrelated with their involvement in the project. Knowing and understanding each person's goals is necessary for you to align the goals of safety and health with their goals, and by extension the goals of the project. For example, the scenic designer may place high value on a super-glossy finish on the stage floor in their design. Knowing and understanding this, you can explore and discuss ways to retain this look while reducing the slipping and fall hazard through the use of specialized paint products or anti-slip applications.

Active listening is a particularly potent skill for discerning such information to gain understanding. The essence of active listening is to make sure what you are hearing is congruent with what the person is intending to express. This process can be envisioned in many ways, one of which involves clarifying what you understood the person to be saying. Asking open-ended questions and paraphrasing what you have heard can achieve this. Reflecting back to the other person your understanding of what you heard gives them the chance to confirm you heard them correctly, or, if not, to correct your understanding. "It is really about paraphrasing . . . to ensure you've heard the person correctly and you reflect back what they've said. Don't just parrot it back—but put it into your own words and include the *feeling* as well as the literal meaning."[9]

For instance, after listening to the scenic designer describe the set, you want to confirm your understanding of the design: "Sounds like you are very interested in a high-gloss finish on the stage floor." A possible clarifying response from the designer might be: "A shiny finish on the floor would be great, but a smooth, uninterrupted look is what I really want; no visible seams or joints."

The Canadian Centre for Occupational Health and Safety's *Health and Safety Report* includes a concise review of active listening skills and describes the process as follows:

- **Make eye contact.** Be attentive, but don't stare.
- **Focus on what is being said.** Do not do other activities at the same time, such as checking emails or texting.
- **Listen and allow the person to speak.** Do not interrupt.
- **Allow pauses.** Do not pressure the person to answer quickly.
- **Ask questions.** If something is not clear, ask for more detail in a friendly and non-judgmental way.
- **Repeat for confirmation.** Repeat what you heard to reduce the chance of misperceptions and confusion.
- **Listen.** Give the other person a chance to correct any misunderstanding.
- **Listen between the lines.** Use visual cues that may reveal how the person is feeling about what they are talking about (posture, facial expressions, eye contact, and body language).[10]

By gaining understanding through your use of communication skills such as active listening comes the ability to effectively have the "Yes, but . . ." conversation from a safety and health point-of-view. The collaboration essential to the success of a theatre production or a performing arts event relies on the ability of all involved to stay in relationship with each other while working toward their common goal with the best outcome. Responding to a design idea or directorial request with a "No, we can't do that" gets in the way of collaboration. Showing support for the request, and its underlying idea, while providing context for what is possible (either in terms of available time or budget, or physics and strength of materials) continues the conversation with a shared exploration of alternatives. This communication technique is referenced in Gillett and Sheehan's book, *The Production Manager's Toolkit*, as a "Yes! No. Yes?" process.[11] Whatever your approach to this communication concept, the important skill to embrace is to be able to express enthusiasm for artistic ideas and requests while engendering an understanding about limitations. This is followed by your commitment to supporting the artistic goal(s) while providing alternatives that are not only possible but that also achieve the underlying concepts of the idea or request.

FINAL THOUGHTS—MY CHARGE TO THE INDUSTRY

The arc of this book returns us to the concept of safety culture: a positive and effective culture of safety and health imbedded in your theatre organization or academic department. "For your organisation's safety culture to develop positively, the whole area of health and safety must become ingrained in how the organization operates. That way, safety is seen as really being key to the organisation's success."[12] I've referenced safety culture at many points throughout this book. I'll elaborate here on what is required to develop, nurture, and integrate a culture of safety into the production process for your theatre or academic department. Organizational culture can be defined as "The values and behaviors that contribute to the unique social and psychological environment of an organization."[13] This and other definitions of organizational culture are often simplified as "the way we typically do things around here."[14] Safety culture is a subset of an organization's or academic department's culture: "The safety culture of an institution is a reflection of the actions, attitudes, and behaviors of its members concerning safety."[15] Or,

> A safety culture is an organisational culture that places a high level of importance on safety beliefs, values and attitudes—and these are shared by the majority of people within the company or workplace . . . A positive safety culture can result in improved workplace health and safety (WHS) and organizational performance.[16]

Establishing safety as a fundamental organizational value places the activities, attitudes, and behaviors related to safety and health on a par with the other values of your organization or department. Doing so aligns safety and health with values such as artistic excellence, professional artistry, inclusive collaboration, or visible diversity. Safety and health moves from an add-on or an afterthought to an essential element of the organization's core values. As a core value, safety and health is integrated into the planning, development, and implementation of everything you do in the same way as other organizational values. A culture of safety addresses the oft-cited concern: "Our theatre company is too small [our academic department has so few members]; we can't hire or designate a single person to be in charge of safety and health." When safety and health becomes simply one of the ways things are done, then everyone is responsible for safety and health in the same way everyone is responsible for the excellence of a show.

In Chapter 3 I discussed two critical aspects of a safety program: management leadership and employee participation. The management of your theatre organization or academic department reinforces the organizational core values through their leadership in support of mission and goals. With safety and health defined as a core value for the organization, consider the creative ways in which the senior managers of your organization or academic department can assure safety is always seated at the production table:

- Reference safety and health in the organization's mission statement.
- Include safety and health as an agenda item at department meetings.
- Leadership individually models safety and health by owning and using PPE.
- Senior management participates in safety inspections.
- Post-incident follow-up for accidents and injuries includes all levels of leadership.
- Safety and health is included as a key aspect of annual reports, quarterly reviews, and reports at board and chair meetings.
- Production schedules reflect concerns for safety and health through a focus on wellness.

By elevating safety and health to the same level of excellence as other core values, the organization's leadership and senior managers exemplify that the responsibility for safety and health is shared by all. "No one can keep an entire organization safe on his or her own. Collaboration is needed to create a healthy atmosphere around safety conversations and a culture where everyone looks out for each other."[17] Supporting and maintaining organizational culture is everyone's responsibility. Therefore, safety is also everyone's responsibility, not just the job of a safety coordinator, the safety manager, or a safety committee.

Related to employee participation, you might imagine such engagement in terms of group activities, like production meetings, safety training, and toolbox talks. But an employee's daily participation in "how we do things around here" in the workplace has a significant impact on your safety culture. Almost 90 percent of what we learn about work and how we are expected to act in the workplace is derived from our experiences on the job, plus the daily feedback we receive from our peers at work.[18] Think about how you approached your work in a new job. Likely you felt confident about the skills and expertise you brought to the job, but you were keenly aware of how things were being done by your coworkers. For instance, when you started your load-in work onstage, if hardhats and safety shoes were being worn, you certainly put yours on. Or, if the craftspeople in the props shop consulted the SDS for chemical products being used before their use, you quickly realized how this practice was integrated into their work practices. This level of employee participation (peer influence) had a great impact on how you perceived the safety culture.

Management leadership is critical for consistency in employees following rules and work practices. As noted above, the safety example set by managers is a key determinate of safety culture. "Lead by example and encourage others to do the same. Workers tend to do what those around them are doing, so it's essential to demonstrate safe behaviors in addition to talking about them."[19] Daily work practices and peer feedback are equally influential on your organization's safety culture. The engagement and participation of employees in your safety and health program will have a positive impact on your organization's safety culture. When each of the stage crew dons their hardhat as they enter the stage area during a load-in, the peer pressure becomes a strong enforcement tool. Routine feedback from coworkers—"Thanks for putting caution tape around the US platform so I know about the hazard there"—provides opportunities to encourage safe work practices.

Organizations and academic departments of all sizes and resources can establish and evolve a positive safety culture using essentially the same tools: garnering management support, and encouraging peer influence through employee participation. The task may seem daunting, especially if the existing organizational culture does not embrace a positive safety culture. (Every organization has a safety culture, but it might not be a positive one. For example, an organizational culture that allows people working during a load-in onstage to wear sandals or work without hardhats is far from a positive safety culture.) But you have to start somewhere. Gaining management support can begin in the form of assessing staffing schedules with safety in mind: Are there sufficient numbers of staff on call for strikes? Is fatigue an issue in light of the scheduled turnaround time? Or, proposing the allocation of funds to initiate a hardhat policy onstage or an eyewear policy in the production shops. Any change is likely to have financial and resource implications. Your research into budgets and expenses is important in preparation for discussions with management related to safety. Context is important, and by aligning safety with the mission and goals of organization you provide your organization's leaders with a means to consider safety an integral piece of the whole. Approach your discussions with management as you would any other budget conversation. Provide realistic estimates, prioritize, and be prepared to evaluate ideas and alternatives.

Compliance is a key aspect of a positive culture of safety. Discussions with management focusing on compliance with legal codes might be off-putting, but compliance considered in the context of organizational reputation, and potential financial costs for a violation, can be meaningful to leadership. An academic department which integrates compliance into its curriculum elevates the level of excellence of the program, and provides students with a fully developed program that can positively affect their future careers. Conversations with employees with a sole emphasis on OSHA or NFPA codes may be the least effective means to build a safety culture. But, when work practices that are in compliance with codes form "the way we do things around here," peer influence will be the most effective means to guarantee daily tasks are completed without concern for violations. For instance, if some means of fall protection (safety net, guardrail, or personal fall arrest system) is routinely implemented whenever a stage trap cover is removed, you do not need to cite OSHA 29 CFR 1910.28(b)(1)(i) to assure compliance.

Changing the work culture among employees can be the most daunting aspect of all we have considered in this book. If the "way we do things around here" has meant not wearing appropriate PPE, working-at-height without fall protection, loading/unloading counterweight without clearing the work area below, or engaging volunteer FOH staff as ushers without sufficient training in emergency procedures, then changing the way we do things will be required as your safety culture evolves. For myself, and from informal conversations with peers and technical theatre people, most of us have experienced situations of being employed on jobs where the way things were done did not seem safe, but we did not feel empowered to change things. As managers and supervisors, we are in positions to make change, but in light of the 90 percent statistic noted above, dictating change simply through pronouncements and hours of safety training will not be as effective as seeking allies among employees to support the change. Be creative in your approaches. For instance, if your hazard assessment indicates the need to require PPE for certain tasks (protective eyewear in the production shops during fabrication) rather than simply purchasing and distributing the PPE, engage employees to research and select PPE with input from their coworkers. The importance of employee engagement is acknowledged and codified by legislation in the UK: the Health and Safety (Consultations with Employees) Regulations 1996 requires employers to consult employees promptly on matters of safety and health at work as issues arise.[20] Ask one of your staff to relate a safety story or to lead a toolbox talk at the start of each work call. Don't hesitate to seek out and engage safety champions[21] among your staff. Such employee engagement taps into many aspects of management theory and personal motivation.[22]

I must close this chapter, and end this book. But endings are simply beginnings in disguise. As a reminder, let's revisit the concept noted in the Preface:

> Safety is a journey; a journey as important as the destination.
> Focus on the journey as you anticipate the destination.

Every journey begins with a single step. You and your theatre organization have already taken many steps on your safety journey. Your challenge is to coordinate these steps into an effective path that builds a positive safety culture.[23] Our industry has done much to provide guideposts and support, but much more needs to be done, within individual organizations, and across the entertainment industry as a whole. We can no longer accept a culture of safety that is not at the same level of artistic creativity and production excellence that prevails across the industry. Collaboration among visionary producers, creative artists, and technical professionals is at the core of what we do; safety and health must be included in this collaboration. My charge to you and to your organization is simple: evolve your safety culture to produce theatre and live entertainment that is risky, but safe.

NOTES

1 Tim Marsh, *Total Safety Culture; Organisational Risk Literacy* (Manchester, England: Ryder Marsh Safety Limited, 2014), 3.
2 Cary Gillett and Jay Sheehan, *The Production Manager's Toolkit: Successful Production Management in Theatre and the Performing Arts* (New York: Focal Press, 2017), 5. Also, Zachary Stribling and Richard Girtain, *The Technical Director's Toolkit* (New York: Focal Press, 2016), 2.
3 Bruce K. Lyon and Georgi Popov, "Communicating & Managing Risk: The Key Result of Risk Assessment," *Professional Safety*, November 2017, 36.
4 Mark Shanda and Dennis Dorn, *Technical Management for the Performing Arts: Utilizing Time, Talent, and Money* (New York: Focal Press, 2016), 41.
5 Jean Schiffman, "The Craft: Listen Up!", *Backstage*, February 21, 2001, accessed April 1, 2019, https://www.backstage.com/news/the-craft-listen-up-active-listening-can-raise-a-performance-to-a-higher-level-in-fact-it-may-be-the-root-of-good-acting/.

6. Robert Faires, "Good Listening: Meryl Streep Talks on the Key to Acting," *The Austin Chronicle*, November 12, 2010, accessed April 1, 2019, https://www.austinchronicle.com/arts/2010-11-12/good-listening/.
7. Gillett and Sheehan, *The Production Manager's Toolkit*, 32.
8. Ralph Nichols and Leonard A. Stevens, *Are You Listening* (New York: McGraw-Hill Companies, 1957).
9. Marsh, *Total Safety Culture*, 196 (emphasis in original).
10. Canadian Centre for Occupational Health and Safety (CCOHS), *Health and Safety Report*, Volume 16, Issue 11, "Tips & Tools: Good Communication Includes Active Listening," accessed April 1, 2019, https://www.ccohs.ca/newsletters/hsreport/issues/2018/11/ezine.html#hsreport-tipstools.
11. Gillett and Sheehan, *The Production Manager's Toolkit*, 13.
12. Richard Byrne, *Be the Best: How to Become a World-Class Health and Safety Professional* (Wigston, Leicestershire, England: IOSH Services Ltd, 2009), 101.
13. Business Dictionary, "Organizational Culture," accessed April 1, 2019, http://www.businessdictionary.com/definition/organizational-culture.html.
14. Marsh, *Total Safety Culture*, 53.
15. American Chemical Society, *Creating Safety Cultures in Academic Institutions: A Report of the Safety Culture Task Force of the ACS Committee on Chemical Safety* (Washington, DC: American Chemical Society, 2012), 4.
16. Department of Justice and Attorney-General, Workplace Health and Safety Queensland, *Understanding Safety Culture*, accessed April 1, 2019, https://www.worksafe.qld.gov.au/__data/assets/pdf_file/0004/82705/understanding-safety-culture.pdf.
17. National Safety Council, "Speaking of Safety, Changing the Atmosphere Around Safety Conversations," *Safety+Health*, May 25, 2017, accessed April 1, 2019, https://www.safetyandhealthmagazine.com/articles/15645-speaking-of-safety.
18. Marsh, *Total Safety Culture*, 54. See also, Princeton University Human Resources webpage "Learning Philosophy," accessed April 1, 2019, http://www.princeton.edu/hr/learning/philosophy/.
19. National Safety Council, "Speaking of Safety," *Safety+Health*, May 25, 2017, accessed April 1, 2019, https://www.safetyandhealthmagazine.com/articles/15645-speaking-of-safety.

20 Health Safety Executive, The Health and Safety (Consultation with employees) Regulation 1996, accessed April 1, 2019, http://www.legislation.gov.uk/uksi/1996/1513/made.
21 Byrne, *Be the Best*, 92.
22 Gillett and Sheehan, *The Production Manager's Toolkit*, 32
23 A positive safety culture can be described as a preventative safety and health culture: "One in which the right to a safe and healthy working environment is respected at all levels; where governments, employers and workers actively participate in securing a safe and healthy working environment through a system of defined rights, responsibilities and duties; and where the principle of prevention is accorded the highest priority," Benjamin O. Alli, *Fundamental Principles of Occupational Health and Safety*, 2nd edition (Geneva: International Labor Organization, 2008), 126.

BIBLIOGRAPHY

Antonsen, Stian. *Safety Culture: Theory, Method and Improvement.* Burlington, VT: Ashgate Publishing Company, 2009.

Byrne, Richard. *Be the Best: How to Become a World-Class Health and Safety Professional.* Wigston: Leicestershire, England: IOSH Services Ltd, 2009.

Gillett, Cary, and Sheehan, Jay. *The Production Manager's Toolkit: Successful Production Management in Theatre and Performing Arts.* New York: Routledge, 2017.

Marsh, Tim. *Total Safety Culture: Organisational Risk Literacy.* Manchester, England: Ryder Marsh Safety Limited, 2014.

Shanda, Mark, and Dorn, Dennis. *Technical Management for the Performing Arts: Utilizing Time, Talent, and Money.* New York: Focal Press, 2016.

Stribling, Zachary, and Girtain, Richard. *The Technical Director's Toolkit: Process, Forms, and Philosophies for Successful Technical Direction.* New York: Focal Press, 2016.

APPENDIX

Additional Resources

William J. Reynolds

CHAPTER 1: INTRODUCTION AND OVERVIEW

Significant Incidents: Theatre and Entertainment

Event Safety Alliance, *2017 Event Structure and Stage Accidents*, list compiled by Rinus Bakker, Rhino Staging Company, https://www.eventsafetyalliance.org/news/2018/1/5/2017-event-structure-and-stage-accidents.

Duval, Robert, *NFPA Case Study: Nightclub Fires*, https://www.nfpa.org/~/media/files/news-and-research/resources/fire-investigations/case_study_nightclub_fires.pdf?la=en.

National Fire Protection Association, *Fires in Nightclubs and Other Assembly Occupancies*, https://www.nfpa.org/Public-Education/By-topic/Property-type-and-vehicles/Nightclubs-assembly-occupancies.

The Station Nightclub Fire

Barylick, John. *Killer Show: The Station Nightclub Fire, American's Deadliest Rock Concert.* Lebanon, NH: University Press of New England, 2012.

NIST NCSTAR 2: Vol. I, *Report of the Technical Investigation of the Station Nightclub Fire*, page iii, https://ws680.nist.gov/publication/get_pdf.cfm?pub_id=100988.

Indiana State Fair Stage Collapse

Witt Associates, *Assessment of 2011 Indiana State Fair Collapse Incident, Part I. Executive Summary*, page 7, https://www.wittobriens.com/wp-content/uploads/2017/09/171758_1883990_3448726_1_6041423_Witt-Associates-Indiana-State-Fair-Report-April-2012.pdf.

Wikipedia, "Indiana State Fair Stage Collapse," https://en.wikipedia.org/wiki/Indiana_State_Fair_stage_collapse.

Indiana State Fair Commission August 13, *2011 Collapse Incident Investigative Report*, prepared by Thornton Tomasetti Inc., http://s3.amazonaws.com/tt_assets/pdf/TT_Indiana_State_Fair_Commission_Investigation_Report.pdf.

Ringling Bros. and Barnum & Bailey Circus Hair-Hang Incident

Occupational Safety and Health Administration (OSHA), *Investigation of the May 4, 2014 Incident at the Ringling Bros. and Barnum & Bailey Performance in Providence, RI, October, 2014*, page 6, https://www.osha.gov/doc/engineering/2014_r_05.html.

CHAPTER 2: SAFETY EVOLVES WITHIN THE ENTERTAINMENT INDUSTRY

Entertainment Industry Organizations

International Alliance of Theatrical Stage Employees (IATSE)
    http://www.iatse.net/
Actors' Equity Association (AEA)
    https://actorsequity.org/
United States Institute for Theater Technology (USITT)
    https://www.usitt.org
Entertainment Services and Technology Association (ESTA)
    https://www.esta.org/
Event Safety Alliance (ESA)
    https://www.eventsafetyalliance.org/

Theatre Production Organizations with Safety and Health Programs

Glimmerglass Festival, Cooperstown, NY
    https://glimmerglass.org/
Goodman Theatre, Chicago, IL
    https://www.goodmantheatre.org/
Milwaukee Repertory Theater, Milwaukee, WI
    https://www.milwaukeerep.com/
Oregon Shakespeare Festival, Ashland, OR
    https://www.osfashland.org/
Yale Repertory Theatre, New Haven, CT
    https://www.yalerep.org/

University Theatre Departments in the United States with Safety and Health Programs and/or Curricula[1]:

- Colby College, ME
- Carnegie Mellon University, PA
- California State University/San Marcos
- Central Wyoming College, WY
- Florida State University School of Theater, FL
- Kansas State University, KS
- Mercer County Community College, NJ
- Princeton University, NJ
- Southern Utah University, UT
- St. Olaf College, MN
- University of the Incarnate Word, TX
- University of Texas/Austin, TX
- University of California/Santa Barbara, CA
- University of Nevada, Las Vegas, NV
- West Virginia University, WV
- Yale School of Drama, CT

CHAPTER 3: SAFETY AND HEALTH PROGRAMS

Safety and Health Program General Resources

Searchable website sources for policies, recommended practices, standard operation procedures (SOPs), and training.

    College and university Environmental Health and Safety offices.

    Manufacturers and vendors of safety and health equipment and supplies.

    Providers for safety training, and safety and health program consultants.

CPWR: Center for Construction Research and Training, A world leader in construction safety and health research and training, https://www.cpwr.com/.

OSHA, *Recommended Practices for Safety and Health Programs*, https://www.osha.gov/shpguidelines/.

OSHA, Safety and Health Programs Publications, https://www.osha.gov/pls/publications/publication.athruz?pType=Industry&pID=183.

OSHA, Safe+Sound, Safety + Health Programs resources website. https://www.osha.gov/safeandsound/safety-and-health-programs.html.

National Institute for Occupational Safety and Health (NIOSH), Total Worker Health, Planning, Assessment, and Evaluation Resources, https://www.cdc.gov/niosh/twh/tools.html.

Theatre Alberta, CA, Programs and Services, Safe Stages-Best Practices, https://www.theatrealberta.com/programs-services/.

University of California, Performing Arts Safety Center of Excellence, *Performing Arts Safety Manual*, https://www.ucop.edu/environment-health-safety/groups-and-programs/centers-of-excellence/performing-arts/index.html.

WorkSafeNB, CA, Guide to Workplace Health & Safety Programs, https://www.worksafenb.ca/docs/WorkSafeNBHSProgramsGuideE.pdf.

Safety and Health Program Resources—Management Leadership

OSHAcademy, Course 113—Introduction to Safety Leadership, and, Course 112—Introduction to Safety Supervision, https://www.oshatrain.org/pages/professional-training-courses.html.

EHSToday, "Safety Leadership," *The best safety cultures are led by business leaders who integrate safety into the business.* https://www.ehstoday.com/safety-leadership.

Safety and Health Program Resources—Employee Participation

Marsh, Tim, Dr., *ASM: Affective Safety Management.* London: International Institute of Risk and Safety Management, 2008.

Karen Price, "Employee Engagement Improves Safety," https://www.coverys.com/knowledgecenter/Articles/Employee-Engagement-Improves-Safety.

Jeff Ross, "Improving Safety Through Employee Engagement," https://www.cashort.com/blog/employee-engagement-is-key-to-improving-workplace-safety.

Safety and Health Program Resources—Hazard Identification and Assessment

OSHA, Hazard Identification Training Tool, https://www.osha.gov/hazfinder/index.html.

The Campbell Institute: Research, *Visual Literacy: How "Learning to See" Benefits Occupational Safety*, https://www.thecampbellinstitute.org/research/.

Safety and Health Program Resources—Hazard Prevention and Control

OSHAcademy, Course 704—Hazard Analysis and Control, https://www.oshatrain.org/courses/mods/704e.html.

Safety and Health Program Resources—Education and Training

CPWR: Center for Construction Research and Training, "Training," https://www.cpwr.com/training/training-offered-cpwr-builds-existing-infrastructure-building-trades-unions-and-2000-joint.

OSHAcademy, Professional Training Courses, https://www.oshatrain.org/pages/professional-training-courses.html.

Safety and Health Program Resources—Coordination and Communication

Joshua Williams, *Improving Safety Communication Skills: Becoming an Empathic Communicator,* http://safetyperformance.com/ImprovingSafetyCommunication.pdf.

Safety and Health Program Resources—Program Evaluation and Improvement

Harvard Center for Work, Health and Well-Being, Workplace Integrated Safety and Health (WISH) Assessment, http://centerforworkhealth.sph.harvard.edu/resources/workplace-integrated-safety-and-health-wish-assessment.

Oakley, Jeffery S., *Accident Investigation Techniques*, 2nd edition. Park Ridge, IL: American Society of Safety Professionals, 2012.

CHAPTER 4: COMPLIANCE

Occupational Safety and Health Administration (OSHA)

United States Department of Labor, Occupational Safety and Health Administration, (OSHA), https://www.osha.gov/.

J. J. Keller & Associates, Inc., *OSHA Safety Handbook*, 8th edition. Neenah, WI: J. J. Keller & Associates, Inc., 2017.

Mancomm, Inc., *OSHA General Industry Regulations, 29 CFR Parts 1903. 1904, and 1910*. Davenport, IA: Mancomm, Inc., 2017.

National Fire Protection Association (NFPA)

National Fire Protection Association, https://www.nfpa.org/.

Cote, Ron, and Harrington, Gregory E., editors, *Life Safety Code Handbook, NFPA 101, 2015 edition.* Quincy, MA: National Fire Protection Association, 2014.

Crowd Manager and Crowd Manager Supervisor Training Resources

International Association of Venue Managers; Trained Crowd Manager (TCM) and Crowd Manager Supervisor (CMS) online training, http://crowdmanagertraining.com/tcm_courses.html.

Fire Marshal Support Services, LLC; Crowd Manager Training online course, https://www.crowdmanagers.com/training.

North Carolina Department of Insurance, Office of the State Fire Marshal; Crowd Manager Training, http://www.ncdoi.com/OSFM/Fire_Safety_Programs/Default.aspx?field1=Crowd_Manager_Training&user=Crowd_Manager_Training.

Commonwealth of Massachusetts, Department of Fire Services; Crowd Manager Regulations and Training Program, https://www.mass.gov/crowd-manager-regulations-and-training-program.

State of Rhode Island, Division of State Fire Marshal, Department of Public Safety; Crowd Management Training, http://fire-marshal.ri.gov/fireacademy/crowdmanagement.php.

Federal Emergency Management Agency (FEMA), Community Emergency Response Team (CERT); CERT Traffic and Crowd Management Module, https://www.fema.gov/media-library/assets/documents/28662.

OSHA Fact Sheet "Crowd Management Safety Guidelines for Retailers," https://www.osha.gov/OshDoc/data_General_Facts/Crowd_Control.html.

International Codes and Standards

Canada

Canadian Centre for Occupational Health and Safety, https://www.ccohs.ca/.

Canadian Standards Association, https://www.csagroup.org/.

Theatre Alberta, *Safe Stages*, https://www.theatrealberta.com/safe-stages/.

Actsafe, https://www.actsafe.ca/.

Ontario Ministry of Labour, Health and Safety, "Performance Industry," https://www.labour.gov.on.ca/english/hs/topics/performance.php.

Ontario Ministry of Labour, Health and Safety, Application of Industrial and Construction Regulations Safety Guidelines for the Live Performance

Industry in Ontario, https://www.labour.gov.on.ca/english/hs/pubs/liveperformance/gl_live_application.php.

Television, Film, Live Performance and Event Electrical Guidelines, ESA Spec-003 R7 2013, https://www.esasafe.com/assets/files/esasafe/pdf/Bulletins/ESA_Spec-003_R7.pdf.

Commission des normes, de l'équité, de la santé et de la sécurité du travail, *Workers: Safety rules for the Québec Film and Video Industry*, https://www.csst.qc.ca/en/Pages/safety_rules_film_video_industry.aspx.

Commission des normes, de l'équité, de la santé et de la sécurité du travail, *Guide de prévention en milieu de travail à l'intention de la petite et moyenne entreprise, 2e edition*, https://www.cnesst.gouv.qc.ca/publications/200/Pages/dc_200_16082.aspx.

Chile

Chile Actúa, "Modernización Integral," http://www.chileescena.cl/index.php?seccion=modernizacion-integral.

Film Commission Chile, *Shoot in Chile, A Practical Guide for a Chile Film Friendly,* https://www.cultura.gob.cl/wp-content/uploads/2015/03/shoot-in-chile_en.pdf.

Website managed by Ministerio de las Culturas, las Artes y el Patrimonio—Gobierno de Chile with links to several documents in Spanish related to risk management, rigging, fall protection, scenery, and lighting: https://issuu.com/consejodelacultura/docs/prevencion_riesgos_vol2.

India

Directorate General, Factory Advice Service and Labour Institutes, http://dgfasli.nic.in/about1.htm.

The Philippines

Department of Labor and Employment, Occupational Safety and Health Council website, http://oshc.dole.gov.ph/.

Department of Labor and Employment, Occupational Safety and Health Standards, as Amended, 1989, http://bwc.dole.gov.ph/images/Downloads/OSH-Standards-Amended-1989.pdf.

Republic of Korea (South Korea)

Korean Occupational Safety and Health Agency, KOSHA, http://english.kosha.or.kr/english/legislation/occupationalSafetyAndHealth.do.

Singapore

Singapore Government, Ministry of Manpower (MOM), "Workplace Safety and Health," https://www.mom.gov.sg/workplace-safety-and-health.

Singapore Government, Workplace Safety and Health (WSH) Council, https://wshc.sg/wps/portal/!ut/p/a1/04_Sj9CPykssy0xPLMnMz0vMAfGjzOJ9_E1MjByDDbzdPUIMDRyNfA08QsyNDYNdzYAKInErcA4zJk6_AQ7gaEBIf7h-FD4IYBeAFeCxwks_Kj0nPwns3UjHvCRji3T9qKLUtNSi1CK90iKgcEZJSUGxlaqBqkF5cUayXnE6kFFQrGpQkF9UgI1bRn5xiX4EVLV-QW5ohEGWaU6Zj6MiABYeP90!/dl5/d5/L2dBISEvZ0FBIS9nQSEh/.

Singapore Civil Defense Force, Fire Safety, https://www.scdf.gov.sg/home/fire-safety.

Singapore WSH Council, Code of Practice for Working Safely at Heights, https://www.wshc.sg/files/wshc/upload/infostop/file/2013/WSH+Code+of+Practice+2013_ebook.pdf.

Singapore MOM, Technical Advisory for Scaffolds, https://www.wshc.sg/files/wshc/upload/cms/file/2014/Technical%20Advisory%20for%20Scaffolds.pdf.

Singapore Standards, Code of Practice for Safe Use of Mobile Elevating Work Platforms, https://www.singaporestandardseshop.sg/Product/SSPdtDetail/b19bf4ff-38f3-49c2-990a-6a84bfcb123a.

Taiwan (R.O.C.)

Taiwan Department of Labor, Occupational Safety and Health Administration, https://www.osha.gov.tw/enhome/.

Occupational Safety and Health Administration, Ministry of Labor, Republic of China (Taiwan), *National Occupational Safety and Health Profile of Taiwan, 2014,* http://she.mcu.edu.tw/sites/default/files/MCU/National%20Occupational%20Safety%20and%20Health%20Profile%20of%20Taiwan.pdf.

Taiwan Association of Theatre Technology (TATT), https://www.tatt.org.tw/english.

United Kingdom

Association of British Theatre Technicians (ABTT), http://www.abtt.org.uk/.
 ABTT Safety Matters archives, http://www.abtt.org.uk/resources/safety-matters/.
 ABTT Codes, Forms, and Updates, http://www.abtt.org.uk/resource/codes-forms-and-updates/.
 ABTT Standards News, http://www.abtt.org.uk/resources/technical-standards-updates/.

ABTT Shop: Books, [including Technical Standards for Places of Entertainment], Codes of Practice, [including Weapons in Theater; Guard rails; and Stage Fog and Smoke Effects], http://www.abtt.org.uk/shop/.

Health Safety Executive (HSE), https://www.hse.gov.uk/.

Health Safety Executive, Guidance, Health and Safety in the Film, Theatre and Broadcasting Industries, http://www.hse.gov.uk/entertainment/theatre-tv/index.htm.

Regulations owned and enforced by the HSE related to theatre production and the entertainment industry can be accessed at the HSE website, http://www.hse.gov.uk/legislation/statinstruments.htm. Regulations to note include:

- Chemicals (Hazard Information and Packaging for Supply) Regulations 2002 (CHIP) (gives effect to EU Directive 67/548/EEC)
- Control of Substances Hazardous to Health Regulations 2002
- Reporting of Injuries, Diseases and Dangerous Occurrences Regulations 2013
- Transport of Dangerous Goods (Safety Advisers) Regulations 1999
- Electricity at Work Regulations 1989
- Lifting Operations and Lifting Equipment Regulations 1998
- The Control of Noise at Work Regulations 2005
- The Construction (Design and Management) Regulations 2015
- The Control of Asbestos Regulations 2012
- Control of Lead at Work Regulations 2002
- Control of Vibration at Work Regulations 2005
- Dangerous Substances and Explosive Atmospheres Regulations 2002
- Safety Representatives and Safety Committees Regulations 1977
- The Confined Spaces Regulations 1997
- The Work at Height Regulations 2005

HSE Books and Documents, https://books.hse.gov.uk/.

CHAPTER 5: INDUSTRY STANDARDS, RECOMMENDED PRACTICES, TRAINING, AND CERTIFICATIONS

Entertainment Services and Technology Association (ESTA)

ESTA, Membership, https://www.esta.org/join/membershipbenefits.html.
ESTA, Entertainment Technician Certification Program, https://etcp.esta.org/.s
ESTA. International Code of Practice for Entertainment Rigging, https://www.esta.org/ESTA/icoper.php.

ESTA Technical Standards Program (TSP)

ESTA TSP, Download Standards, https://tsp.esta.org/tsp/documents/published_docs.php.
ESTA TSP, Public Review Documents, https://tsp.esta.org/tsp/documents/public_review_docs.php.
ESTA TSP, Working Groups, https://tsp.esta.org/tsp/working_groups/index.html.

Event Safety Alliance (ESA)

Event Safety Alliance, List of Safety Resources, https://www.eventsafetyalliance.org/safety-guidance-and-resources.
Event Safety Alliance, Education, Event Safety Summit, https://www.eventsafetyalliance.org/esaess.
Event Safety Alliance, Education, Severe Weather Summit, https://www.eventsafetyalliance.org/severe-weather-summit-annual.
Event Safety Alliance, Education, Crowd Safety Symposium, https://www.eventsafetyalliance.org/crowd-safety-symposium-workshops.
Event Safety Alliance, Education, Event Safety Access Training, https://www.eventsafetyalliance.org/event-safety-access-training-esat.
Event Safety Alliance, Education, Event Safety University, https://www.eventsafetyalliance.org/event-safety-university-esau.

CHAPTER 6: POLICIES AND PROCEDURES: SPECIFIC HAZARDS

General

Actsafe Safety Association, https://www.actsafe.ca/.
Theatre Alberta, *Safe Stages*, https://www.theatrealberta.com/safe-stages/.
United States Institute for Theater Technology, Education & Training, https://www.usitt.org/master/.

University of California, Office of the President, Safety Loss and Preventions, Performing Arts Safety Center of Excellence, https://www.ucop.edu/safety-and-loss-prevention/environmental/program-resources/performing-arts/index.html.

Personal Protective Equipment

OSHA, Personal Protective Equipment Overview, https://www.osha.gov/SLTC/personalprotectiveequipment/.

OSHA, Personal Protective Equipment, OSHA 3151, https://www.osha.gov/Publications/osha3151.pdf.

National Institute for Occupational Safety and Health, Personal Protective Equipment Overview, https://www.cdc.gov/niosh/ppe/.

Canadian Centre for Occupational Health and Safety, OSH Answers Fact Sheets, Personal Protective Equipment, https://www.ccohs.ca/oshanswers/prevention/ppe/designin.html.

Fall Prevention and Fall Protection

OSHA Publications, Fall Prevention/Protection, https://www.osha.gov/pls/publications/publication.athruz?pType=Industry&pID=402.

Washington State Department of Labor & Industries, Fall Protection, Fall Restraint and Fall Arrest, http://www.lni.wa.gov/Safety/Topics/AtoZ/fallprotect/.

CPWR—Center for Construction Work and Training, Fall Protection, https://www.cpwr.com/search/search_by_page/fall%20protection.

Stage Fog and Haze

Actors' Equity, Theatrical Smoke and Haze Regulations, https://www.actorsequity.org/resources/Producers/safe-and-sanitary/smoke-and-haze/.

Ontario, CA, Ministry of Labour, Fog and Smoke Safety Guideline for the Live Performance Industry in Ontario, https://www.labour.gov.on.ca/english/hs/pubs/liveperformance/gl_live_fog.php.

Health Safety Executive, UK, "Smoke and Vapour Effects Used in Entrainment," http://www.hse.gov.uk/pubns/etis3.pdf.

Stage Weapons and Stage Combat Policies

Contract Services Administration Trust Fund (CSATC, "administers a variety of programs for the benefit of the motion picture and television industry"), *Safety Bulletins*, https://www.csatf.org/bulletintro.shtml.

Actors' Equity Association (AEA), https://actorsequity.org/resources/Producers/safe-and-sanitary/safety-tips-for-use-of-firearms/#, and, https://actorsequity.org/resources/Producers/safe-and-sanitary/aea-firearms-questionnaire.pdf.
Health and Safety Executive, UK, http://www.hse.gov.uk/pubns/etis20.pdf.
Association of British Theatre Technicians (ABTT), Code of Practice 06, Weapons in Stage Productions, 2019.
Actssafe Safety Association, *Performing Arts Bulletins*, https://www.actsafe.ca/?s=Performing+Arts+Bulletins, and *Motion Picture Bulletins*, https://www.actsafe.ca/?s=Bulletins.
Weapons of Choice, https://weaponsofchoice.com/extras/on-the-ue-of-prop-firearms/.
Yale University Undergraduate Productions, https://up.yalecollege.yale.edu/regulations/prop-weapon-and-stage-combat-policy.
Ontario, CA, Safety Guidelines for Live Performance, https://www.labour.gov.on.ca/english/hs/pubs/liveperformance/gl_live_combat.php.
Inouye, Kevin, *The Theatrical Firearms Handbook.* Burlington, MA: Focal Press, 2014.

Live Flame Onstage

NFPA 160, Standard for the use of Flame Effects before an Audience, https://www.nfpa.org/codes-and-standards/all-codes-and-standards/list-of-codes-and-standards/detail?code=160.
Ontario, CA, Flame Effects Safety Guideline for the Live Performance Industry in Ontario, https://www.labour.gov.on.ca/english/hs/pubs/liveperformance/gl_live_flame.php.

Fire and Life Safety

National Fire Protection Association (NFPA), https://www.nfpa.org/.
NFPA, "Codes and Standards," https://www.nfpa.org/Codes-and-Standards.
NFPA, NFPA 101 Life Safety Code, https://www.nfpa.org/codes-and-standards/all-codes-and-standards/list-of-codes-and-standards/detail?code=101.
International Code Council (ICC), International Fire Code, https://codes.iccsafe.org/content/IFC2018.

Patron Alerts and Notifications

Health Safety Executive (HSE), "Managing Crowds Safely," http://www.hse.gov.uk/event-safety/crowd-management.htm.
Live Performance Australia, *Audience and Crowd Management Hazard Guide*, http://members.liveperformance.com.au/uploads/files/

(Final)%20Audience%20and%20Crowd%20Management%20-%20Feb18-1519008281.pdf.

Incident Reporting and Recording

OSHA, "Safety and Health Topics, Incident Investigation," https://www.osha.gov/dcsp/products/topics/incidentinvestigation/index.html.

Previsor Insurance, Sample Accident Reporting Policy, http://previsorinsurance.com/wp-content/uploads/policy-accident-reporting.pdf.

EHSToday, "Accident Investigation: Back to Reality," https://www.ehstoday.com/news/ehs_imp_32816.

CHAPTER 7: BORROWING SAFETY IDEAS

Checklists

Gawande, Atul, *The Checklist Manifesto: How to Get Things Right*. New York: Metropolitan Books, 2009.

Operational Inspections

Occupational Safety and Health Administration (OSHA), "Operating the Fork-lift: Pre-Operation," https://www.osha.gov/SLTC/etools/pit/operations/servicing.html.

WorksafeBC, "Safety Inspections," https://www.worksafebc.com/en/search#q=safety%20inspections&sort=relevancy&f:language-facet=[English].

WorksafeBC, *Safety Inspections Workbook*, https://www.worksafebc.com/en/resources/health-safety/books-guides/safety-inspections-workbook?lang=en.

Identification of Hazards

Occupational Safety and Health Administration (OSHA), "Hazard Identification and Assessment," https://www.osha.gov/shpguidelines/hazard-Identification.html.

OSHA, Hazard Identification Training Tool, https://www.osha.gov/hazfinder/game/manual.html.

Campbell Institute, *A Second Look: Update on Visual Literacy*, https://www.thecampbellinstitute.org/research/.

Cal/OSHA, Sample Forms and Checklists, Hazard Assessment Checklist, https://www.dir.ca.gov/dosh/etools/09-031/tools.htm.

Canadian Centre for Occupational Health and Safety (CCOHS), "Hazard Identification," https://www.ccohs.ca/oshanswers/hsprograms/hazard_identification.html.

Center for Chemical Process Safety, "Introduction to Hazard Identification and Risk Analysis," https://www.aiche.org/ccps/topics/elements-process-safety/understand-hazard-risk/hazard-identification-and-risk-analysis/introduction.

Alone (Lone) Work Policy

Health Safety Executive (HSE), *Working Alone,* http://www.hse.gov.uk/pubns/indg73.htm.

National Safety Council, "Lone Worker Safety," *Safety+Health*, https://www.safetyandhealthmagazine.com/articles/12628-lone-worker-safety,

Ohio State University, Working Alone Safety Program, https://ehs.osu.edu/sites/default/files/working_alone_safety_program.pdf.

Prevention through Design (PtD)

Center for Disease Control (CDC), "Prevention through Design," https://www.cdc.gov/niosh/topics/ptd/default.html.

David I. Walline, "Prevention through Design; Proven solutions from the Field," *Professional Safety*, November, 2014, https://www.nafe.org/assets/HollywoodEdSeminar/prevention%20through%20design12152014.pdf.

Risk Assessments

Health and Safety Workbook, *Risk Assessments,* https://www.eastcambs.gov.uk/sites/default/files/health_safety/risk_assessment_31396.pdf.

EHSToday, "On Acceptable Risk," https://www.ehstoday.com/news/ehs_imp_35066.

European Agency for Safety and Health at Work, Risk Assessment Tool, https://osha.europa.eu/en/tools-and-publications/publications/promotional_material/rat-essentials/view.

Field Level Hazard Assessments

OSHA, *Job Hazard Analysis, OSHA 3071*, https://www.osha.gov/Publications/osha3071.pdf.

OSHAcademy, "Introduction to Job Hazard Analysis (JHA)," https://www.oshatrain.org/pages/professional-training-courses.html.

Examples of Field Level Hazard Assessment forms can be found at: https://www.uregina.ca/hr/hsw/assets/docs/pdf/Procedures/Facilities%20Management%20Field%20Level%20Hazard%20Assessment%20Procedure%20and%20toolbox%20form.pdf,

or, http://www.bildalberta.ca/uploads/files/PDF/2017/Safety/Field%20Level%20Hazard%20Assessment%20card%20May%202017.pdf,

or, https://wssolutions.ca/wp-content/uploads/2016/05/Field-Level-Hazard-Assessment-Form-WSS.pdf,
or, http://www.tollestrup.com/images/safety/Field%20Level%20Hazard%20Assessment.pdf.

Visual literacy and the identification of hazards, "Seeing Safety in a New Way," *Safety+Health*, https://www.safetyandhealthmagazine.com/articles/17952-seeing-safety-in-a-new-way.

The Campbell Institute, Research, "A Second Look: Update on Visual Literacy," https://www.thecampbellinstitute.org/research/.

Serious Injury and Fatality (SIF) Prevention

Krauss Bell Group, "Serious Injuries & Fatalities Prevention," https://krausebellgroup.com/category/serious-injuries-fatalities/.

Campbell Institute, *Serious Injury and Fatalities Prevention: Perspectives and Practices*, https://www.thecampbellinstitute.org/research/.

CHAPTER 8: PUTTING IT ALL TOGETHER: SAFETY CULTURE

Communication

Susan Vargas, "Speaking of safety, Changing the atmosphere around safety conversations," *Safety+Health*, https://www.safetyandhealthmagazine.com/articles/15645-speaking-of-safety.

OSHA, "Better Safety Conversations," *Safe+Sound*, https://www.osha.gov/safeandsound/docs/SHP_Better-Safety-Conversations.pdf.

Marsh, Tim, Dr., *Talking Safety*. Burlington, VT: Gower Publishing Company, 2013.

Safety Culture

Antonsen, Stian., *Safety Culture: Theory, Method and Improvement*. Burlington, VT: Ashgate Publishing Company, 2009.

Marsh, Tim, Dr., *Total Safety Culture: Organisational Risk Literacy*. Manchester, England: Ryder Marsh Safety Limited, 2014.

NOTE

1 A non-inclusive list based on a college or university having theatre safety curricula listed online for their academic programs, or safety training noted as part of their student requirements.

GLOSSARY OF SAFETY AND HEALTH TERMS

^Accident[1]: An unplanned event that results in harm to people, damage to property, or loss to process.

^Accident Investigation: The process of systematically gathering and analyzing information about an accident. This is done for the purposes of identifying causes and making recommendations to prevent the accident from happening again.

*ACGIH[2]: American Conference of Governmental Industrial Hygienists. A professional organization devoted to worker health protection. In particular, the organization publishes "Threshold Limit Values for Chemical Substances in the Work Environment" and the "Documentation of TLVs." The TLV booklet is one source which may be used in hazard determination. www.acgih.org.

*Acute: An adverse effect on the human body with symptoms of high severity coming quickly to a crisis. Acute effects are normally the result of short-term exposures and short duration.

*Acute Toxicity: "Adverse effects occurring following oral or dermal administration of a single dose of a substance, or multiple doses given within 24 hours, or an inhalation exposure of 4 hours." Acute toxicity is considered a health hazard under OSHA's Hazard Communication Standard at 29 CFR 1910.1200.

^Administrative Controls: A category of hazard control that uses administrative/management involvement in order to minimize employee exposure to the hazard. Some examples are: job enrichment; job rotation; work/rest schedules; work rates; periods of adjustment.

*Aerosol: This is a solid or liquid particulate, natural or man-made, which can remain suspended in air. Paint spray and smoke are examples of aerosols.

*Asphyxiant: A chemical, usually in a gas or vapor state, which displaces oxygen or prevents its use in the body by other chemical means.

Authorized Person: A person approved or assigned by the employer to perform a specific type of duty or duties or to be at a specific location or locations at the jobsite. **[OSHA]**[3]

^**Barrier Cream:** A cream designed to protect the hands and other parts of the skin from exposure to harmful agents. Barrier cream is also known as protective hand cream.

***Carcinogen (OSHA):** "A substance or a mixture of substances which induce cancer or increase its incidence." A cancer is characterized by the proliferation of abnormal cells, sometimes in the form of a tumor. Examples of carcinogens include asbestos, vinyl chloride, and benzene.

***CAS Number:** The CAS Number is an identification number assigned by the Chemical Abstracts Service (CAS) of the American Chemical Society. The CAS Number is used in various databases, including Chemical Abstracts, for identification and information retrieval.

***Ceiling (ACGIH):** The Threshold Limit Value Ceiling (TLV-C) is "the concentration that should not be exceeded during any part of the working exposure."

***CFR:** Code of Federal Regulations. This is the collection of rules and regulations originally published in the Federal Register by various governmental departments and agencies. OSHA regulations are found in 29 CFR; EPA regulations are in 40 CFR; and Department of Transportation regulations in 49 CFR.

***Chronic:** An adverse effect on the human body with symptoms which develop slowly over a long period of time or which frequently recur. Chronic effects are the result of long-term exposure and are of long duration.

Close Call: An incident that could have caused serious injury or illness but did not. SEE ALSO: NEAR-MISS.[4]

Code: A systematic and comprehensive compilation of laws, rules, or regulations that are consolidated and classified according to subject matter. Many states have published official codes of all laws in force, including the Common Law and statutes as judicially interpreted, that have been compiled by code commissions and enacted by legislatures. The U.S. Code (U.S.C.) is the compilation of federal laws.[5]

Competent Person: One who is capable of identifying existing and predictable hazards in the surroundings, or working conditions which are unsanitary, hazardous, or dangerous to employees, and who has authorization to take prompt corrective measures to eliminate them. **[OSHA]**

*Compliance: This is the state of meeting all the requirements of the law. The best way to be assured of being in compliance with OSHA is to be familiar with OSHA's regulations and expectations.

Construction Work: Work for construction, alteration, and/or repair, including painting and decorating. [OSHA]

Culture; Safety Culture: "The safety culture of an organisation is the product of individual and group values, attitudes, perceptions, competencies, and patterns of behaviour that determine the commitment to, and the style and proficiency of, an organisation's health and safety management. Organisations with a positive safety culture are characterised by communications founded on mutual trust, by shared perceptions of the importance of safety and by confidence in the efficacy of preventive measures."[6]

*Dermal: Relating to the skin.

*Documentation: Documentation is the record of compliance that a company should maintain. The Hazard Communication Law prescribes that certain requirements be met including employee information and training. Complete training records should be kept to prove compliance in the event of an inspection. Other areas where documentation should be maintained include the written program, SDS maintenance, hazard determination, and quality assurance audits.

^Due Diligence: The taking of every precaution reasonable in the circumstances for the protection of the health and safety of workers.

^Engineering Controls: A category of hazard control that uses physical/ engineering methods to eliminate or minimize the hazard. Examples of engineering controls include: ventilation, isolation, elimination, enclosure, substitution, and design of the workplace or equipment.

*EPA: Environmental Protection Agency. Responsible for enforcing regulations related to the Resource Conservation and Recovery Act, Toxic Substance Control Act, Superfund, and others.

^Ergonomics: An applied science that studies the interaction between people and the work environment. It focuses on matching the job to the worker.

*Evaporation Rate: A measure of the length of time required for a given amount of a substance to evaporate, compared with the time required for an equal amount of ether or butyl acetate to evaporate. The evaporation rate of toluene is 2.24 (butyl acetate = 1).

*Exposed (OSHA): means that an employee is subjected to a hazardous chemical, substance, or environment in the course of employment through any route of entry (inhalation, ingestion, skin contact or absorption, etc.), and includes potential (e.g., accidental or possible) exposure.

Fall Protection: "any equipment, device, or system that prevents an employee from falling from an elevation or mitigates the effect of such a fall." **[OSHA]**

Fire Watch: "The assignment of a person or persons to an area for the express purpose of notifying the fire department, the building occupants, or both of an emergency: preventing a fire from occurring; extinguishing small fires; or protecting the public from fire or life safety dangers."[7]

Flame Retardant: "A flame retardant is a product that can be applied to fabrics, set pieces, props and costumes to inhibit their ability to burn. A flame retardant will keep the fire from burning for more than a few seconds, thus reducing the chance of spreading."[8]

*Flammable Limits (FL): The range defined by the lower (LFL) and upper (UFL) flammability limit. May sometimes be referred to as explosive limits (LEL and UEL) in other sources of information. This is the range of concentrations in air that may readily ignite when exposed to a flame or spark.

*Flashpoint (OSHA): "means the minimum temperature at which a liquid gives off vapor in sufficient concentration to form an ignitable mixture with air near the surface of the liquid, as determined by a method identified in Section B.6.3" of OSHA's Hazard Communication Standard at 29 CFR 1910.1200.

^Fog: Suspended droplets of a liquid that are produced by condensation or by the breaking up of a liquid (e.g. by splashing or foaming).

^Fume: Finely divided solid particles that are formed when a hot metal vapor cools and condenses. Fumes are usually associated with molten metals (e.g. copper, lead, or zinc) and are often accompanied by a chemical reaction such as oxidation.

^Guarding: Use of any device or combination of devices designed to keep any part of a worker's body out of the danger zone of a machine during its operating cycle. This usually involves guarding the point of operation, guarding power transmission components by fixed enclosures, and/or protecting the operator and nearby workers from flying fragments.

Guardrail System: A barrier erected along an unprotected or exposed side, edge, or other area of a walking-working surface to prevent employees from falling to a lower level. **[OSHA]**

Hazard: "A hazard is anything with the potential to cause harm.

- A hazard is any condition, event, or circumstance which could induce an accident (EUROCONTROL ESARR 4).
- A hazard is any existing or potential condition that can lead to injury, illness, or death to people; damage to or loss of a system, equipment, or property; or damage to the environment.
- A hazard is a condition that might cause (is a prerequisite to) an accident or incident. (FAA AC 120–92A: Safety Management Systems for Aviation Service Providers)."[9]

^**Hazard:** The potential of any machine, equipment, process, material (including biological and chemical) or physical factor that may cause harm to people, or damage to property or the environment.

***Hazard Category (OSHA):** "means the division of criteria within each hazard class, e.g., oral acute toxicity and flammable liquids include four hazard categories. These categories compare hazard severity within a hazard class and should not be taken as a comparison of hazard categories more generally." This definition refers to the Hazard Communication Standard at 29 CFR 1910.1200.

***Hazard Class (OSHA):** "means the nature of the physical or health hazards, e.g., flammable solid, carcinogen, oral acute toxicity." This definition refers to the Hazard Communication Standard at 29 CFR 1910.1200.

***Hazard Communication Standard:** The purpose of OSHA's Hazard Communication Standard, also known as HCS or HazCom, is to address the issue of classifying the potential hazards of chemicals and to ensure that employers and employees can identify and understand hazardous chemicals in the workplace, the physical and health hazards associated with them, and how to take protective action. Hazard communication is achieved by recognition and evaluation of workplace hazards, accurate labeling of hazards, and effective training of employees about proper handling and use of those hazardous materials in the workplace. The OSHA Hazard Communication Standard describes how employers are to inform employees of workplace chemical hazards. The OSHA standard is enforced under the regulations found in 29 CFR 1910.1200.

***Hazard Not Otherwise Classified (HNOC) (OSHA):** "means an adverse physical or health effect identified through an evaluation of scientific evidence during the classification process that does not meet the specified criteria for the physical and health hazard classes addressed in this section. This does not extend coverage to adverse physical and health effects for which there is a hazard class addressed in this section, but the effect either falls below the cut-off value/concentration limit of the hazard class or is under a GHS hazard category that has not been adopted by OSHA (e.g., acute toxicity Category 5)." This definition refers to the Hazard Communication Standard at 29 CFR 1910.1200.

Hazard Statement: "means a statement assigned to a hazard class and category that describes the nature of the hazard(s) of a chemical, including, where appropriate, the degree of hazard." This definition refers to OSHA's Hazard Communication Standard at 29 CFR 1910.1200.

^**Health and Safety Policy:** A policy is a statement of intent, and a commitment to plan for coordinated management action. A policy should provide a clear indication of a company's health and safety objectives. This, in turn, will provide direction for the health and safety program.

^**Health and Safety Program:** A systematic combination of activities, procedures, and facilities designed to ensure and maintain a safe and healthy workplace.

Health Hazard (OSHA): "means a chemical which is classified as posing one of the following hazardous effects: acute toxicity (any route of exposure); skin corrosion or irritation; serious eye damage or eye irritation; respiratory or skin sensitization; germ cell mutagenicity; carcinogenicity; reproductive toxicity; specific target organ toxicity (single or repeated exposure); or aspiration hazard." This definition refers to the Hazard Communication Standard at 29 CFR 1910.1200.

Hierarchy of Controls: There can be multiple safeguards to control any one hazard. Each level of these safeguards serves to protect employees. Some safeguards or controls are more effective than others. The Hierarchy of Controls outlines the controls used to mitigate a hazard from most effective to least effective. The Hierarchy of Controls is typically listed as: elimination (most effective), substitution, engineering controls, administrative controls, and PPE (least effective).[10]

HMIS: Hazardous Materials Identification System. This is an integrated approach to working with hazardous materials. The system includes information on assessing hazards, labeling, and training. It was devised by the National Paint and Coatings Association.

*Immediate Use (OSHA): "means that the hazardous chemical will be under the control of and used only by the person who transfers it from a labeled container and only within the work shift in which it is transferred." Employers are not required to label containers designated for an "immediate use" purpose.

Incident: A work-related event in which an injury or ill-health (regardless of severity) or fatality occurred, or could have occurred.[11]

^Industrial Hygiene: A science that deals with the anticipation, recognition, evaluation, and control of hazards in the workplace. These hazards may cause sickness, harm to employee health, discomfort, and inefficient performance on the job.

Infeasible: Impossible to perform the construction work using a conventional fall protection system (i.e. guardrail system, safety net system, or personal fall arrest system) or technologically impossible to use any one of these systems to provide fall protection. **[OSHA]**

*Ingestion: Chemicals which enter the body by this route of entry may have local effects and/or may be absorbed into the bloodstream through the small intestine.

*Inhalation: Chemicals which enter the body by this route of entry may have local effects and/or may be absorbed into the bloodstream through the lungs.

*Inventory: A list or inventory of hazardous chemicals known to be present in the workplace is a required component of the written hazard communication program. This list is to be cross-referenced with the SDS and the label.

*Irritant: A chemical that produces reversible damage to the skin following the application of a test substance for up to four hours.

*Job Hazard Analysis (JHA): This is a process by which a job is studied to determine the hazards involved and ways to safely complete the job by procedures and/or personal protective equipment.

*Label (OSHA): "means an appropriate group of written, printed, or graphic information concerning a hazardous chemical that is affixed to, printed on, or attached to the immediate container of a hazardous chemical, or to the outside packaging." Containers in the workplace must be labeled in accordance with section (f) of OSHA's Hazard Communication Standard at 29 CFR 1910.1200.

***Language Requirements [OSHA]:** All labels and other forms of warning are to be in English. The label may also present the information in a different language in addition to English.

***LC50:** Lethal concentration 50. This is the concentration in air of a toxic substance that was required to cause the death of half the test animal population under controlled administration. This evaluates inhalation as a potentially harmful route of entry. LC50 data is used to assess the toxicity of a chemical.

***LD50:** Lethal dose 50. This is the dose or amount of toxic substance that was required to cause death of half the test animal population under controlled administration. Either ingestion or skin contact may be evaluated. LD50 data is used to assess the toxicity of a chemical.

***Material Safety Data Sheet:** The material safety data sheet (MSDS) has been replaced by the safety data sheet (SDS) in accordance with OSHA's 2012 revisions to its Hazard Communication Standard. ALSO SEE: SDS.

^**Mist:** Small droplets of a liquid that can remain suspended in air. Mists can form when a vapor condenses back to its liquid state, or when a liquid breaks up (e.g. by splashing or atomizing).

***MSHA:** Mine Safety and Health Administration.

***Mutagen:** A substance which causes genetic mutations. ALSO SEE: REPRODUCTIVE TOXINS.

***NAICS Codes:** North American Industry Classification System codes. NAICS codes use a six-digit hierarchical coding system to classify all economic activity into 20 industry sectors and 1,170 industries. OSHA began using NAICS codes in its data in 2003. ALSO SEE: SIC CODES.

National Consensus Standard: "means any standard or modification thereof which (1) has been adopted and promulgated by a nationally recognized standards-producing organization under procedures whereby it can be determined by the Secretary of Labor or by the Assistant Secretary of Labor that persons interested and affected by the scope or provisions of the standard have reached substantial agreement on its adoption, (2) was formulated in a manner which afforded an opportunity for diverse views to be considered, and (3) has been designated as such a standard by the Secretary or the Assistant Secretary, after consultation with other appropriate Federal agencies."[12]

*NFPA: National Fire Protection Association. NFPA is a non-profit organization which provides information on fire protection and prevention. Among the publications the NFPA develops is the 704 Standard for the Identification of the Fire Hazards of Materials. This publication describes a hazard warning system suitable for labels on containers. See www.nfpa.org.

*NIOSH: National Institute for Occupational Safety and Health. NIOSH is involved in research on health effects due to workplace exposures. Research is used to make recommendations for reducing or preventing worker exposures. NIOSH is also responsible for testing and certifying respirators. See www.cdc.gov/niosh.

Near-Miss: An occurrence in a sequence of events that had the potential to produce an accident.[13] ALSO SEE: CLOSE CALLS.

^Occupational Safety: The maintenance of a work environment that is relatively free from actual or potential hazards that can injure employees.

*OSHA: Occupational Safety and Health Administration. See www.osha.gov.

*Oxidizer (OSHA): "means a chemical other than a blasting agent or explosive as defined in section 1910.109(a), that initiates or promotes combustion in other materials thereby causing fire either of itself or through the release of oxygen or other gases." The law considers an oxidizer to be a physical hazard.

*PEL: Permissible Exposure Limit. The PEL refers to the maximum air contaminant concentration a worker can be exposed to on a repeated basis without developing adverse effects. The PELs are listed in 29 CFR 1910.1000 Tables Z-1, Z-2, Z-3. Also see CFR 29 Section 1910 Subpart Z.

*Penetration: This is the passage of a chemical through an opening in a protective material. Holes and rips in protective clothing can allow penetration as can stitch holes, space between zipper teeth, and open jacket and pant cuffs.

*Permeation: Permeation is the passage of a chemical through a piece of clothing on a molecular level. If a piece of clothing is permeated, the chemical may collect on the inside, increasing the chance of skin contact with that chemical. Permeation is independent of degradation. Permeation may occur even though the clothing may show no signs of degradation.

Personal Fall Arrest System (PFAS): A system used to stop an employee in a fall from a working level. It consists of an anchorage, connectors, a body harness, and may include a lanyard, deceleration device, lifeline, or suitable combinations of these. As of January 1, 1998, using a body belt for fall arrest is prohibited. **[OSHA]**

Personal Fall Protection System (PFPS): Means a system (including all components) an employer uses to provide protection from falling or to safely arrest an employee's fall if one occurs. Examples of personal fall protection systems include personal fall arrest systems, positioning systems, and travel restraint systems. **[OSHA]**

*Physical Hazard (OSHA): "means a chemical that is classified as posing one of the following hazardous effects: explosive, flammable (gases, aerosols, liquids, or solids); oxidizer (liquid, solid, or gas); self-reactive; pyrophoric (liquid or solid); self-heating; organic peroxide; corrosive to metal; gas under pressure; or in contact with water emits flammable gas." This definition refers to the Hazard Communication Standard at 29 CFR 1910.1200. Any chemical which can be classified as a physical hazard is considered to be a hazardous chemical under the law.

*Pictogram (OSHA): "means a composition that may include a symbol plus other graphic elements, such as a border, background pattern, or color, that is intended to convey specific information about the hazards of a chemical." Eight pictograms are designated under OSHA's Hazard Communication Standard for application to a hazard category.

*Portable Containers: Portable containers need not be labeled if they are for "immediate use." ALSO SEE: IMMEDIATE USE.

*ppb: parts per billion.

*ppm: parts per million.

^Practice: A set of guidelines that are helpful in carrying out a specific type of work.

*Precautionary Statement (OSHA): "means a phrase that describes recommended measures that should be taken to minimize or prevent adverse effects resulting from exposure to a hazardous chemical, or improper storage or handling." This definition refers to OSHA's Hazard Communication Standard at 29 CFR 1910.1200.

*Product Identifier (OSHA): "means the name or number used for a hazardous chemical on a label or in the SDS. It provides a unique means by which the user can identify the chemical. The product identifier used shall permit cross-references to be made among the list of hazardous chemicals required in the written hazard communication program, the label and the SDS." This definition refers to OSHA's Hazard Communication Standard at 29 CFR 1910.1200.

*psi: pounds per square inch.

*Pyrophoric Liquid (OSHA): "means a liquid which, even in small quantities, is able to ignite within five minutes after coming into contact with air." OSHA considers pyrophoric liquids to be physical hazards under its Hazard Communication Standard at 29 CFR 1910.1200.

Qualified Person: One who, by possession of a recognized degree, certificate, or professional standing, or who by extensive knowledge, training, and experience, has successfully demonstrated his ability to solve or resolve problems relating to the subject matter, the work, or the project. **[OSHA]**

Recommended Practice: "any specification for physical characteristics, configuration, material, performance, personnel or procedure, the uniform application of which is recognized as desirable in the interest of safety, regularity or efficiency."[14]

Registered Professional Engineer: A person who is registered as a professional engineer in the state where the work is to be performed. However, a professional engineer registered in any state is deemed to be a "registered professional engineer" within the meaning of this standard when approving designs for "manufactured protective systems" or "tabulated data" to be used in interstate commerce. **[OSHA]**

*Reproductive Toxins (29 CFR 1910.1200, Appendix A): Chemicals that have adverse effects on sexual function and fertility in adult males and females and/or adverse effects on the development of offspring. Examples of reproductive toxins include lead and DBCP.

*Respirator Use: Respirators are commonly used to protect workers from hazardous vapors and gases and particulates. There are respirators that remove hazards and those which supply the worker with air. Each type has limitations and advantages. Proper selection and correct use is essential to worker health. OSHA and ANSI provide guidance for respirator use.

*Right-to-Know Law: This is a term applied to a variety of laws and regulations enacted by municipal, county, and state governments that provide for the availability of information on chemical hazards. This also includes the OSHA Hazard Communication Standard. The different laws that have been enacted around the United States vary greatly from the OSHA Standard. Some require that information be made available not only to employees, but also to emergency personnel and the community as a whole. Many of the local and state laws require submission of work area surveys as well as annual activity reports. The basic intent of these laws is the same as the OSHA Standard. ALSO SEE: HAZARD COMMUNICATION.

^**Risk:** The probability of a worker suffering an injury or health problem, or of damage occurring to property or the environment as a result of exposure to or contact with a hazard.

Risk Assessment: "a process that commences with hazard identification and analysis, through which the probable severity of harm or damage is established, followed by an estimate of the probability of the incident or exposure occurring, and concluding with a statement of risk."[15] A hazard's risk level can be assessed based on the product of the likelihood of occurrence times the severity of consequences: Risk = Likelihood × Severity.

^**Root Cause:** The real or underlying cause(s) of an event. Distinguished from immediate cause(s), which are usually quite apparent.

^**Route of Entry:** The method by which a contaminant can enter the body. There are four main routes of entry. Contaminants can be breathed in, swallowed, absorbed through the skin, or injected into the bloodstream.

Safety: Relative freedom from danger, risk, or threat of harm, injury, or loss of personnel and/or property, whether caused deliberately or by accident.[16]

***SDS (OSHA):** "means written or printed material concerning a hazardous chemical that is prepared in accordance with paragraph (g) of" OSHA's Hazard Communication Standard at 29 CFR 1910.1200. Safety data sheets have a specified 16-section format that chemical manufacturers, importers, and other employers responsible for preparing SDSs must follow as of June 1, 2015.

^**Sensitizer:** A substance which on first exposure causes little or no reaction in humans or test animals. However, on repeated exposure, it may cause a marked response not necessarily limited to the contact site. Skin sensitization (e.g. to a metal such as nickel) is the most common form of sensitization in the workplace. Respiratory sensitization to a few chemicals (e.g. isocyanates) is also known to occur.

***SIC Codes:** Standard Industrial Classification Codes. OSHA has transitioned to the use of the newer six-digit NAICS Codes for industry identification, but several OSHA data sets are still available with four-digit SIC-based data. ALSO SEE: NAICS CODES.

*Signal Word (OSHA): "means a word used to indicate the relative level of severity of hazard and alert the reader to a potential hazard on the label." The signal words used in OSHA's Hazard Communication Standard at 29 CFR 1910.1200 are "danger" and "warning." "Danger" is used for the more severe hazards, and "warning" is used for the less severe.

*Skin Sensitizer (29 CFR 1910.1200, Appendix A): "A chemical that will lead to an allergic reaction following skin contact."

Standard: "means a standard which requires conditions, or the adoption of one or more practices, means, methods, operations, or processes, reasonably necessary or appropriate to provide safe and healthful employment and places of employment." **[OSHA]**

*STEL: Short Term Exposure Limit. This is a term used by the ACGIH to denote "a 15-minute time-weighted average exposure which should not be exceeded at any time during a work day even if the eight hour time-weighted average is within the TLV." As with the TWA-TLV, the STEL is only a recommendation. ALSO SEE: TLV, TWA.

^Substitution: The replacement of toxic or hazardous materials, equipment, or processes with those that are less harmful.

^Synergistic Effects: The health effects of two or more substances or agents that are greater than the sum of their separate effects.

*Teratogen: A substance which causes birth defects as a result of exposure during fetal development. ALSO SEE: REPRODUCTIVE TOXINS.

*TLV: Threshold Limit Value. The TLVs are a group of recommended concentrations established by the ACGIH for worker protection. They are based on toxicity data generated from human and animal studies and industrial experience. TLVs are only recommendations to industry, whereas OSHA enforces the PELs. ALSO SEE: ACGIH, CEILING, PEL, STEL, TWA.

*Toxicity: The measure of the adverse effect exerted on the human body by a poisonous material.

*TWA: Time-weighted average. This type of Threshold Limit Value established by the ACGIH is "the time-weighted average concentration for a normal 8-hour day and 40-hour workweek, to which nearly all workers may be repeatedly exposed, day after day, without adverse effect." ALSO SEE: ACGIH, TLV.

^Vapor/Vapour: The form that a gas or liquid takes when it evaporates into the air.

*Vapor Pressure: A measure of the volatility of a liquid, usually given in millimeters of mercury (mmHg). The vapor pressure of toluene at 68°F is 22 mmHg and 760 mmHg at 231°F (the boiling point). ALSO SEE: VOLATILITY.

^Ventilation: The supplying and exhausting of air at the same time to an enclosed machine, room, or an entire building. There are two types of ventilation:

- General or Dilution: The air contaminants are diluted by natural or mechanical air exchange in the plant. This method is not appropriate for highly toxic contaminants.

- Local Exhaust: The contaminant is captured at its source, usually by the use of hoods, ducts, or vents located near or directly over the source. This is the preferred method where toxic contaminants are released and there is the potential for worker exposure.

*Volatility: A measure relating the tendency of a liquid to change to a vapor at a specific temperature. ALSO SEE: EVAPORATION RATE.

Walking-Working Surface: Any surface on which an employee walks or works, including, but not limited to, floors, roofs, ramps, bridges, runways, formwork, and concrete reinforcing steel, but not including ladders, vehicles, or trailers, on which employees must be located in order to perform their job duties.

^Work Practices: Procedures for carrying out specific tasks which, when followed, will ensure that a worker's exposure to hazardous situations, substances, or physical agents is controlled by the manner in which the work is carried out.

*Workplace (OSHA): "means an establishment, job site, or project, at one geographical location containing one or more work areas."

^Workplace Hazardous Materials Information System (WHMIS): An information system implemented under the [Canadian] federal Hazardous Products Act and provincial occupational health and safety laws to ensure communication of information on hazardous materials. The information delivery system under WHMIS requires 1) labels, 2) material safety data sheets (MSDSs), and 3) worker education and training programs. The WHMIS is Canada's national hazard communication standard. The key elements of the system are hazard classification, cautionary labeling of containers, the provision of safety data sheets (SDSs), and worker education and training programs.[17]

NOTES

1. Disclaimer: The definitions marked with ^ are obtained from the Glossary of Occupation Health & Safety Terms by the International Accident Prevention Association (now Workplace Safety & Prevention Services [WSPS]). WSPS does not warrant nor guarantee the accuracy or completeness of the definitions or that they are up to date. The definitions made available do not represent any partnership, endorsement, or recommendations with/by WSPS, and in no event will WSPS be liable to you or anyone else for any decision made or action taken in reliance on the definitions in this book. IAPA Glossary accessed April, 4, 2019, http://www.iapa.ca/pdf/iapa_glossary.pdf.
2. Definitions marked with * are from Safety.BLR.com; used with permission, accessed December 10, 2018, https://safety.blr.com/workplace-safety-news/safety-administration/safety-general/Safety-101-Glossary-of-Workplace-Safety-Terms-1163-116341/.
3. Definitions noted with **[OSHA]** are from OSHA Construction eTools, Construction Home-Glossary, accessed December 11, 2018, https://www.osha.gov/SLTC/etools/construction/glossary.html, and from OSHA 29 CFR 1910 Occupational Safety and Health Standards, accessed December 11, 2018, https://www.osha.gov/laws-regs/regulations/standardnumber/1910.
4. OSHA. *Incident [Accident] Investigations: A Guide for Employers*, page 2, accessed April 14, 2019, https://www.osha.gov/dte/InclnvGuide4Empl_Dec2015.pdf.
5. *West's Encyclopedia of American Law, edition 2*, "Code," accessed May 27, 2019, https://legal-dictionary.thefreedictionary.com/code.
6. *ACSNI Human Factors Study Group: Third report, Organising for Safety*, HSE Books 1993, accessed December 11, 2018, http://www.hse.gov.uk/humanfactors/topics/common4.pdf.
7. National Fire Protection Association, NFPA 101—Life Safety Code, 2018, Section 3.3.108.
8. Theatre Effects, "Flame Retardant," accessed April 7, 2019, http://www.theatrefx.com/funfacts51.html.
9. SKYbrary, "Hazard Identification-Definitions," accessed May 28, 2019, https://www.skybrary.aero/index.php/Hazard_Identification.
10. Safety Talk Ideas, "Hierarchy of Controls," accessed December 11, 2018, https://www.safetytalkideas.com/safetytalks/hierarchy-of-controls/.

11 OSHA. *Incident [Accident] Investigations: A Guide for Employers*, page 2, accessed April 14, 2019, https://www.osha.gov/dte/InclnvGuide4Empl_Dec2015.pdf.

12 OSHA. Regulations (Standards-29 CFR 1910.2(g)), accessed June 6, 2019, https://www.osha.gov/laws-regs/regulations/standardnumber/1910/1910.2.

13 Jeffrey S. Oakley, *Accident Investigation Techniques*, 2nd edition (Park Ridge, IL: American Society of Safety Professionals, 2012), 117.

14 Wikipedia, "Standards and Recommended Practices," accessed March 26, 2019, https://en.wikipedia.org/wiki/Standards_and_Recommended_Practices.

15 ANSI/ASSE Z590.3-2011 (r2016) "Prevention through Design: Guidelines for Addressing Occupational Hazards and Risks in Design and Redesign Processes, as quoted in *Professional Safety*, November, 2017, 35.

16 Business Dictionary, "Safety," accessed April 4, 2019, http://www.businessdictionary.com/definition/safety.html.

17 Government of Canada, Occupational Safety and Health, "Workplace Hazardous Materials Information System (WHMIS)," accessed April 4, 2019, https://www.canada.ca/en/health-canada/services/environmental-workplace-health/occupational-health-safety/workplace-hazardous-materials-information-system.html.

BIBLIOGRAPHY

Antonsen, Stian. *Safety Culture: Theory, Method and Improvement*. Burlington, VT: Ashgate Publishing Company, 2009.

Barylick, John. *Killer Show: The Station Nightclub Fire, American's Deadliest Rock Concert*. Lebanon, NH: University Press of New England, 2012.

Byrne, Richard. *Be the Best: How to Become a World-Class Health and Safety Professional*. Wigston: Leicestershire, England: IOSH Services Ltd, 2009.

Casner, Steve. *Careful: A User's Guide to Our Injury-Prone Minds*. New York: Riverhead Books, 2017.

Cooper, Donald C., editor. *The Event Safety Guide*, created by the Event Safety Alliance. New York: Skyhorse Publishing, 2014.

Cote, Ron, and Harrington, Gregory E., editors. *Life Safety Code Handbook, NFPA 101, 2015 edition*. Quincy, MA: National Fire Protection Association, 2014.

Gawande, Atul. *The Checklist Manifesto: How to Get Things Right*. New York: Metropolitan Books, 2009.

Gillett, Cary, and Sheehan, Jay. *The Production Manager's Toolkit: Successful Production Management in Theatre and Performing Arts*. New York: Routledge, 2017.

Heinrich, H. W. *Industrial Accident Prevention: A Scientific Approach*. New York: McGraw-Hill Book Company, 1931.

Inouye, Kevin. *The Theatrical Firearms Handbook*. Burlington, MA: Focal Press, 2014.

J. J. Keller & Associates, Inc. *OSHA Safety Handbook*, 8th edition. Neenah, WI: J. J. Keller & Associates, Inc., 2017.

Mancomm, Inc. *OSHA General Industry Regulations, 29 CFR Parts 1903. 1904, and 1910*. Davenport, IA: Mancomm, Inc., 2017.

Marsh, Tim, Dr. *ASM: Affective Safety Management*. London: International Institute of Risk and Safety Management, 2008.

Marsh, Tim, Dr. *Talking Safety.* Burlington, VT: Gower Publishing Company, 2013.

Marsh, Tim, Dr. *Total Safety Culture: Organisational Risk Literacy*. Manchester, England: Ryder Marsh Safety Limited, 2014.

Oakley, Jeffery S. *Accident Investigation Techniques*, 2nd edition. Park Ridge, IL: American Society of Safety Professionals, 2012.

O'Doherty, David, and Judge, Chris. *Danger Is Everywhere: A Handbook for Avoiding Danger*. New York: Little, Brown and Company, 2014.

Rogoff, Gordon. *Theater Is Not Safe: Theatre Criticism 1962–1986*. Evanston, IL: Northwestern University Press, 1987.

Rossol, Monona. *The Health and Safety Guide for Film, TV, and Theater*, 2nd edition. New York: Allworth Press, 2011.

Shanda, Mark, and Dorn, Dennis. *Technical Management for the Performing Arts: Utilizing Time, Talent, and Money*. New York: Focal Press, 2016.

Stribling, Zachary, and Girtain, Richard. *The Technical Director's Toolkit: Process, Forms, and Philosophies for Successful Technical Direction*. New York: Focal Press, 2016.

Sutherland-Cohen, Robert I. *Introduction to Production: Creating Theatre Onstage, Backstage & Offstage*. New York: Routledge, 2018.

van Beek, Marco. *A Practical Guide to Health and Safety in the Entertainment Industry*. Cambridge, England: Entertainment Technology Press Ltd., 2000.

INDEX

Note: *Italic* **page numbers indicate figures.**

A
accidents, injuries, deaths (example cases) xvi, *xviii*, 2–3
   Indiana State Fair, stage collapse 2, 16
   Ringling Bros. and Barnum & Baily Circus, hair-hang accident 2–3, 18
   Station, The, nightclub fire, Rhode Island 2, 124
   weapon-related 139
Actors' Equity Association (AEA) 14–15, 136–137, 162
   AEA venue inspections 15
   Equity contracts (AEA's safe and sanitary workplace rules), 14–15
   Equity-League Pension and Health Trust Funds 14
   stage fog and haze health hazard investigations 15, 136–138
alone (lone) work, policies (safety strategies) 166–168
   policy development 167–168
   examples 166–167
   OSHA standards 167
   UK Health and Safety Executive (HSE), *Working Alone* guidance 167

The Yale School of Drama's Safety Handbook 2018 167–168; *see also* safety strategies
American National Standards Institute (ANSI) 90, 109
ANSI-accredited standards 15, 112–113, 114–119
accreditation/revision process 16, 109–110, 113, 120
ANSI A92 (mobile elevating work platforms) 134
ANSI E1.2–2012 (aluminum trusses and towers) 114–115
ANSI E1.32–2012, R2017 (incandescent lamp luminaires) 117
ANSI E1.4–1–2016 (manual counterweight rigging systems) 115–116
ANSI E1.46–2016 (fall prevention/protection) 118–119, 133–134, 173–174, *174*, 176
ANSI E1.47–2017 (rigging system inspections) 116
ANSI E1.53–2016 (overhead luminaires, lighting accessories, portable devices) 117

ANSI/ASSP Z590.3-2011, R2016 (prevention through design guidelines) 172–173
ANSI/ISEA 121–2018 (dropped objects) 136
publication 113, 114
standards developing organizations (SDOs) 109–110
asbestos 12
   General Industry Standard (29 CFR 1910) *74*, 75
   OSHA's Asbestos Standard, 1972 12
Association of British Theatre Technicians (ABTT) 139–140; see also United Kingdom (UK)

B
Barnes, J. H. 139

C
Campbell Institute of the National Safety Council 180
Canada 90–91; see also international codes
CFR; see codes of federal regulations (CFR), legal requirements
checklists (safety strategies) 158–162
   checklist for checklists 160, *161*
   The Checklist Manifesto: How to Get Things Right 159
   content 159, 162
   formats (DO-CONFIRM, DO-READ) 160
   testing, modification, review 161; see also safety strategies
Chile 91–93; see also international codes
codes of federal regulation (CFR), legal requirements: definition 66
   distinction from industry standards 66–67
   hierarchy of safety controls 68, *68*
   international codes 90–100 (see also international codes)
   National Fire Protection Association (NFPA) codes 82–90 (see also NFPA codes)
   Occupational Health and Safety Administration (OSHA) standards 70–82 (see also OSHA standards)
collaboration: collaborative character theater productions 4, 170–171, 182, 190, 192, 197
   cooperation creative/technical team and safety/health program 8, 39, 158, *158*, 170, 182, 194, 197
compliance (codes, standards, procedures) 3, 13, 19, 129, 133
   fire codes and standards 82–90 (see also NFPA codes and standards)
   industrial standards 15, 112–113, 114–119 (see also ANSI-accredited standards)
   international codes 90–100 (see also international codes)

compliance, key aspect of safety culture 195–196
legal codes 68–70, 72–82 (*see also* OSHA standards)
policies and procedures for specific hazards (*see* policies and procedures)
Construction Standard (29 CFR 1926, OSHA standards) 71–72, 167
  example: Subpart C, employer responsibilities 80
  theatre-relevant subparts 79–82; see also OSHA standards
culture of safety; *see* safety culture
current state safety health program development, survey, 2017 12–19

D
Davis, Phil 54
death; *see* fatalities
Deming, W. Edwards *39*, 40

E
employee: coordination/communication, multi-employer worksite 57–59
  education, training 54
  International Alliance of Theatrical Stage Employees (IATSE) 7
  job satisfaction in secure environment 7
  open hazard reporting, Right-to-Know 44, 46
  OSHA code protection 67 (*see also* employer responsibilities, legal regulations)
  safety and health program, participation 7, 43–46, 47
  safety program evaluation, improvement 59, *60*
  sample whistleblower protection policy 46
employer responsibilities, legal duties: OSH Act, 1970: General Duty Cause (industry standard enforcement) 111–112
  OSHA 29 CFR 1904: recordkeeping 72, 80–82, *81*, 145, *146*
  OSHA 29 CFR, 1910.30: fall hazard training 76–77
  OSHA 29 CFR 1926.20: safe work environment (provision) 80
  OSHA 29 CFR 1926.21: safe work environment (training) 80
  OSHA codes, employee safety, employer duties 67
Entertainment Services and Technology Association (ESTA) 14, 15, 90, 112–114, 119, 120–121, 122, 137
Entertainment Technician Certification Program (ETCP) 15, 110–112, 122, 135
  safety and health standards (*see* ANSI-accredited standards)
  Technical Standards Program (TSP) 90, 112–114
entertainment/theatre industry organizations 14–18; *see also* Actors' Equity Association (AEA); Entertainment Services and

Technology Association (ESTA); Event Safety Alliance (ESA); International Alliance of Theatrical Stage Employees (IATSE); United States Institute for Theatre Technology (USITT)
ENVIRON Corp. (stage fog investigation) 15, 137, 138
Equity; see Actors' Equity Association (AEA)
ESTA; see Entertainment Services and Technology Association (ESTA)
Event Safety Alliance (ESA) 14, 15–16, 120–121
   Event Safety Guide 16, 120
   Event Safety Summit 16, 120–121
   Severe Weather Summit 16, 120

F

fall prevention/protection (FP/FP) 13, 27, 129, 133–136, 173
   ANSI E1.4-1–2016 (manual counterweight rigging systems) 115–116
   ANSI E1.46–2016 (theatrical stages, raised performance platforms) 118, 118–119, 133–134, 173–174, 174, 176
   ANSI/ISEA 121–2018 (dropped objects) 136
   duty to fall protection 133
   fall hazards 7, 27–28, 49–50, 76, 118–119, 134, 165
   FP/FP policy/program development 134, 135
   International Code of Practice for Entertainment Rigging (ICOPER) 135
   OSHA 29 CFR, 1910.28 (fall and falling object protection) 75–76
   OSHA 29 CFR, 1910.29 (protection systems) 76
   OSHA 29 CFR, 1910.30 (fall hazard training) 76–77
   OSHA Letter of Interpretation, 1997 13
   personal fall protection systems (PFPS) 134–135
fatalities 13, 81, *150*
   serious injury and fatality (SIF), prevention 179–182
   accident data 180
field level hazard assessment (FLHA) (safety strategies) 176–179, *178, 179*; see also hazards
fire and life safety 15, 27, 28, 66, 82–90, 142–144, *143*
   authority having jurisdiction (AHJ) inspection/approval 142
   codes and standards 82–90 (see also NFPA 101 (Life Safety Code); NFPA codes and standards)
   incidents form *143*
   policy/program development 142–144
   safety and health handbook 144
   scenic design 143; see also live flame onstage; policies and procedures; Station, The, nightclub fire, Rhode Island
fixed hazards 27, 48–50, 119, 165
   definition 4–5, 7

examples 7
safety policies requirements 7
fluid hazards 4–5, 7, 8, 27, 48–50, 119, 165
   definition 4–5, 7
   examples 8
   safety procedure demands 8
fog; *see* stage fog, haze

G

Gawande, Atul 159–160, 161, *161*
General Industry Standard (29 CFR 1910, OSHA standards) 71, 131–133
   example: Subpart D, walking-working surfaces 75–77
   theatre-relevant subparts 72–79, *73*, *74*; *see also* OSHA standards
Glerum, Jay 112
Glimmerglass Festival, Cooperstown, New York, safety and health strategies 19–22
Glover, Anna 38
Goodman Theatre, Chicago, safety and health strategies 19, 22–23, 41–42, 70

H

Heinrich, H. W.: Safety Triangle 180–181
habituation, safety risk 47
hazards: categorization (fixed, fluid) 4–5, 7, 27, 48–50, 119, 165
   definition 165
   education, training 56
   field level hazard assessment (FLHA) 176–179, *178*, *179*
   habituation, olfactory fatigue 47
   identification, assessment 46–50, *49*, 165–166, *166*
   management, Hazard Control Plan Management Cycle 53
   mitigation: hierarchy of controls *51*
   OSHA Hazard Communication Standard (HCS) (29 CRF 1910.1200) 44
   OSHA Hazard Identification Training Tool 47–48
   prevention, control 51–54
   reporting (Right-to-Know) 44–45
   theatre's hazardous nature 1; *see also* risk (of hazards) assessments; safety strategies
haze; *see* stage fog, haze
Heinrich, H. W. 180–181, *181*
hierarchy of safety controls: codes 68
   industry standards *110*
   policies, procedures *130*
   recommended practices, training, certification *111*
human capital 6, 54
Huneycutt, Bryan (Disney Parks) 160

I

incident reporting and recording 145–150, *150*
   codes, legal requirements (*see* Recordkeeping Regulation (OSHA 29 CFR 1904))
   data analysis, trend determination, incident prevention 145, 147, 149
   Incident [Accident] Investigations: A Guide for Employers 147

INDEX **239**

National Emphasis Programs (NEPs) 147
National Institute for Occupational Safety and Health (NIOSH) reports 147
National Safety Council 149
near misses reporting 5, 44, 46, 59, *60*, 148, 148–149, 149, *150*
policy development 148–149
qualitative data records, root cause detection 147, 148
quantitative data records (OSHA 300 log) *146*, 147–148, 148
India 93–94; *see also* international codes
Indiana State Fair, stage collapse 2, 16
industry recommended practices 119–121
  Event Safety Alliance (ESA): Event Safety Summit 120
  Event Safety Alliance (ESA): Severe Weather Summit 120–121
  Event Safety Alliance (ESA): *The Event Safety Guide* 120
  implementation in safety and health programs 125
  International Code of Practice for Entertainment Rigging (ICOPER) 121; *see also* hierarchy of safety controls
industry standards (nature and development) 109–119, *111*
  standard accreditation, American National Standards Institute (ANSI) 109
  standard development process 109–110
  Standards Developing Organizations (SDOs) 109, 110, 112
  voluntary nature vs legal enforceability (OSH Act, 1970: General Duty Cause) 109, 110, 111–112; *see also* ANSI-accredited standards
industry standards (training and certification) 110–111, 121–125
  Entertainment Technician Certification Program (ETCP) 15, 110–111, 122, 125, 135
  Essential Skills for Entertainment Technicians (eSET) certificate 110–111, 121–122
industry standards (U.S. entertainment industry): development, technical standards program (TSP) working groups 112, 119
  ESTA as primary standard developing organization 90, 112
  examples 112–113, 114–119 (*see also* ANSI-accredited standards)
  implementation in safety and health programs 119
  maintenance, re-approval 113
  publication, review 113
  scope 114; *see also* Entertainment Services and Technology Association (ESTA); hierarchy of safety controls

International Alliance of Theatrical Stage Employees (IASTSE) 13, 14, 16–17, 123
   IATSE Training Trust Fund (TTF) 17, 123
International Association of Venue Managers (IAVM) 124–125
international codes: Canada 90–91
   Chile 91–93
   India 93–94
   International Building Code (IBC) 69, 83, 92–93
   International Code of Practice for Entertainment Rigging (ICOPER) 121
   International Fire Code (IFC) 69
   Philippines, The 94–95
   Republic of Korea (South Korea) 95–96
   Singapore 96–97
   Taiwan (R.O.C.) 97–98
   United Kingdom 98–100

L
legal requirements; *see* codes of federal regulations (CFR), legal requirements
Life Safety Code (NFPA 101); *see* NFPA 101 (Life Safety Code)
live flames onstage 21, 130, 141–142, 143, *143*, 166

M
Michaels, David 13
Milwaukee Repertory Theater, Wisconsin, safety and health strategies 19, 23–25
Minnesota Theater Alliance Statewide Theater Conference, Minneapolis, 2017 11
mobile elevated work platform (MEWP) 134
Mount Sinai School of Medicine, New York 137, 138

N
NAICS; *see* North American Industry Classification System (NAICS) codes
National Fire Protection Association (NFPA) 66–67, 68, 82–90, 123–124; *see also* NFPA codes and standards
National Institute for Occupational Safety and Health (NIOSH) 147
   health hazard investigations (stage fog) 136–137, 138
   prevention through design (PtD) program 168–172
   safety and health programs, assessment tools 60
National Safety Council 149
near-misses, reporting 5, 44, 46, 59, *60*, 148–149, *150*; *see also* incident reporting and recording
New York Times, The 148
NFPA 101 (Life Safety Code), built structures 83, 84–86, 88, 90, 123–124, 141, 142
   chapter overviews 85–86
   scope, purpose, terminology 84
   theatre-relevant regulations (chapters 12, 13, 43) 86–90
NFPA codes and standards 82–90
   coverage 68, 69
   legislative adoption and enforcement 82–83

NFPA 101 (*see* NFPA 101 (Life Safety Code))
NFPA 160: Standard for the Use of Flame Effects Before an Audience 141
theatre-relevant codes (buildings) 83–84
theatre-relevant codes (productions) 83
Nixon, Richard M. 12
North American Industry Classification System (NAICS) codes 81, *81*, 82, 180
Nunnally, Tracy 122

O

Occupational Health and Safety Administration, The (OSHA) 12–13, 17, 18, 26, 30
  Consultant Program 20
  General Industry classes 31
  OSHA Recommended Practices for Safety and Health Programs, 2016 39–40, 40, *40*, 62
  Recommended Practices guide 39–40; *see also* OSHA standards
Occupational Safety and Health (OSH) Act, 1970 12, 55, 67, 70–71, 80, 111
operational inspections (safety strategies) 162–164
  common aspects 163
  fire and life safety 142, 143
  hazard identification 47–50, *49*, 53, 165
  implementation in safety and health programs 163
  mechanical systems, equipment 114–116, 117, 162–163, 182; *see also* safety strategies
Oregon Shakespeare Festival, Ashland, safety and health strategies 19, 25–29
organization model, theatre/academic department 158, *158*
OSHA; *see* Occupational Health and Safety Administration, The (OSHA)
OSHA standards/Codes of federal regulation (CFR); *see* codes of federal regulations (CFR), legal requirements; Occupational Safety and Health (OSH) Act, 1970
  applicability 13, 70
  coverage 26, 70–71
  definition 71
  enforcement (inspection, legislation, court) 13–14, 111, 112
  identifying syntax 71
  OSHA State Plans 26, 71
  theatre-related: Construction Standard (29 CFR 1926) 71–72, 79–80, 167
  theatre-related: General Industry Standard (29 CFR 1910) 71, 72–75, *73*, *74*, 131–133
  theatre-related: Recordkeeping Regulation (29 CFR 1904) 72, 80–82, *81*, 145, *146*
OSHA State Plans 26, 70; *see also* OSHA standards (federal)

P

patron alerts and notifications: crowd management training

(IAVM, Fire Marshal Support Services, Fire Services) 123–125
patron interactions and customer service 144–145
policy/program development 144
single signs 144
stage fog, haze exposure 138; *see also* policies and procedures
Philippines 94–95; *see also* international codes
policies and procedures: fall prevention/protection (FP/FP) 13, 27, 129, 133–136, 173
fire and life safety 15, 27, 28, 66, 82–90, 142–144, *143*
incident reporting and recording (*see* incident reporting and recording)
live flame onstage 21, 130, 141–142, 143, *143*, *166*
patron alerts and notifications 144–145
personal protective equipment 129, 130–133
stage fog and haze 15, 129, 136–138, 144
stage weapons 31, 129, 138–141, 144, *166*; *see also* hierarchy of safety controls
prevention through design (PtD) (safety strategies) 156, 168–172, 181–182
definition, potential 169, 171
examples 171–172 (*see also* safety strategies)
hierarchy of controls 169, *170*
production process (theatre/live event) 156–157

R

Recordkeeping Regulations (OSHA 29 CFR 1904) 72, 80–82, *81*, 145, *146*
forms for reports 82
partially exempt industries *81*
theatre-relevant subparts 81; *see also* incident reporting and recording; OSHA standards
Republic of Korea (South Korea) 95–96; *see also* international codes
Rignold, William 139
Ringling Bros. and Barnum & Baily Circus, hair-hang accident 2–3, 18
risk (of hazards) assessments 119, 156, 172–176
acceptable risk, concept 176
assessment methods 173–174
definition (ANSI/ASSE Z590.3-2011, R2016) 172–173
risk assessment documentation form *175*
risk assessment matrix, ANSI E1.46–2016 173–174, *174*; *see also* safety and health programs, OSHA recommended core elements; safety strategies
Rogoff, Gordon 1
Rossol, Monona 1

S

safety and health programs: congruency to production process 38–39
definition 38
Plan–Do–Study–Act *39*, 40
proactive character 38–39
survey, 2017 11–12

safety and health programs
(core elements, OSHA
recommended) 39, 40, *40*
  coordination/communication,
    multi-employer worksite
    57–59
  education and training 54–57
  employee participation 43–46
  hazard identification,
    assessment 46–50, *49*
  hazard prevention, control
    51–54, *51*, *53*
  management leadership
    41–43
  program evaluation and
    improvement 59–61, *60*
  whistleblower protection policy,
    sample 46
safety and health programs
  (development/
  implementation support):
  OSHA Recommended
  Practices for Safety and
  Health Programs, 2016
  39
  OSHA Safe + Sound: *10 Ways
    to Get Your Program Started*
    61–62
  OSHA Safety and Health
    Program Management
    Guidelines, 1989 39
safety culture 3–4
  collaboration, creative/
    technical–safety/health 8,
    39, 158, *158*, 170, 182, 194,
    197
  communication 132, 178–179,
    188–192
  compliance (*see* compliance
    (codes, standards,
    procedures))
  definition 192
  employee participation, peer
    influence 7, 43–46,
    193–194, 195
  management leadership 41–43,
    194
  organizational culture, values
    192–193
  safety and health programs
    (*see* safety and health
    programs)
  work culture, changing 196
safety risks/breaches, effects:
    career longevity 6
  death, injuries 5
  financial risks 6
  morale, job satisfaction 6–7
  production process interruption
    5–6
safety strategies: alone (lone)
    work policy 166–168
  checklists 158–162
  field level hazard assessment
    (FLHA) 176–179, *178*,
    179
  hazard identification 46–50, *49*,
    165–166, *166*
  operational inspections 47–50,
    53, 114–117, 142–143,
    162–164, 165
  prevention through design
    (PtD) 156, 168–172, *170*,
    181–182
  risk assessments 119, 156,
    172–176
  serious injury and fatality (SIF),
    prevention 179–182, *181*
serious injury and fatality
  (SIF), prevention (safety
  strategies) 179–182, *181*
  Campbell Institute of the
    National Safety Council,
    data report 180–181

H. W. Heinrich: Safety Triangle 180–181
  policy/program development 181
  root causes 180
Singapore 96–97; *see also* international codes
South Korea (Republic of Korea) 95–96; *see also* international codes
stage fog, haze 15, 129, 136–138, 144
  health hazard investigations (NIOSH, Mount Sinai/ENVIRON) 15, 136–137
  policy/program development 136, 137–138
  recommended practice: chemical restrictions 138
  recommended practice: exposure levels, limits 137
stage weapons 31, 138–141, 144, *166*
  Macbeth, accidental stabbing (Theatre Royal, London, 1882) 139
  stage weapons policy, elements 140–141
standard operating procedures (SOPs) 45, 56, 160
standards adoption, implementation 18–34
  Glimmerglass Festival, Cooperstown, New York 19–22
  Milwaukee Repertory Theater, Wisconsin 19, 23–25
  Oregon Shakespeare Festival, Ashland 19, 25–29
  Yale School of Drama/Yale Repertory Theatre, New Haven, Connecticut (YSD/YRT) 29–34

standards developing organizations (SDOs) 109, 110, 112; *see also* industry standards (nature and development)
Station, The, nightclub fire, Rhode Island 2, 124

T
Taiwan (R.O.C.) 97–98; *see also* international codes
Technical Standard Program (TSP), ESTA 90, 112–114, 120
  TSP working groups 113, 120
Theatre Is Not Safe (Gordon Rogoff) 1
toolbox talks 178–179, 194, 196; *see also* field level hazard assessment (FLHA)
training and certification 110–111, 121–125
  crowd management training (IAVM, Fire Marshal Support Services, Fire Services) 123–125
  Entertainment Technician Certification Program (ETCP) 15, 110–111, 122, 125, 135
  Essential Skills for Entertainment Technicians (eSET) certificate 110–111, 121–122
  IATSE Training Trust Fund (TTF) 17, 123
  OSHA 29 CFR, 1910.30 76–77
  OSHA-10 General Industry card, course 123
  United States Institute for Theatre Technology (USITT) 17–18, 121–122, 123

U

United Kingdom (UK) 98–99, 120, 139, 167, 172, 173, 196; *see also* Association of British Theatre Technicians (ABTT); international codes

United States Institute for Theatre Technology (USITT) 17–18, 121–122, 123

V

van Beek, Marco 172

W

walking, working surfaces security (ladders, stairs, rails) 75–76

water 7–8, 92

weapons; *see* stage weapons

whistleblower protection policy, sample 46

wind-caused accidents xviii, 2; *see also* Indiana State Fair, stage collapse

working alone; *see* alone (lone) work, policy

Y

Yale Insights 54

Yale School of Drama (YSD)/Yale Repertory Theatre (YRT), New Haven, Connecticut, safety and health strategies 19, 29–34, 38, 53, 54, 57–58, 62, 69, 129

The Yale School of Drama's Safety Handbook 2018 167–168

Yale School of Management 54

Young, Andrew 122

For Product Safety Concerns and Information please contact our EU
representative GPSR@taylorandfrancis.com
Taylor & Francis Verlag GmbH, Kaufingerstraße 24, 80331 München, Germany

www.ingramcontent.com/pod-product-compliance
Lightning Source LLC
Chambersburg PA
CBHW081804300426
44116CB00014B/2235